LIFE ON TELEVISION

Content Analyses of U.S. TV Drama

COMMUNICATION AND INFORMATION SCIENCE

A series of monographs,
treatises, and texts

Edited by
MELVIN J. VOIGT

University of California, San Diego

HEWITT D. CRANE • The New Social Marketplace: Notes on Effecting Social Change in America's Third Century
RHONDA J. CRANE • The Politics of International Standards: France and the Color TV War
GLEN FISHER • American Communication in a Global Society
BRADLEY S. GREENBERG • Life on Television: Content Analyses of U.S. TV Drama
JOHN S. LAWRENCE AND BERNARD M. TIMBERG • Fair Use and Free Inquiry: Copyright Law and the New Media
ROBERT G. MEADOW • Politics as Communication
VINCENT MOSCO • Broadcasting in the United States: Innovative Challenge and Organizational Control
KAARLE NORDENSTRENG AND HERBERT I. SCHILLER • National Sovereignty and International Communication: A Reader

In Preparation

HERBERT S. DORDICK, HELEN G. BRADLEY, AND BURT NANUS • The Emerging Network Marketplace
WILLIAM H. MELODY, LIORA R. SALTER, AND PAUL HEYER • Culture, Communication, and Dependency: The Tradition of H. A. Innis
ITHIEL DE SOLA POOL • Retrospective Technology Assessment of the Telephone
CLAIRE K. SCHULTZ • Computer History and Information Access

LIFE ON TELEVISION
Content Analyses of U.S. TV Drama

by

BRADLEY S. GREENBERG

in collaboration with

Charles K. Atkin
Pilar Baptista-Fernandez
Nancy Buerkel-Rothfuss
Nadyne Edison
Carlos Fernandez-Collado
David Graef
Laura Henderson
Mary Hines
Linda Hogan
Felipe Korzenny
Kimberly A. Neuendorf
Marcia Richards
Katrina W. Simmons

Ablex Publishing Corporation
Norwood, New Jersey 07648

Printed in the United States of America.

Library of Congress Cataloging in Publication Data

Greenberg, Bradley S
    Life on television.

    (Communication and information science)
    Bibliography: p
    Includes indexes.
    1. Television series—United States.   I. Title.
II. Title: Content analyses of U.S. TV drama.
III. Series.
PN1992.8.S4G7   302.2′3   80-14478
ISBN 0-89391-039-2
ISBN 0-89381-062-7 (PBK.)

ABLEX Publishing Corporation
355 Chestnut Street
Norwood, New Jersey 07648

CONTENTS

PREFACE

In December 1978, according to the Roper organization, for the first time in its 17 years of examining television usage, the average American watched television more than three hours each day. In 1978, according to the Nielsen raters, television sets were on an average of more than seven hours each day in each house. Whatever the precision of those estimates, give or take a half-hour in either direction, a lot of television gets turned on and a lot of television gets watched. In fact, if you figured out how much free time a person has available on a weekday—subtracting time for work inside or outside the home, sleeping, eating, car errands, and other professional and family obligations—you'd come up with about six hours. That's the time that the typical American can give to playing games, handiwork, social visits, parties, reading, going to the movies, taking a night class—or watching television. It's fair to say that the American decision has been to watch TV; that choice consumes one-half of our free time.

This book, then, is about what we watch and what we get to watch on American television. It is the first book-length report which concurrently examines several major kinds of television content and does so for more than a single season. Typically, when we wanted systematically to determine the attributes of a special kind of TV content, we did so for either two or three television seasons. That trend information lends a dynamic quality to data which otherwise would be overly descriptive and time bound.

The primary purpose of this effort has been to identify, document, and trace some major dimensions of television content. The singular criterion used to determine what dimensions to search out was whether the content area was judged to have significant potential social implications. That is, was this content, if presented in certain amounts and forms, likely to have social effects on issues of some significance both to policy makers and to individual American families? We think the areas studied meet this criterion. Others we have not yet been able to study would also qualify.

Some brief background may be useful in explaining what has been done in the last four years. In 1975, the Office of Child Development in the Department of Health, Education, and Welfare made a one-year grant to Michigan State University for a project to focus on issues related to "Parental Mediation of Social Learning from Television." Professors Charles K. Atkin and Bradley S. Greenberg of the Department of Communication were codirectors of the project. The original grant proposal outlined two additional years of work, and subsequent grants were received in 1976 and 1977. The project took the acronym, Project CASTLE (Children and Social Television Learning). Three distinct elements were outlined in the project. First, commercial television content was to be systematically and thoroughly analyzed in four specific content areas: the presentation of antisocial and prosocial behaviors; the portrayal of black Americans; the portrayal of the American family; and the portrayal of the sexes. The content analysis each season consisted of videotaping one episode of each fictional series available in prime time (8–11 p.m.) and on Saturday morning (8 a.m.–1 p.m.) during one selected week in the fall, and supplementing that with replacement series that had emerged by early winter. Typically, it took about three weeks to accumulate one episode of each series, because of preemptions. Each sample week included about 60 hours of television, representing 80–90 different series. Excluded were public affairs programs, variety shows, game shows, and movies. The focus was on regularly appearing fictional characterizations created specifically for commercial television. This first phase of the project grew from the original four content elements to include half a dozen more—another minority group, added social behaviors, drinking and drugging, and so on, as shown in the separate chapters in this book. As these multiple content analyses began to accumulate, we realized that there was a special opportunity to present this information all together, in a single package, rather than distributing it among a dozen different academic journals. Concurrent presentation ought to provide a broader examination and a more comprehensive cultural depiction than had heretofore existed.

But this was the first component of a larger research project. The content-analytic results were to be used in subsequent research phases.

The second of those phases was a series of field surveys of young people and their mothers. What relationship was there between watching pro- and antisocial behaviors on television and the youngster's own parallel behaviors? What relationship was there between watching portrayals of television families, black people, and male and female sex roles with the youngster's own attitudes, aspirations, and expectations about these groups and the social roles they represented? And how did these relationships vary in different family settings, among parents who guided or mediated their children's television behaviors differently. The answers to these questions will not be reported in this book. What is central is recognition that the results of the content analyses played a key role in formulating the substance of the field surveys. The content analyses defined and isolated the basic themes, values, and messages of television. They stipulated what the sexes were doing to each other and saying about each other; they related how minorities were being presented differently; they captured the essential characterizations of fictional TV families. As these patterns began to emerge across programs, as we could identify characteristics, behaviors, and values that occurred frequently, persistently, and consistently, we could say, "Hey, that's what television is saying and showing." By finding content patterns that were representative of a good share of programs, that were repeated and repeated and repeated, we would argue that these were likely to be the television texts most capable of being learned by the viewer. In this way, the content-analysis results contributed to the design of the field surveys.

Phase three of Project CASTLE turned to field experimental research. Once we could understand the content of television and some of the relationships between exposure to that content and the subsequent responses of young viewers, in the context particularly of different parenting styles and parental guidance about television, then it was time to determine whether and how intervention in that system might be effective. Specifically, could one provide some kinds of information in that social context which would be effective in facilitating some presumably positive effects of certain television content and in truncating some presumably negative effects of other content segments? During this phase, we directed several exploratory experiments. In one, a television guide was specially created for children and distributed to them and/or their parents. It recommended certain shows, disapproved others, and talked about certain kinds of television portrayals, e.g., how men and women are shown, how real that is, etc. In another, parents agreed to make a special effort to provide guidance to their children about certain kinds of program content, to be compared with others not asked to do anything special. We also began to examine guidance systems outside the home. Two special in-school curriculum modules were designed and implemented with elementary and middle-school youngsters, five sessions for about 45 minutes each. The behaviors and attitudes of children who received and did not receive this training program were compared. Another study was keyed to using the media themselves as possible mediating systems in coping with youngsters' understanding of, and response to, television content. A radio series was produced, a set of newspaper columns written, and television public service announcements created.

These examples describe the process and logic of the research project. A dozen other studies were conducted within this framework. Several of the field studies have been described in both published research reports and in academic journals. The task of drawing together the results of the field experimentation awaits us.

Content examinations remain the initial entry in the necessary set of clues as to what television is about and its potential consequences for individuals and for society. To isolate effects that may be worth examining, one must find content statements that are prominent, emphatic, frequent, and seldom contradicted. An interesting counter-approach is suggesting that if something is absent from television, then that absence stamps the "thing" as without much value in society, given the judged importance of television among the American public. But here we prefer to concentrate on explicit statements found in the media, rather than more implicit abstractions.

This book offers specific details about selected aspects of television fictional program content. At the same time, it carries a larger message—it says something about the structure of television, about the writers' orientations, about the American public's preferences and tolerances, and about television's repetitiveness and susceptibility to change.

ACKNOWLEDGMENTS

The chapter authors are both faculty and student colleagues who played major roles in the conceptualization and execution of the individual subprojects.

Dr. Maizo Bryant was for three years the project officer from the Office of Child Development (now the Agency for Children, Youth, and Families) in the Department of Health, Education, and Welfare. He was a friend of the project, as well as a critic and monitor.

Dr. Charles Atkin, codirector of the project, managed other major components of Project CASTLE; I directed the content analyses.

Two colleagues did so much of the data analysis that they deserve special credit. Felipe Korzenny and Kim B. Neuendorf performed analyses well beyond the data for which they themselves were responsible or even interested. Katrina Simmons organized the first setups for the data analysis. Carlos Fernandez-Collado served as a most trusted research assistant.

Ken Zgraggen, Mike Zgraggen, and Mary Taber coordinated data collections, compiled the data archives, organized the videotaping, and performed other administrative tasks without which a large project such as this would fall under its own weight. Myles Rich became a master coder on several of the subprojects.

At Michigan State Universtiy, superb secretarial support came from Joy Mulvaney, Paula Place, Julie Dingee, Cindy Spiegel, Betty Gingas, Betty Holmer, and Michelle Torres. Nearly half of this manuscript was written while I spent a sabbatical at the East-West Center in Honolulu, in its Communication Institute. There, one superb secretary, Cherylene Hidano, produced better manuscripts than I had drafted. One month at the Annenberg School of Communication at the University of Southern California also helped significantly.

During this project, more than 100 individuals served as content coders. Some were volunteers, some were paid, some were doing it for academic credit. They spent thousands of hours watching television, rewatching it, in a dismal room, with continuous equipment noises around them, with forms, pencils, supervisors, other coders, etc. Watching television could not have been made less enjoyable. It was work for them, drudgery perhaps. Every single bit of information collected originated with them. No comprehensive record of who they were was kept. Many names have been forgotten. If one were to set up a memorial to the unknown coder, I should be the one most indebted to that effort. Rather than take the easy way and omit all the names, here are the names of coders and staff workers that the study directors could supply. Thanks to those whom we can recall, and thanks to those we have, in our ignorance, forgotten:

John Barry
Edward Bellefeuille
Fred Bosbus
Rich Brink
Nancy Buerkel-Rothfuss
Karen Cottledge
Jan Crosby
Barbara Day
Jim Day
Mary Lou Dudley
Marie Evans
Laura Frizzell
Vicky Garret
Howard Giese
David Graef
Jeff Green
Ellen Hadley
Nancy Hale
Carrie Jill Heeter
Darci Hemleb
Kim Hicks
Mary Hines
Clare Jewell
Martin Jones

Carol Keith

Chris Kesserling

Susie Kheder

Melody Lees

Sandra Mackey

Michelle McFarlin

Elizabeth Meyers

Kim Neuendorf

Denise Ott

Nicholas Palain

Karol Plachta

Lenora Proft

Myles Rich

Marcia Richards

Mary Lou Riley

Linda Rodrigues

Jesse Rosenbaum

Graham Ross

Michel Sawicki

Susan Schimmel

Helen Short

Chip Steinfield

Tina Stock

Mary Taber

Steve Vondale

Bruce Wherman

Thomas Wigton

Melanie Williams

Kevin Wilson

Bev Wood

Nora Zeagler

Ken Zgraggen

Mike Zgraggen

Then, there are the four ladies who make my personal life worthwhile and my professional life worth the effort—Dee, Beth, Shawn and Debbie. Thank you all.

B.S.G.

ABOUT THE AUTHORS

Bradley S. Greenberg is Professor of Communication and Tele-communication and Chairman of Communication at Michigan State University.

Charles K. Atkin is Professor of Communication at Michigan State University.

Pilar Baptista-Fernandez is a graduate student in Sociology at Michigan State University.

Nancy Buerkel-Rothfuss is Assistant Professor of Speech and Dramatic Arts at Central Michigan University.

Nadyne Edison is Assistant Professor of Journalism at New York University.

Carlos Fernandez-Collado is a graduate student in Sociology at Michigan State University.

David Graef is a graduate student in Communication at Michigan State University.

Laura Henderson is Assistant Professor of Communication at the University of Southern Maine.

Mary Hines is a graduate student in Counseling, Personnel Services, and Educational Psychology at Michigan State University.

Linda Hogan is a former graduate student in Communication at Michigan State University.

Felipe Korzenny is Assistant Professor of Communication at Michigan State University.

Kimberly A. Neuendorf is a graduate student in Communication at Michigan State University.

Marcia Richards is a social researcher for ABC-TV in New York City.

Katrina W. Simmons is Assistant Professor of Speech and Dramatic Arts at Central Michigan University.

LIFE ON TELEVISION
Content Analyses of U.S. TV Drama

I
PEOPLE
ON TELEVISION

1

HISPANIC-AMERICANS: THE NEW MINORITY ON TELEVISION

BRADLEY S. GREENBERG
PILAR BAPTISTA-FERNANDEZ

What images of Mexicans and Latinos do you recall from movies and from television? Parhaps you can remember a string of Westerns with Mexican bandits, all of whom wore two belts of bullets crossed over protruding bellies. These same bandits went into animation as the Frito Bandito and José Carioca. If your forte was musical comedies, you can recall Carmen Miranda shaking her bananas and assorted fruit hats, with Xavier Cugat not too distant in the background. For those inclined to romance, the Latin lover image often was reflected by Fernando Lamas and Ricardo Montalban, chasing fruitlessly after non-Latin women. Television's distinctly Hispanic lead characters included "The Cisco Kid" in the 1950s, and Desi Arnaz a half decade later. Some noteworthy movies in this period focused on the portrayal of Puerto Rican gangs in urban centers, e.g., *West Side Story,* and *Young Savages.* The 1960s included no television Hispanic-Americans of star rank; that brings us to the contemporary popular characterizations of Chico ("Chico and the Man"), Epstein ("Welcome Back Kotter"), and Ponch ("CHiPs"), others who have lasted more than a single television season are more difficult to recall.

In the 1960s, the civil rights movement focused heavily on attempts to seek equity for black Americans. The Kerner Commission report cited media portrayals and coverage of blacks as a special locus of needed attention; it called for fairer and more comprehensive coverage. This was seconded by the Federal Communications Commission and other non-black national agencies.

Less strident, but emerging during this same period, were parallel complaints from Hispanic-American groups. Actually, the first major complaint about mass media portrayals of Hispanic-Americans occurred much earlier. In the 1930s, the Mexican government banned importation of films that perpetuated the "greasy bandit" image of the Mexican (Whitney, 1978). That same portrayal prompted a state-side effort in the late 1960s when the Frito-Lay company used the Frito Bandito as the centerpiece of its advertising campaign. This character ". . . had a Spanish accent, a long handlebar mustache, a huge sombrero, a white suit tightly covering a pot belly and he used a pair of six-shooters to steal corn chips from unsuspecting victims. . . ." (U.S. Civil Rights Commission, 1977). Similar characters were used by Granny Goose, the A.J. Reynolds Tobacco Co., Frigidaire, and Arrid in their advertising (Martínez, 1968–69). Partly because of efforts by the Mexican-American Anti-Defamation Committee, the Frito-Lay commercials were banned.

One can anticipate an increasing effort from Hispanic-Americans to focus attention on their television portrayals in the 1980s. That assumes that there exists a basis similar to that offered by black civil rights groups for arguing for more portrayals, for better portrayals, and for a greater variety of them. This analysis was designed to provide preliminary information as to just how often and in what ways television has portrayed Hispanic-Americans in its entertainment programming. For our purposes, the term *Hispanic-Americans* includes Mexican-Americans, Puerto Ricans, Cubans, and other people of Latin American or Spanish origin now living in the United States.

The U.S. Census Bureau tells us, in 1978, that almost 20 million people of Hispanic origin live in the United States. By the end of the 1980s, estimates indicate that Hispanic-Americans will be the largest minority group in the United States, exceeding blacks, and will still be growing most rapidly. Increasing their current numbers by 50 percent by the start of the twenty-first century is not an uncommon estimate. How commercial television can or should accommodate to this changing population composition becomes an important question of public policy. Although part of that accommodation must be in TV employment and advertising practices, as well as marketing to a large audience subgroup, the concern here is with the content aspect and its potential social influence. In the same way that many Americans have had early, or even primary, experiences with blacks only vicariously—through television—so the opportunity exists for distinctive and lasting impressions about Hispanic-Americans to develop. Because many of the Hispanic media examples from films are quite dated, and because television is only beginning to use Hispanic characters, this is a most appropriate time and opportunity to consider emerging Hispanic-American imagery in commercial television.

Here, we are not yet concerned principally with the nature of social learning that may be accruing from television's portrayals of this ethnic subgroup. Our anticipation of a very small number of characterizations and of an even smaller number of significant characterizations tends to diminish that interest. Of course, the sheer omission or ignoring of a large minority group may itself have implications for both majority group evaluations of that minority and for the minority group's self-estimate. If being on television confers status, omission implies lower status. Nevertheless, we are at an earlier stage of inquiry. Given that we expect these portrayals to increase greatly in incidence and importance during the next decade, we wish to provide the background against which those changes may occur.

Cedric Clark suggests that the evolution of minority groups in mass media entertainment occurs in a distinct sequence (1969). Although this sequence contains some overlapping phases, the initial exclusion of the minority constitutes a first stage of *nonrecognition* or invisibility; the minority group is neither seen nor heard from very much. Then, often, an early form of visibility occurs as *ridicule,* where the minority group portrayals consist largely of buffoons, fall guys, and other objects of derision. In 1969, Clark suggested that Mexican-Americans were then in the stage where, ". . . particularly in its commercials, the medium reinforces the American stereotype of Mexicans and Mexican-Americans as lazy, dirty and socially unproductive." Today, Epstein ("Welcome Back, Kotter") might qualify. A further evolution occurs with the increasing prominence of minorities in *regulatory* roles, or roles related to legal activities. Clark conceived of these primarily as roles on the "right" side of society, where ". . . characters have some connection with an organization devoted to the maintenance of law and order. . . ." It is not far-fetched to conceive of the antithetical role type—that of lawbreaking—as one likely to accompany this stage. Thus, we believe that roles as both cops and robbers are likely to emerge concurrently. Finally, the sequence leads to what might be termed *egalitarian* roles, which Clark refers to as roles of "respect." This means that the roles given to minorities become more representative of a wider variety of statuses, occupations, and responsibilities. The minority roles blend into the fabric of media messages in both minority-related and nonminority contexts and situations. The characters develop broader dimensions and are not so differentiated from the roles given to majority ethnics. There is some strong degree of assimilation as well as of contrast.

This sequence of events is not to be taken too literally; one phase is not likely to end abruptly and the next begin. This brief review of earlier media treatment of Hispanics suggests a small overall presence and, within that minimal recognition, a focus on ridiculous and bandit characters; co-occurrence is more likely than strict sequencing.

These ideas provide a background for the quantitative and qualitative analysis of Hispanic-Americans, an analysis of the new minority on television.

METHODS

For each of three television seasons (1975–76, 1976–77, and 1977–78) a sample week of all commercial fictional television series was constructed. This yielded 255 separate episodes on videotape and 3549 television characters with speaking roles.

For this analysis, the demographic breakdown of all speaking television characters was used to isolate the characters categorized as *Hispanic-American.* All tapes of episodes containing identified Hispanic-Americans, both the prime-time (8–11 p.m.) and Saturday morning samples in all three seasons, were reviewed and analyzed. Only commercial series of fictional episodes were used, thus excluding such variety series as "Tony Orlando and Dawn," which may have featured Hispanics.

The original demographic analysis generated certain kinds of information, i.e., age, sex, occupation of the characters, program types. Other elements were added especially for this subanalysis. These included physical characteristics, goal orientations, and a descriptive synthesis of each character's role, including its importance. Since we knew from the general demographic analysis that the total number of Hispanic characters would be well under 100, this analysis was designed as a comprehensive depiction of Hispanic-Americans on television, rather than tables of information based on very small frequencies.

FINDINGS

Distribution

In this population of 3549 television characters, we found 53 different individuals who could reliably be identified as Hispanics. Thus, we begin with a very small collection of people. They constitute slightly less than 1.5 percent of the population of speaking TV characters. To some, it may seem gratuitous to do a detailed analysis of such a small group. But since the basic purpose of this analysis was to establish a sound baseline from which subsequent trends may be examined, the analysis was pursued.

First, note the relative smallness of the group by comparison with

1978 Census estimates. Then, some 12 million Hispanic-Americans were recorded, and the Census Bureau estimated that there were some 7.4 million additional "undocumented" Hispanics. The former comprises slightly less than 6 percent of the United States population and both together account for 9 percent. Thus, Hispanic-Americans are significantly underrepresented in the TV population. Furthermore, the trend has not been positive: the most recent sample week, from the 1977–78 season, yielded only 12 characters, by comparison with twenty and twenty-one in the sample weeks from two previous seasons.

Second, only two of the characters were carried in more than one of the three seasons analyzed. Chico, from "Chico and the Man," and Epstein, from "Welcome Back, Kotter," were the only Hispanic characters on shows successful enough to be renewed. As this was being written, the trend for the 1979–80 season did not appear to be any stronger for successful Hispanic characters, with only Ponch, from "CHiPs," likely to be seen again.

Third, the distribution of characters identifies a basic concentration or skewness across programs. Half the characters identified appeared on just four shows: "Quest," "Joe Forrester," "Delvecchio," and "Popi." Each of these had five or more characters. Their appearance on the first three of these was unusual in that they were not part of the regular casting. The particular episodes featured stories that centered on illegal aliens and criminal elements that would not reoccur. Any parallel sample weeks would, however, be expected to include such relatively rare episodes from other series which do not regularly feature Hispanics. The point is that large clusters of Hispanic-Americans appeared together in a small number of shows dealing with gangs or barrios. In only one of these, "Popi," would they be seen again, and not for very long there, given the early cancellation of that series. In contrast, 17 shows had a single Hispanic character, two had two, and two had three scattered through the story.

Across these three seasons, average adult viewing hovered at the three hours per day mark. Therefore, in a typical week, the average viewer might see five or six Hispanic-American characters.

Demographic and Social Characteristics

Two ethnic subgroups dominated this character array—Mexican-Americans and Puerto Ricans. There were 29 Mexican-Americans, 14 Puerto Ricans (half of them from "Popi"), 6 Mexicans, 3 Uruguayans, 1 Cuban, and 1 Spaniard. The two dominant subgroups on television do correspond to the majority subgroups in the United States Hispanic population, aside from illegal aliens.

The distribution of Hispanic-American television characters by sex was even more disproportionately male than is found in television overall. Of the 53 characters, 44 were males, a ratio of nearly 5 to 1. The typical ratio of males to females on television, documented in a dozen separate content analyses, is 3 to 1. The Hispanic-American female has been virtually nonexistent in TV fiction.

Perhaps of most interest in the demographic analysis of these characters is their occupational portrayal. A typical set of occupational categories, e.g., professional, semiprofessional, skilled, etc., is inadequate. The most common vocation among the 53 characters was that of crook. A dozen of the characters were identified as bandits, thieves, junkies, extortionists, and other sorts of criminals. Nearly an equal number—10—were cast as law enforcers, e.g., sheriff, inspector, patrolman. Thus, the most common work context in which Hispanics could be seen on television for three seasons with any consistency, was in a regulatory or anti regulatory role, either breaking the law or helping to maintain it.

For the record, the full range of legal jobs held by Hispanic-Americans excluding law-related ones in the three sample weeks were:

Animal trainer	Fireman
Bartender	Foreman
Baseball player	Handyman
Building inspector	Housewife (2)
Butcher	Mechanic (3)
Car washer	Receptionist
Chauffeur	Restaurant owner (3)
Construction worker (3)	Sailor
Doorman	Student
Farmer	Waiter

Using standard occupational classification criteria, the three restaurant owners would be placed in the highest category of "professionals and manager," where one usually expects to see doctors, lawyers, bankers, etc. The next most advanced set of jobs for Hispanics included building inspector, fireman, foreman, animal trainer, and detective.

Programming Characteristics

Next, we examined details of the programming context in which these characters appeared. It is important to note that none of the Hispanics appeared on Saturday morning shows, for largely child audiences, during either of the first two seasons in the sample; only two appeared on Saturday morning in the third season. Thus, at the times of very large child audiences, and with programming targeted for children, Hispanics could not be seen. The 51 remaining characters were divided unevenly during the evening; half of them appeared in the first of the prime-time hours, 8 to 9 p.m., the rest from 9 to 11 p.m. Thus, this group has been absent from Saturday morning and heavily concentrated in the early evening time slot.

Further, the distribution across networks has been uneven. ABC accounted for only five of the 53 characters, with CBS and NBC sharing the remainder nearly equally. Earlier studies had shown that ABC had programming with a disproportionately large share of black Americans; for this new minority, they were less inclusive.

The two primary types of television programs, aside from Saturday cartoons, are situation comedies and crime-adventure shows. Situation comedies are most frequent, usually as half-hour shows; crime-adventure shows tend to be hour-long episodes, and contain more characters per episode. Twenty-three of the characters analyzed here were found in situation comedies, and 28 in crime-adventure shows. Each character's role portrayal was assessed as essentially serious or essentially comic. The assessment placed 22 Hispanic-Americans in comic roles and 31 in serious roles. Twenty-two of the serious characterizations, however, were either as lawbreakers or as law enforcers. Thus, by subtraction, not more than 10 characters were in serious role portrayals unrelated to the legal system. There emerge from this three major role characterizations—the *funny Hispanic,* the *crooked Hispanic,* and the *Hispanic cop.*

What of *role importance,* rather than merely how many there are to be seen? Here, that means whether the character had a major, secondary, or minor role in the episode analyzed. *Major roles* were those central to the development of the story line in that particular episode. Although that may change from week to week, it is likely that regularly appearing characters in a series have major roles. In this analysis, 10 of 11 identified major roles were performed by regular characters in TV series. Capsule descriptions of those ten follow here. They provide a certain depth to the findings presented so far and add understanding of what "star" roles for Hispanics have been.

. . . *Chico Rodriguez* of "Chico and the Man": The original Chico was a tall, dark, happy-go-lucky Mexican-American in his early twenties. Working as a mechanic in a garage, with little formal education, he works hard, works well and has his primary interaction with the white, aging, griping garage owner. He is witty, jokes much of the time, and appears to have no orientation to the future, no strong aspirations. His home is his decorated van in the garage. He deals successfully with the problems of neighborhood people.

. . . *Raúl* of "Chico and the Man": This chubby pre-teen was Chico's successor in the series, an illegal alien from Mexico who crossed over in the trunk of the garage owner's car. This is the standard, overly cute and all-knowing, outspoken child star, except that his outspokenness is accompanied by a thick accent. He wants to earn money to send to his mother and to go to school in the United States. He works hard at jobs around the garage and at fibbing. He is trying to improve himself.

. . . *Hector Fuentes* from "On the Rocks": This jailhouse show featured a group of convicts and Hector was one of them. A thirty-ish Puerto Rican, with heavy accent, and seemingly ignorant, he is concerned about his family. He is verbally aggressive and full of advice to all around him.

. . . *Chano* of "Barney Miller": Part of the original group of precinct house detectives, Chano later disappeared from the group. The character was reserved, perhaps shy and somewhat lazy or at least languid. The intended character of a sporty Puerto Rican failed to develop.

. . . *Epstein* of "Welcome Back, Kotter": His mother is Puerto Rican and his father Jewish. Epstein is loud and obnoxious as a high school student interested primarily in how to get out of school. He is just hanging around without apparent ambitions or aspirations. When funny, it's typically a putdown of someone else. His major social relationships are with the rest of his classmates, the Sweathogs.

. . . *Ponch* of "CHiPs": Here is a tall, dark, handsome, youthful (late twenties or early thirties) California highway motorcycle cop. As a Mexican-American, he works hard at what he does, mingles in integrated and nonintegrated settings both professionally and socially. Ponch is a brave cop, getting into lifesaving scrapes in each episode with his Anglo-American sidekick. Ponch is a would-be lover, always chasing after beautiful women, with what seem to be normal levels of failure and success. All these behaviors enhance his deliberately macho image. He is gregarious, dedicated, community-oriented without any apparent interest in moving up in the ranks.

. . . *Popi* from the show of the same name: There were four regular major characters in this Puerto Rican family situation comedy. Abraham, the widower, holding down several jobs simultaneously to earn enough to support his youngsters and to get something better for them, was generally happy, active, and interested in educational opportunities. *Lupe,* the possible stepmother for the children, has not been married, but her own job is either unspecified or noncentral. Her goal-directed future certainly includes Popi and perhaps some higher ambitions as well. Then, there are *Junior* and *Luis,* Popi's nine-year-old and seven-year-old sons. Both are strongly attached to their father, and it may be stretching matters to consider them major roles. Certainly, the series did not last long enough for any of the characters to become memorable.

From this full set of major characters, Chico and Ponch become individual stars, with Epstein a weak third. The tragedy of Chico (Freddy Prinze) is well known, and we have yet to determine the longevity of "CHiPs." However, it is likely that the growing core of teenage and preteen fans for Ponch will continue him in central TV roles.

The eleventh major role characterization identified in the three-season sample was not of a regular character, but the portrayal of an extortionist on "Delvecchio."

Noticeable is the absence of any major female Hispanic characters, aside from Lupe. Some secondary female roles included a receptionist to "Doc," and Hector Fuentes's sister who visited him in prison. But no Hispanic-American female character has yet been portrayed on commercial television in a continuing fashion since Marcus Welby brought Consuelo to his office as a nurse-receptionist.

Let us close this analysis with a more personal qualitative summary, a kind of summing up of what you could expect to find if you had studied the portrayal of Hispanic-Americans on commercial television during this time period:

1. They're hard to find. If you watched 300 different television characters, say, you'd find less than a handful of Hispanics;

2. They're males, of dark complexion, with dark hair, most often with heavy accents. Women are absent and insignificant.

3. They're gregarious and pleasant, with strong family ties. Half work hard, half are lazy, and very few show much concern for their futures. Most have had very little education, and their jobs reflect that fact.

4. In essence, it seems that television has yet to do much with, or for, the Hispanic-American either as a television character or as a viewer. It might be improper to characterize them as invisible, but the portrayal is blurred or certainly hard to follow. To the extent that blacks felt themselves maligned by the media through the twin processes of being ignored or cast in nonfavorable roles, the same situation exists here.

This first systematic analysis of Hispanics on United States commercial television can be used by programmers to establish objectives for more comprehensive and varied inclusion of a major segment of this country's population in subsequent programming. It can be used by critics who sense shortcomings in the portrayals of Hispanics, but who have lacked adequate documentation to present their case. As for social researchers, who might wish to study the impact of Hispanic TV portrayals on either Hispanic or non-Hispanic children, it is probably premature to expect to trace consistent outcomes. The portrayals seem neither to have reached a critical mass in quantity, nor even enough outstanding instances. Perhaps it would be better to begin to project just what kinds of portrayals, in what kinds of settings and contexts, could yield the most positive social outcomes. From such projections, an agenda for regular, frequent, and substantive portrayals might be crystallized. If implemented over the next few years, accompanying social research on the impact of that programming would be appropriate and desirable.

2

THE CONTEXT, CHARACTERISTICS AND COMMUNICATION BEHAVIORS OF BLACKS ON TELEVISION

Pilar Baptista-Fernandez
Bradley S. Greenberg

The most recent and comprehensive attempt to map the portrayal of blacks on commercial television was directed by Franzwa for the US Commission on Civil Rights (1977). She commissioned a secondary analysis of data collected from 1969 through 1974 by George Gerbner and his associates in their continuing profile of violence on television. Thus, the original purposes for the data bore no relationship to a study of blacks on television, and the data's shortcomings in doing that are evident from the limited analysis that could be executed. Essentially the commission's report of that analysis verified earlier studies; these showed that blacks were on half of the TV dramas (Dominick and Greenberg, 1970), that about 10 percent of all television characters were black (Seggar, 1977), and that blacks were in less pretigious jobs, or unemployed or poorer (Northcott, Seggar, and Hinton, 1975). In new descriptions, the report indicated that blacks were younger than white TV characters, proportionately more likely to be heroes; black men were less likely to be married and equally likely to commit crimes.

Other researchers have added to this lore of information with studies that indicated that blacks were being portrayed as equally industrious, competent, and physically attractive as whites, but that blacks were more moral and kind (Hinton et al., 1974). In terms of interracial interaction, blacks were dominating whites in situation comedies in which they co-appeared, with the opposite pattern in crime dramas (Lemon, 1977).

13

The present study had three purposes:

      1. To continue to document the physical and social characteristics of the portrayal of blacks on commercial television so that trends may be examined;

      2. To expand the level of inquiry to include a comprehensive examination of the context in which blacks are portrayed,

      3. To make an initial attempt to examine the content of those portrayls in terms of the social communication interactions that occur within and between the races on television.

Here, those interactions will be examined in terms of their frequency, their content, and their major topics.

In addition, research in this area is designed to contribute to two central issues related to social learning. First, what do black viewers, particularly young ones, learn about or believe about themselves from the portrayals they see and how, if at all, does that contribute to their emerging or changing self-concept? Second, what do white viewers, again with young ones as a special focus, learn about blacks from fictional television images? A content analysis addresses these social learning issues by providing empirical evidence on what is systematically available on television that may lead to learning. Such an analysis constitutes a first necessary stage in any attempt to derive social learning effects from television content.

Previous research provides clues to the general proposition that exposure to television portrayals will produce corresponding changes in role orientations of young viewers. A majority of white youngsters with the least direct contact with blacks reported that television was their basic source of information about the physical appearance, speech, and dress of blacks (Greenberg, 1972). Black youngsters held perceptions of blacks on TV that were more positive in terms of beauty, activity, and strength than their perceptions of whites (Atkin, Greenberg, and McDermott, 1978). In another study, black youngsters said that blacks on television were more true-to life than did white children (Greenberg and Atkin, 1978).

All these findings nave been in the context of general exposure to blacks on television, without pinpointing specific programs or characters. Two studies of "Sesame Street," however, provide evidence of positive changes in racial attitude. An early field survey showed that white children who had viewed for two years were more positive toward other races (Bogatz and Ball, 1971). More recently, an experiment with white nursery school youngsters manipulated segments of that program containing nonwhite characters. One-third of those in the control group subsequently picked minority playmates from photographs; more than two-thirds of those exposed to the multiracial segments chose minority playmates (Gorn, Goldberg and Kanungo, 1976).

Thus, there is an initial assembly of modest evidence that television contributes to the socialization of both black and white youngsters, much as Bandura's general social learning propositions suggest (1977). Social learning, however, can accrue only from the available content, from the available role models. For such research to flourish more fully, one needs to document a fuller range of the content attributes which depict blacks and to collate comparable information about white portrayals.

All earlier content analyses have compared black portrayals with the full range of whites on television. In contrast, the present study compares the characteristics and behaviors of TV blacks with TV whites who appear on the same programs as those blacks, for two reasons. First, it would be well to determine whether white characters coappearing with blacks are substantially similar to white characters on shows without minority representation. Second, and more important from the social learning perspective, white characters appearing with blacks constitute an immediate, proximate reference frame. The viewer is not likely to examine characters in isolation from other characters, but by primary comparisons with adjacent images and behaviors. Similarity and contrast with concurrent characterizations should provide more precise information from which to posit possible social learning about blacks than more abstract comparisons with the totality of whites on television.

METHODS

A sample week of prime time and Saturday morning commercial television series was videotaped in the fall, 1977, excluding sports, news, specials, variety shows, and movies. The week encompassed 81 fictional series episodes, of which 43 had one or more black speaking characters. The total number of black characters on these shows was 101; the same shows had 484 white speaking characters. A random sample of 101 whites was drawn from the 484 available and used for all comparisons in this analysis.

Coding was done by three trained persons, working in pairs. When training sessions resulted in minimum reliabilities of .80 on all content variables, the formal coding began. Periodically, reliabilities were computed to reaffirm that level of agreement.

Three major sets of content variables were defined: (1) physical and social attributes; (2) programming context variables; (3) social interaction attributes.

Physical and Social Attributes. Recorded were the characters' *sex, age* (assessed to nearest year), *job* (using 13 categories for those of working age with an identifiable job), and *socioeconomic status* (lower, middle, and upper, using visible signs of affluence within the historical and/or cultural setting of each show).

In addition, coders judged the *physique* of each character, as ectomorphic (lean, skinny, or slightly built, e.g., J.J. on "Good Times"), mesomorphic (well-developed or solid musculature, e.g., "Rhoda," "Wonder Woman"), and endomorphic (characterized by prominence of the abdomen or other soft body parts, e.g., Archie Bunker, Lou Grant); the predominant *clothing style* of the characters, as flashy, casual, conservative, in uniform, or in costume;[1] whether the character was primarily in a *serious* or *comic* role; and whether the character was predominantly a *good* or *bad* person on that episode.[2]

Programming Context Variables. In this category, coders recorded the *duration* of the show (30 minutes or longer); the *time of day* the show was telecast (8–9 p.m., after 9 p.m., Saturday morning); the *network* originating the show; the *program type* (situation comedy, crime, action-adventure, family drama, Saturday morning cartoon, Saturday morning noncartoon).

In addition, coders recorded the racial composition of each show, i.e., for each black and white character, the frequency of other black and white characters appearing on each show was identified.

Social Interaction Attributes. Here were coded the ethnicity of each participant in communicative interactions, the topics of conversations. An *interaction* began with something being said between one or more of the sample characters and ended when one of the characters left the scene, or a new character entered; then the ethnic composition of that current interaction was newly recorded. Six *topics of conversation* were coded: love, courtship, and sexual relationships; domestic matters, exclusive of sexually intimate issues; business matters; crime; race-related issues; and public affairs, exclusive of any which fell into the prior categories. The *content* of the conversations was analyzed for seven behaviors: giving, seeking, and receiving advice; giving and receiving orders; and giving and seeking information.

RESULTS

The depiction of blacks on commercial television was analyzed in terms of their physical and social characteristics, the programming context in which they were portrayed, and their patterns of

---

[1]*Flashy dressers* wore clothes of colors that did not contrast, or that conflicted, and unconventional accessories; *casual clothes* were jeans, slacks, sweaters; *conservative* included suits, sport coats; *uniforms* included sports, military, hospital, and restaurant uniforms; *costumes* were from another era or location, e.g., space clothes, Egyptian garb.

[2]For these last two variables, a mixed category was included.

social interaction. Comparisons were made with an equal-size sample of white TV characters drawn from the set of 43 shows which included black characters.

Physical and Social Characteristics. This analysis permits the following conclusions:

1. The typical black character was substantially younger. Blacks averaged 28 years of age in their portrayals; whites averaged 34.5 ($p < .05$). A three-way age breakdown of the entire pool of characters located 62 percent of the Black characters and 38 percent of the white characters in the youngest age category (under 23).[3]

2. Blacks were less likely to have an identifiable job (50 percent vs. 33 percent); whites were more likely to be professionals, administrators and managers (25 percent vs. 10 percent, $p < .01$).

3. The job differences carried over into general socio-economic status assessments. Using three SES levels, blacks comprised 75 percent of the lowest level and 22 percent of the upper; whites were the complementary proportion at each level ($p < .001$). This large SES difference existed within each major age subgroup.

4. Two-thirds of the blacks and three-fourths of the whites were males, a difference that was not statistically significant.

5. Assessment of physiques identified blacks as more likely to be ectomorphic (69 percent), with equivalent distributions of mesomorphs and endomorphs ($p < .05$). This was especially so among young adults.

6. Blacks and whites also differed in dress. Whites constituted 61 percent of the conservative dressers and 68 percent of those in costumes; Blacks comprised 79 percent of the "flashy" dressers ($p < .01$). When age was controlled, these differences diminished, indicating that age was a more important determinant of dress style than race.

7. Only one black character was judged a "bad" person, compared to 14 whites ($p < .001$); the two races had equal proportions of "good" and "mixed" characters.

8. Blacks were 42 percent of the serious characters, but 71 percent of the partly or wholly comical characters ($p < .001$), especially among the youngest television character portrayals.

Programming Context. The analysis of programming and scheduling variables permits the following conclusions:

1. Large racial differences existed in type of show. Nearly half the blacks were cast in situation comedies, and an additional one-fifth in Saturday cartoons; one-third of the whites had roles in crime shows, one-fifth in action-adventure stories, and one-fifth in situation comedies ($p < .001$). This disparity occurred although equivalent proportions (57 percent to 64 percent) of all major program types, save one (Saturday cartoons, 33 percent) had at least one black

---

[3]Given this difference in average age, and its potential influence on other content variables, e.g., physical appearance or SES, subsequent analyses that indicated racial differences were accompanied by age breakdowns to determine whether race or age accounted for the difference. Three age groups were used, as nearly equivalent in overall size as the distribution permitted: 4–22 ($n = 63$), labeled *young people;* 23–36 ($n = 61$), labeled *young adults;* and 37 and over ($n = 70$), labeled *adults.*

character. Thus, although a majority of all shows had some blacks, they were located far more frequently on certain types of shows than others.

2. The intense concentration of black characters among other blacks is partly identified in Table 2.1. Forty-one percent of the blacks and none of the whites appeared in shows with four or more other black characters. Table 2.1a demonstrates a clear bimodal distribution of black characters, either as a single black in a program, or as part of an extensive group. Six among the 43 shows with black characters contained 41 percent of all the black characters identified in the sample week ("Fat Albert," "Good Times," "Muhammed Ali," "Sanford Arms," "The Jeffersons," and "What's Happening"). Table 2.1b shows the direct contrast: 41 percent of the blacks were in shows without any white characters; three-fourths of the white characters were on shows with a dozen or more whites. These findings did not vary within different age groups.

3. Of the Saturday morning characters, 61 percent were black; of the 9–11 p.m. characters, 61 percent were white ($p < .01$).

4. Blacks were disproportionately overrepresented on half-hour shows (75 percent) and underrepresented on longer shows (31 percent), ($p < .01$).

5. The distribution of black and white characters did not differ by commercial network.

TABLE 2.1
Racial Context of Ethnic Portrayals

1a. Appearance with Black Characters

	Blacks (%)	Whites (%)
Other Blacks		
1–2	43	90
3–4	16	10
> 4	41	0
	($X^2 = 58.9$, df = 2, $p < .001$)	

1b. Appearance with White Characters

	Blacks (%)	Whites (%)
Other Whites		
0	41	0
1–10	31	26
11–20	14	41
> 20	14	33
	($X^2 = 61.04$, df = 3, $p < .001$)	

Social Interaction. This analysis focused on the frequency and content of social interactions between and within the races. The major results were as follows:

1. Inasmuch as the sample of white characters and the census of black characters were imbedded among nearly 400 additional white characters, it is not surprising that whites averaged 7.6 conversations or social interactions with other whites, whereas blacks averaged 2.9 separate interactions with other blacks ($p < .001$), and this was so, in all age groups. As for cross-race interactions, blacks averaged three interactions with whites for every one that whites had with blacks ($p < .001$).

2. Table 2.2 identifies the frequency of occurrence of various topics of conversation among these characters. Domestic issues dominated; business matters were discussed heavily; racial discussions were very infrequent. Whites were more likely to discuss crime and business issues than blacks ($p < .05$); although the black rates were higher for all other topics of conversation coded, none was significantly larger.

TABLE 2.2
Topics of Conversation (rate per person)

Topics	(f)	Black rate	White rate	(p)
1. Domestic matters	(366)	1.80	1.70	n.s.
2. Business	(196)	.72	1.20	< .05
3. Crime	(71)	.22	.47	< .05
4. Love and courtship	(61)	.40	.19	n.s.
5. Public issues	(59)	.45	.12	n.s.
6. Racial issues	(30)	.20	.08	n.s.

3. The final analysis examined the kinds of content interaction among the participants, in terms of giving, seeking, or receiving advice, information, or orders. For all eight content variables examined, the results were the same—no significant difference between black and white characters on any of these content characteristics, and no uniform trend across the variables.

DISCUSSION

A brief mapping of these findings seems in order before discussing them. First, observed differences between blacks and whites on the same shows paralleled earlier comparisons of televised blacks with the larger set of all whites on television. In other words, whites look alike in whatever racial context they appear.

Visually, blacks on television were found to be younger, leaner, funner, and flashier. Economically, they were poorer, jobless or in jobs below the top echelons. There was an avoidance of portraying them as villains. The distribution of male and female blacks was similar to that of whites.

There was maximum inclusion of blacks in situation comedies and thus in half-hour shows. Furthermore, the distribution of blacks was heavily skewed—about half of all those found in a sample week were in virtually all-black shows, with the remainder spread out one to a show, in tokenlike fashion.

This initial examination of their social interactions showed that the content of the conversations by race did not differ, in terms of giving or receiving advice, information, or orders. Whites talked to other whites on this subset of shows with black characters at a rate (7.6 per person) more than twice that of any other racial combination. Conversations among blacks occurred at the same rate (3 per person) as black characters' conversations with whites, whereas the average number of conversations that whites had with blacks was less than one. In subsequent research, we would merge these two sets of data and compare the content of same-race interactions with those of cross-race conversations. Finally, differences in topics of conversations—whites were more likely to discuss business and crime matters—perhaps stemmed from differences in distribution of the races by type of program.

These findings can be interpreted in several ways in order, subsequently, to study the impact of these portrayals on viewers. Black youngsters may see an imagery of desirable physical attributes but be disenchanted with the continuing low status features. White youngsters may learn to perceive blacks as buffoons who, by and large, stick to themselves, or else get lost in a white crowd. Or perhaps both sets of youngsters may be impressed by the equity in verbal exchanges, giving and getting as many orders, giving and getting as much advice. Even more subtle would be the lesson that blacks interact as much with whites as they do with each other. These possibilities cannot be resolved from the present data, but the data identify critical questions for research.

An important design change can be advocated for further research in this area if the primary goal continues to be the focus on possible social learning from observing televised blacks. About half the black characters, and an equivalent proportion of whites, were identified as major characters. It is proposed that major characters are far more likely to serve as role models than a transient panorama of minor characters, seen once or perhaps twice. Rather than document the characterization of all blacks on television, we would argue for more intensive analysis of that subset of 20–30 black characters appearing in regular, weekly, major roles. Examination of these characters during a longer period, rather than analysis of a single episode, should yield more definitive information about characters likely to be evaluated and emulated by both races of viewers. Further, it is possible to reduce the set of shows for analysis even further; preliminary determination of which shows are heavily watched by black and white youngsters could lead to an even more precise content-analytic focus on those shows most likely to have impacts because they are watched regularly. Why divert analytic effort to major and minor characters who go unwatched?

Absent from the present study, and particularly germane to the study of blacks on television, are those very special instances when television provides a strong dose of racial content, within the entertainment format, but outside of the weekly series. Surely, "critical instances" of viewing such programs as "Roots," or "The Autobiography of Miss Jane Pittman," can leave strong and lasting impressions on young minds. Yet, the evidence for that is minimal. The balancing of race role information from weekly, regurgative images with the occasional spectacular presentation must also be assessed.

It is curious that the overall population of blacks on television remains so stable at the 10 percent level, a figure reached nearly a decade ago with trivial variation since. That level came about after the Kerner Commission's lament about the representation of blacks in the media. Perhaps a built-in sensor (or censor?) system stipulated that when blacks achieved parity with their census proportion, that would be sufficient to deal with critics. Perhaps it was decided that the most palatable way to portray blacks for a largely white audience would be as young and funny, rather than as adults with serious goals. Indeed, there is a substantial number of blacks on television, but if you don't choose to watch them in shows in which there are whole families of blacks, they may go unnoticed in most other shows. More than 30 years ago, Berelson and Salter (1946) provided this still timely comment:

> Minority problems in the United States are serious and deep-rooted. They will not be solved alone by symbols, but symbols might help.

3

TRENDS IN THE PORTRAYAL OF THE ELDERLY

BRADLEY S. GREENBERG
FELIPE KORZENNY
CHARLES K. ATKIN

Concerns about the role of the mass media in the lives of the aging have been expressed in a number of ways in recent years. These concerns have related to the amount of time older people spend with the media, particularly television, their media content preferences, the impact of the media on their attitudes, knowledge levels and behaviors, and the means by which the media could be used to improve the delivery of information services to older people (Atkin, 1976). Another major concern, and the focus of this investigation, is with how older people are portrayed on television programs.

Careful content analyses of the quantity and quality of portrayal of older persons on television entertainment programs are essential if one wishes to study whether those portrayals have important impacts on viewers. Hunches or hypotheses about possible impacts are best preceded by thorough examination of the values, themes, and emphases of the content available to be viewed. Possible impacts of commercial television can be articulated for two primary viewing groups—the aging themselves and young audience members. For example, if the television portrayls are stereotyped or deviant from real-life information, older viewers seeing such presentations may derive implications for their own self-images, for norms regarding appropriate social behavior for themselves

The original version of this article appeared under the title, "The Portrayal of the Aging: Trends on Commercial Television," by Bradley S. Greenberg, Felipe Korzenny, and Charles K. Atkin, published in *Research on Aging*, Vol. 1 No. 3 (Sept. 1979) pp. 319–334 and is reprinted herewith by permission of the publisher, Sage Publications, Inc.

or for expectations about the realities of old age. For young viewers, particularly children, who have had few experiences with older people, mass media portrayals may be significant in influencing their orientations toward the aged. Such messages may influence their notions of how older people think, talk, behave, and act toward others, and in turn their own actions toward older people may be affected. All such possible effects of the portrayal of older people on television hinge on identifying significant content emphases.

The most frequent research on the media and the aging does not deal with content portrayals; it deals with patterns of media exposure (Atkin, 1976). The abundant content analyses of mass media messages provide very few which have separated out the findings in terms of the age of the characters. And when television content in particular is of interest, the relevant studies dwindle further, as do the substantive findings of those studies.

Aronoff (1974) analyzed video tapes from network TV drama, sampled from 1969–71. The "elderly" (no ages specified) comprised 5 percent of the male characters and 5 percent of the female characters in the total pool of 2741 TV characters. Compared to younger age groups, elderly males were more likely to be characterized as "bad guys" and less likely as "good guys"; elderly females were cast more frequently as failures than as successes. Aronoff concluded, "In a world of generally positive portrayals and happy endings, only 40 percent of older male and even fewer female characters are seen as successful, happy and good."

Petersen (1973) sampled 30 commercial network half-hours between 8 and 11 p.m. in 1972. She counted as old people those whose real-life age was at least 65 and those playing roles judged by an observer to be at least 65. In all, she located 32 old people, three of whom were women. Old people comprised 13 percent of that TV population, substantially discrepant from the Arnoff study, but based on a much smaller sample. Petersen hypothesized that the image of old people would be distinctly unfavorable. She had observers rate the characters on 21 bipolar, seven-point adjective scales, e.g., friendly-unfriendly, high-status–low status, smart-stupid. Overall, 18 percent of the ratings were negative, 23 percent were neutral, and 59 percent were positive. She provided no evidence about these ratings for other age groups of characters, precluding a comparative analysis of whether old people were portrayed as better or worse than anyone else.

Francher (1973) assessed a sample of 100 television commercials for their age content, and found only two commercials with any older characters. Further, a majority of the commercial messages focused on youth, youthful appearance, or the energy to act youthful.

This paucity of research on the portrayal of the aging on television, the limited examination of personal characteristics, the even more limited examination of manifest social behaviors, and the dependence on observer ratings signify a need for more thorough analysis over time. This study attempts to serve that need, as a precursor for studies of the impact of such portrayals on audience groups.

METHODS

Each season, the coding team consisted of four to six persons. Supervised training of all coders in multi-hour practice sessions was followed by independent viewing and coding of a fixed subsample of shows. After inter-coder reliability of at least .80 was attained for the demographic and program variables reported in this chapter, independent viewing and coding of the sampled shows began.

Each speaking character in each series was in the analytic framework. For the three years, the numbers of characters coded were 1212, 1120, and 1217, successively.

The critical variable of *age* was created by coder assessment of age to the nearest full year. Other manifest attributes coded included:

1. *Gender;*
2. *Ethnic identity,* coded as Native American, Asian, Black, Spanish, and other White, for United States characters;
3. *Program time,* subdivided among Saturday morning shows, those on from 8–9 p.m., and those on from 9–11 p.m.;
4. *Program types,* including situation comedies, crime shows, Saturday cartoons, Saturday noncartoons, family dramas, medical dramas, and adventure series;
5. Whether the character's portrayal was a *regular role* in the series, or a *guest role;*
6. Whether the character was identified as a *lawbreaker* in the episode;
7. *Social class.*[1]

In addition, a subset of the social behaviors performed by these characters was also coded and analyzed. This coding was done by different coding teams undergoing lengthy and intensive training to achieve acceptable levels of inter-coder reliability. Subsequently, the data set from the demographics coding was merged with the data set from the

---

[1]Social class was coded from occupational information in the shows. Four SES groups were constructed: upper SES, based on professional jobs; upper-middle SES, based on managerial jobs; lower-middle based on jobs in sales and crafts, or as operatives and service workers, including police and firemen; and lower, based on jobs as private household workers and laborers.

social behaviors coding. From among a larger set of *positive social behaviors* coded, two will be illustrated here because of their relevance to consideration of portrayals of the aging. These were acts of *altruism,* operationally defined as instances of helping, sharing, and cooperating with others in nonillicit situations, and acts of *affection,* in the form of overt display or offer of positive emotions toward people or animals either physically or verbally, e.g., hugging, kissing, holding hands, and statements of affection. From among a larger set of *negative social behaviors,* two will be presented here because they occurred often enough to enable elaborated analysis. These were acts of *physical aggression,* operationally defined as overt behaviors intended to or resulting in fright, injury, or damage to oneself, another person, an animal, or physical property, and acts of *verbal aggression,* heard as messages of rejection, verbal threat, or hostility toward another person.

RESULTS

The purpose of the analyses was to provide social profile and social behavior information about the portrayal of the aging on commercial television.

Table 3.1 presents the distribution of fictional television characters by major age groups, for each of three seasons, and presents census data for these same age groups, as a point of comparison. The two ends of the age range—children and the elderly—were most noticeably lacking, compared to their presence in the census population. Clearly, in these three seasons, persons in the 65+ age group have not been increasingly visible on television; of more than 3500 characters analyzed across the three years, barely 100 were in this age bracket, or approximately 3 percent.

In contrast, the television world is overpopulated by those in the

TABLE 3.1
Age Distribution of TV Characters for Three Seasons

		(%) 1975–76	*(%) 1976–77*	*(%) 1977–78*	*(%) 1970 Census*
Age:	0–12	4	4	5	(29)*
	13–19	8	10	15	(9)
	20–34	31	33	32	(20)
	35–49	37	39	32	(17)
	50–64	17	11	14	(15)
	65+	4	3	2	(10)
		(*n* = 1212)	(*n* = 1120)	(*n* = 1217)	

*The first two census age categories are 0–14, and 15–19.

20–34 and 35–49 age brackets, constituting two-thirds of all TV characters, but only a little more than one-third of the census population. The only change trend in the composition of the TV population across the three seasons was a consistent increase in the frequency of portraying teenagers. Older adults, the 50–64 group, were reflected on television proportionately to their representation in the population.

For the remaining analyses, two seasons of data were used with three age regroupings. Those 50–59 and those 60 and over were grouped as separate age categories. This was necessary because the frequency of those 65 and over, by itself, was insufficient for the elaborated analyses done. Those under 20 years of age also were combined.

Table 3.2 indicates when viewers could view programs with the different age groups of television characters. Young characters, under 20, were predominantly found on Saturday morning and in the early evening. For all other age groups, a majority were located in the 9–11 p.m. time slot during the second season analyzed; this was essentially so in the 1975–76 shows as well.

By time of program, the most prominent shifts occurred in the two oldest age categories. Larger percentages of the older characters appeared on Saturday morning during the second season, and larger percentages of those same characters appeared later at night. Significantly fewer of the older adults were found from 8–9 p.m.

Three of the standard program type categories for fictional television series—situation comedies, crime shows, and Saturday cartoons—contained more than 70 percent of the programming hours, 80 percent in the 1975–76 sample, and 72 percent in the 1976–77 and 1977–78 samples. They also contained more than 70 percent of all characters. Table 3.3 identifies the age distribution in these three series types.

One noteworthy difference among program types was the lesser

TABLE 3.2
Program Time by Age of TV Characters for Two Seasons

| | | Saturday Morning | | 8–9 p.m. | | 9–11 p.m. | |
		(%) 75–76	(%) 76–77	(%) 75–76	(%) 76–77	(%) 75–76	(%) 76–77
Age:	< 20	40*	54	44	30	15	16
	20–34	11	9	37	33	52	59
	35–49	18	14	32	29	49	57
	50–59	11	20	35	18	54	62
	60+	16	20	43	27	41	53

*This entry means that 40 percent of those under 20 were located in Saturday morning shows in the 1975–76 programs.

TABLE 3.3
Major Program Types by Age of TV Characters

Age:		Situation Comedies (%) 75–76	(%) 76–77	Crime Shows (%) 75–76	(%) 76–77	Cartoons (%) 75–76	(%) 76–77
	< 20	26	27	20	3	25	19
	20–34	28	28	47	41	8	4
	35–49	21	25	50	41	13	10
	50–59	21	24	52	37	8	7
	60+	36	33	44	29	7	10

representation of young people, under 20, in crime shows and their overrepresentation in cartoons, during both seasons. During the second season, this age group was virtually absent from crime shows.

The older age groups were also located differentially by program type. First, the 60-and-over characters were more often found in situation comedies than any other age group. Second—although all age groups dropped in representation in crime shows during the second season because fewer crime shows were broadcast—the two oldest age groups decreased in crime shows by 15 percent compared with 7 percent in the 20–34 and 35–49 age groups. In summary, the oldest characters on television were found in equivalent proportions in situation comedies and crime shows; all other adults were found primarily on crime shows.

Table 3.4 provides information about other attributes of these age groups, primarily in terms of demographic and role characteristics. They further describe whether the elderly were portrayed similarly or differently from other major groups. In terms of ethnic identification, older and younger adults were similarly portrayed, averaging more than 80 percent white characters. Only children deviated significantly in both seasons; nonwhites were more likely to be children or teenagers than any other age group.

TABLE 3.4
Selected Attributes of TV Characters by Age

Age	< 20	20–34	35–49	50–59	60+
1. White	74/68*	79/81	84/81	90/89	88/82
2. Female	34/39	41/43	22/19	14/19	17/29
3. Regular role	70/68	43/42	34/33	29/38	30/39
4. Lawbreaker	5/5	11/16	12/14	8/8	6/6
5. a. Upper class	**	44/31	31/34	39/32	36/25
b. Lower class	**	18/15	20/10	15/9	19/21

*The lefthand figure in each pair is for 1975–76; the righthand figure is for 1976–77.

**Too few in this age group had jobs to warrant computation.

As for the sex of the characters, across all of television, 26 percent of the characters were female in 1975–76 and 29 percent in 1976–77. In the former season, the two oldest age groups were even more heavily male-biased than the overall level, but the discrepancy was largely dissipated in the second season; larger proportions of the older characters were women, particularly in the over-60 group. Nevertheless, television's portrayal of the elderly remained distinctly male; only the two youngest age groups displayed females in less than a three-to-one male proportion.

The second season indicated greater parity for the older age groups in terms of regular appearances in TV series. Both older groups increased their representation in regular roles to levels equivalent to other TV adults. There were a third more regular roles among the older characters in the second season analyzed.

Young adults were twice as likely to be lawbreakers (14 percent) as the older adults (7 percent), with no major differences between the two seasons.

The final demographic characteristic in Table 3.4 was an assessment of social class, with information about portrayals as upper-and lower-class characters. The results changed only for the 60-and-over group between the two years: In year 1, upper-class characterizations predominated over lower-class ones by 2:1 to 4:1 margins for all age groups. This continued in year 2 for all age groups save those 60 and over, where the proportions of upper-class and lower-class characters were nearly equal. Thus, television's portrayal of the aging moved in the direction of portraying them as poorer than other age groups.

The final two analyses focused on the social behaviors of television characters. Each character was capable of initiating or receiving social behaviors, and the analyses maintained this distinction. Table 3.5 identifies two positive social behaviors—affection and altruism—as they occurred in roles either as agents or targets of these behaviors. The tabled data also indicate both the average rate of occurrence of these behaviors per character and the proportion in each group who performed *none* of each behavior.

Most noteworthy in Table 3.5 was the absence of any strong systematic differences among the age groups in terms of displaying or receiving either affection or altruism. The sharpest difference was among those in their 50s, a greater proportion of whom were less likely to be targets of altruisitic behavior, in both seasons. Similarly, they were least likely to initiate acts of altruism. Those 60 and over, however, were equivalent to the younger groups in giving and receiving these behaviors.

TABLE 3.5
Positive Social Behaviors by Age of TV Characters

	< 20	20–34	35–49	50–59	60+
I. As Agent					
A. Altruism					
1. Rate	.8/.8	.8/.6	.7/.5	.6/.5	.8/.5
2. Percent doing none	58/61	63/69	62/70	69/72	61/65
B. Affection					
1. Rate	.3/.3	.5/.4	.5/.3	.4/.5	.2/.4
2. Percent doing none	82/82	77/76	81/84	83/78	81/74
II. As Target					
A. Altruism					
1. Rate	.7/.7	.7/.5	.7/.4	.6/.3	.8/.6
2. Percent receiving none	72/72	71/73	75/79	79/86	69/71
B. Affection					
1. Rate	.5/.4	.5/.5	.4/.3	.4/.4	.4/.4
2. Percent receiving none	70/80	77/76	84/86	82/83	77/82

A parallel analysis for negative social behaviors is in Table 3.6. There was a sharp distinction in the commission of acts of physical aggression, with the two oldest age groups much less likely to perform any such acts and to perform them at a lesser rate. But the older age groups were equally likely to be targets of physically aggressive acts on television. In contrast, during both seasons, the older TV characters were more likely to be engaged in verbally aggressive situations than younger age groups: Those 50–59 and 60 and over, particularly, were more likely to be agents of verbal aggression.

TABLE 3.6
Negative Social Behaviors by Age of TV Characters

	< 20	20–34	35–49	50–59	60+
I. As Agent					
A. Physical Aggression					
1. Rate	.6/.5	.6/.7	.7/.7	.6/.3	.2/.3
2. Percent doing none	74/75	76/72	74/73	81/84	86/88
B. Verbal Aggression					
1. Rate	1.3/.8	1.0/.9	1.4/1.1	1.9/1.3	1.7/1.3
2. Percent doing none	51/64	58/64	51/65	57/71	56/63
II. As Target					
A. Physical Aggression					
1. Rate	.7/.4	.5/.6	.6/.4	.4/.3	.4/.3
2. Percent receiving none	69/78	78/72	75/80	85/82	78/80
B. Verbal Aggression					
1. Rate	1.2/.8	1.2/.9	1.3/.9	1.5/1.1	1.2/.9
2. Percent receiving none	52/60	56/64	53/68	54/69	61/59

SUMMARY

The portrayal of the elderly as fictional television characters, during the 1975–76 and 1976–77 seasons, had these primary attributes:

. . . a very small number of characters in the 65-and-over group, averaging about 3 percent of all characters, with no trend of an increase;

. . . an increasing distribution of older characters into Saturday morning and late evening programs;

. . . a disproportionately high placement of older characters in situation comedies;

. . . a distinctly male bias in portrayal of the elderly;

. . . increased casting into regular, rather than guest roles;

. . . increasing representation of the elderly in lower-class portrayals;

. . . the giving and getting of acts of altruism and affection at rates equivalent to other age groups;

. . . the commission of acts of physical aggression at lower rates, while equally likely to be the targets of such acts,

. . . the commission of acts of verbal aggression at higher rates than other age groups.

DISCUSSION

These findings provide a basis for considering whether the portrayal of the aging in television fiction can stimulate social learning about them. Although a definitive answer depends on field and/or experimental studies directly addressed to that question, these results suggest key issues to examine.

Most striking is the paucity of total portrayals of older people. From 1975 to 1977, the elderly were portrayed in no greater numbers than Aronoff found from 1969 to 1971 (Aronoff, 1974). In a given week of prime-time and Saturday morning television, in any of three recent seasons, one could find perhaps 30–50 representations of older people, among more than 1200 total characters. Since that figure comes from competing program hours, a viewer may be exposed to perhaps half a dozen old people in a week's viewing. Although what constitutes a "critical mass" of exposure experiences for purposes of social learning is not known, this level may be inadequate. Furthermore, one can argue that regular portrayals, repeated weekly, would be more important for potential social learning to occur. Over time, viewers can come to identify with a character, learn his or her strengths and frailties. About one-third of the TV elderly each season had regular roles, or about a dozen characters in all. With such limited opportunity, a single viewer was likely to be watching no more than two or three old people in regular TV roles throughout the season.

For the three seasons examined, these characters included classical crotchety old men, such as the old man in "Chico and the Man," and Fred Sanford of "Sanford and Son," kindly grandparents on "The Waltons," and such action-oriented men, as Rockford's father and Barnaby Jones. These examples, with but a single female, point out that regular roles for older women were nearly nil during the three seasons examined, something not so apparent in the results section. The paucity of older women in regular roles on TV could distort perceptions of reality. It is possible that young viewers, for example, would seriously err in estimating the relative incidence or distribution of older men and women in society, based on their television experiences.

Nevertheless, the limited portrayal of older people in regular roles suggests that social learning researchers might more appropriately focus on exposure to regularly appearing characters, rather than be concerned with the full mass of portrayals of the elderly. This would argue for seeking out the "critical instances" of television exposure to older characters, including precise examination of viewing patterns of those specific shows which regularly feature older persons, and those few special programs, e.g., "The Autobiography of Miss Jane Pittman," which give special emphasis to them. From those specific characters to which the viewer is regularly exposed, one would posit different outcomes in terms of orientations toward the elderly. Fans of Barnaby Jones should develop different impressions than fans of "Soap," with its senile old soldier. Useful experimentation could be done comparing the same actor in very different portrayals, e.g., Jack Albertson in his role as "Grandpa Goes to Washington," vs. his role in "Chico and the Man," or Buddy Ebsen as "Barnaby Jones," vs. his role in reruns of "The Beverly Hillbillies."

Our findings, and those in earlier studies cited, do not identify the portrayal of older people on television as uniformly or predominantly negative. They perform positive social acts of altruism and affection and receive those acts, similarly to other age groups. They are less physically aggressive and more verbally aggressive; they are represented in varied social classes and across the major program types. Thus, the comparatively few messages available are mixed in evaluation, reemphasizing the need to examine more closely specific characterizations on the more popular shows over time.

Finally, the present evidence shows that TV characters in their 50s more closely correspond in attributes and behaviors to older characters than to younger ones. This may well indicate the television writer's orientation to that age group. It also suggests that parallel research be conducted among young viewers to determine what cues they use in assessing a person's or a television character's age. The young viewer may merge several age categories into the concept of "old." Perhaps the focus should be less on chronological age categories of television characters, as assigned by research workers, and more on empirically derived groupings of characters, among specific audiences of interest. If Maude, Archie Bunker, George Jefferson, and Lou Grant are perceived to be "old" by young viewers, then those characters become part of the content panorama to be examined for social learning purposes. Arbitrarily defining old people by age or other physical indicators, may be inadequate to isolate and study the relevant portrayals which trigger impressions, attitudes, and information about older people.

4

THE DEMOGRAPHY
OF FICTIONAL TV CHARACTERS

BRADLEY S. GREENBERG
KATRINA W. SIMMONS
LINDA HOGAN
CHARLES K. ATKIN

How are people portrayed in fictional television stories? Prior studies investigating such characteristics as ethnicity, occupations, sex roles, and age have verified that TV characters are systematically different from their counterparts in the general population. For example, a chronology of research on the portrayal of blacks on commercial television could begin with Clark's report (1969) that "all black characters had some connection with maintenance of law and order." Dominick and Greenberg (1970) reported an increase in minority roles on programs over three seasons but still a smaller proportion of black characters than blacks in the general population. Seggar and Wheeler (1973) found that minority roles were overrepresented in lower-status positions and in brief appearances of less than three minutes. Gerbner *et al.* (1976) reported proportions of nonwhite major characters that ranged from 23 percent (in 1967–68) to 5 percent (in 1971), with a trend approaching 13 percent over the eight-year study. More recently, Simmons *et al.* (1977) analyzing the 1975–76 seasons, found the sheer incidence of blacks on TV equivalent to their proportion in the population, but their role portrayals confined to a narrow band of program types—not the crime shows that Clark identified eight years earlier, but to situation comedies. Other minorities, e.g., Spanish-Americans, remain virtually absent from the screen.

The original version of this article appeared under the title, "Three Seasons of TV Characters," published in *Journal of Broadcasting*, copyright, 1980 by the Broadcast Education Association.

A parallel synthesis could be made for research examining portrayal of the sexes on television. Although women comprise slightly more than half the general population, they have represented a much smaller proportion of the population of television characters on prime-time television. Studies in the early 1950s by Symthe (1954) and Head (1954) reported up to twice as many men as women. Levinson (1973), Long and Simon (1974), and McArthur and Resko (1976) all documented the disproportionate quantity of males on television, and the US Commission on Civil Rights (1977) recently reported that women comprise less than one-fourth (23%) of all major characters. Further, these same studies demonstrated that roles played by female characters generally have been younger than their male counterparts, better-groomed, and more physically attractive. Female roles have had a more limited scope than male roles; Levinson (1973) and Long and Simon (1974) reported that the status of women was primarily defined in terms of their relationships to males. McArthur and Resko (1976) determined that women's roles in television commercials were as consumers, males held roles as authorities, even for products primarily used by women.

Fewer studies have focused on occupational or age characteristics, but the major trends from such studies support similar conclusions, despite differences in program samples, time frames, and different coding schemes across a wide span of television years. The characterizations show the important people on television as predominantly male, white, unmarried, upper-middle class, and in an age range from 20–40 years.

So why another study of similar characteristics? First, few studies have done a comprehensive analysis of major demographic characteristics. They typically choose this characteristic or that, but not a broad set. By concurrently analyzing a fuller range of such characteristics, it is possible to look for interactions among the characteristics. Second, the networks claim that they are making significant efforts in their portrayals of women, of minorities, and of the aged. Verification of these claims is possible using recent data, comprehensively collected. Third, by using virtually the same coding scheme and procedures for three consecutive years, we can make more precise and reliable trend comprisons. This is far more rigorous than comparing a single study with prior studies that used alternative procedures. Fourth, by adding certain other attributes and program information to the demographic information, one can make a more complete mosaic of these portrayals. For example, knowing whether a character's role was regular or as a guest, and on what type of program he/she appeared, usefully supplements demographic descriptions. Fifth, the present effort is related to concerns with what kinds of role images are available to be learned from television. If there is a conspicuous absence of one race, or the conspicuous presence of one sex in occupational groupings, or the regular confinement of some group by program type, then the projection is that viewers may develop values and beliefs about such groups that are consonant with the TV portrayals. As a prerequisite for determining whether learning and acceptance of TV's character emphases occur among young viewers, it first is imperative to document exactly what portrayals are consistently available to be learned.

This study describes the demographic composition of TV's fictional population.

Character Attributes

Each speaking character was identified in the demographic analysis. In 1975–76, 1212 characters were coded; 1120 in 1967–77; and 1217 in 1977–78. The coders identified each *speaking character* by name or by description, in order of speaking appearance on the show. *Gender* was specified and the character's *age* in years was estimated to the nearest full year. *Ethnic identity* for United States characters was coded as Native American, Asian, Black, Spanish, and other White.

Occupation was recorded as specifically as possible. After all shows were coded, occupations were assigned numerical codes developed from the United States Census Codes by the Institute for Social Research at the University of Michigan. The occupation codes were organized into 13 major classifications, ranging from "professional, technical and related workers," to "laborers." Eight of these categories were retained in this analysis; the remainder occurred among less than 1 percent of the characters. An additional category (lawbreaker) was added to account for the characters whose only occupation in a show was judged to be outside the law, e.g., prostitute, bandit, or robber. Finally, the character was identified as having a *regular* or a *guest role* in the series.

Program Types

Each evening show was classified according to type of program. During the first season analyzed, the types were family drama, medical drama, situation comedy, and action/crime. Saturday morning shows were divided into "cartoon" shows and "noncartoon" shows.

A *family drama* was a show primarily concerned with a serious presentation of problems within the context of a family, e.g., "Beacon Hill," "The Waltons," or "Little House on the Prairie." *Medical dramas* presented noncomic problems surrounding a hospital or medical setting, e.g., "Doctor's Hospital," "Medical Story," or "Emergency." *Situation comedies* appeared in a variety of settings (home, office, hospital), but were primarily designed to be humorous, e.g., "Sanford and Son," "Maude," or "M*A*S*H." *Action/crime* shows were concerned with law enforcement by public (police) or private agencies, e.g., "Kojak," "Starsky and Hutch," or "The Rockford Files." Saturday morning shows were subdivided into Saturday cartoons, e.g., "Pink Panther," "Scooby Doo," and "Bugs Bunny," and Saturday noncartoon shows, e.g., "Shazam/Isis," and "Uncle Croc's Block."

During the second season analyzed, medical dramas had largely disappeared and did not increase during the third year. One program type—*adventure* series, like "Grizzly Adams," which did not fit the crime series typology—was added.

Coder Training

Each season the coding teams consisted of four to six undergraduate students. Supervised training was provided for each team during a multi-hour practice coding session. When coders had completed the practice session, they independently viewed and coded the same set of shows until inter-coder reliabilities reached .80 for all variables. Thereafter, shows were viewed by a single coder. Periodically, multiple coders were instructed to code the same show to provide further reliability checks.

RESULTS

First, the attributes of the population of TV characters in terms of their marginal distributi n on each of the coded variables will be identified. Second, the key demographic variables will be cross-tabulated with selected other characteristics.

Overall Characteristics. The distribution of television characters for each of the coded variables is in Table 4.1. United States Census data from 1970 have been included as a referent for those same variables, where available. The data in Table 4.1 permit the following conclusions:

1. In each of the three years, males outnumbered females by approximately three to one with no apparent trend across that time period. In the 1970 census, females were a slightly larger proportion of the United States population than males.

2. The proportion of blacks in the television population was fairly constant in the three seasons analyzed, at about 10 percent. This is identical to the 1970 census proportion of blacks.

3. By age distribution, there has been a distinct increase in the proportion of teenagers in the fictional television population. At the same time, there has been no trend for more frequent portrayal of the elderly, either those 50–64 or those over 65. In fact, during the last two seasons, the proportion in those older age categories was less than it was three years ago. The age distribution of television characters is substantially discrepant from that of the 1970

TABLE 4.1
Demographic and Role Attributes of TV Characters

	1975–76 (n = 1212) (%)	1976–77 (n = 1120) (%)	1977–78 (n = 1217) (%)	1970 Census (%)
A. Sex				
Female	27	29	29	(51)
Male	73	71	71	(49)
B. Race				
Black	10	11	9	(10)
White	86	85	86	(89)
C. Age				
0–12	4	4	5	(29)*
13–19	8	10	15	(9)
20–34	31	33	32	(20)
35–49	37	39	32	(17)
50–64	17	11	14	(15)
65+	4	3	2	(10)
D. Lawbreakers	10	11	11	—
E. Job**				
Professional	37	32	29	(15)
Managerial	11	14	22	(10)
Clerical	6	5	9	(18)
Sales	2	2	2	(3)
Craftsmen	6	10	10	(14)
Operatives	6	2	4	(18)
Service workers	26	31	22	(11)
Private household	4	4	1	(2)
Laborers	2	0	2	(7)
F. Role				
Regular	40	41	50	
Guest	60	59	50	
G. Program types				
Sitcoms	20	24	23	
Crime	41	32	23	
Family drama	8	3	9	
Saturday live	4	9	4	
Saturday cartoons	19	16	26	
Adventure	—	7	15	
Others***	8	9	—	

*The first two census age categories are 0–14, and 15–19.
**Here, the base *n*'s for the three years were 728-620-630. Those omitted include children, lawbreakers, and those without identifiable jobs.
***These included medical dramas in year 1, and segments of miniseries in year 2.

census, and the largest discrepancy occurs in the youngest age category. Television characterizations cater about equally to portrayals of people in their 20s, 30s, and 40s. Whereas this is one-third of the real population, it is two-thirds of the TV population. Adults of retirement age are substantially underrepresented in the television population.

4. Across the three seasons, approximately 10 percent of television characters were lawbreakers. According to 1976 federal crime statistics, one-half of 1 percent of the population committed a violent crime, e.g., murder, rape, aggravated assault, and 4.8 percent committed a property crime, e.g., burglary, larceny, vehicle theft.

5. The job world on television is heavily that of professionals, managers, and service workers, and all three are far more likely to be found on television than in the real world. The across-time data indicate some drop-off in professional positions, accompanied by a parallel increase in managerial role presentations. Police-related occupations primarily account for the substantial presentation of service workers on television. The two most underrepresented occupations on television are those of clerks and operatives. Finally, it is useful to note that the proportion of characters with any identifiable job decreased from 60 percent in year one to 55 percent in year two to 52 percent in year three.

6. If anything, the third season indicates there were more likely to be regular roles than guest roles in series. This trend comes from series with larger casts of regularly appearing performers.

7. The final portion of Table 4.1 identifies the program types in which television characters are most likely to appear. During the first two years analyzed, the proportion of characters on crime shows surpassed that of any other program type. That proportion was smaller during the second year of analysis, and for the third year had dropped to a level equivalent to two other program types. For the 1977–78 season, the origin of characters was equivalent for situation comedies which have remained constant over the three years, crime shows where the number of characters dropped over the three years, and Saturday cartoons in which the number of characters increased. In addition, a new program type introduced in the second year of this analysis, adventure programs, was providing approximately 15 percent of all characters by the third season. Thus, crime shows no longer predominate in character presentations to the same extent as they did in the first two seasons analyzed.

Ethnic Comparisons. This section cross-tabulates the race of the television characters by other demographic and role characteristics. The findings are in Table 4.2. As noted earlier, blacks comprise 10 percent of the TV characters, and this proportion serves as a baseline for the tabled comparisons. The analysis permits the following conclusions:

1. By sex, the proportions of black females and black males have been consistent and equal.

2. By age, younger blacks were much more likely to be seen on television than their representation in the population of television characters would lead one to expect. More than one-third of the under-20 age group has been black, and this proportion is nearly four times their representation in the TV population. Further, they are systematically underrepresented during each season in the mature adult category, 50–64.

3. Across the three seasons, there was a sharp drop in the presentation of blacks as lawbreakers. Whereas in the first year analyzed, the proportion of blacks as lawbreakers was higher than the proportion of blacks in the total sample, by this third year, it was comparable.

4. Blacks have consistently been underreflected in higher-level jobs; this was most evident in the third season analyzed. Their representation in service and other jobs has been more equivalent to their proportion in the TV population.

5. Blacks constituted a larger proportion of regular television characters than as series guests, and those proportions have been marginally larger than their representation in the total television population.

TABLE 4.2
Race of TV Characters by Selected role
Characteristics (percent black)

		1975–76 (%)	1976–77 (%)	1977–78 (%)
I.	Total sample	10	11	9
	A. Sex			
	Female	10	10	10
	Male	11	12	9
	B. Age			
	< 20	37	38	38
	20–34	13	11	10
	35–49	9	11	7
	50–64	4	3	3
	65+	12	8	6
	C. Lawbreakers	14	12	8
	D. Job			
	Professional	7	8	4
	Manager	6	6	6
	Service	12	9	13
	All Others	13	10	9
	E. Role			
	Regular	14	13	12
	Guest	8	10	7
	F. Program type			
	Sitcoms	17	17	17
	Crime	9	7	6
	Family drama	7	0	3
	Saturday live	2	9	6
	Saturday cartoons	11	26	10
	Adventure	—	3	7

6. Blacks are, and have been, significantly more likely to be cast in situation comedies than in most other types of programming. Their second most active program type has been Saturday cartoons, with a distinctly higher rate of being featured in 1976–77 than either the year before or the year after. Blacks are distinctly underrepresented in family dramas and their representation in crime and adventure shows is less than their proportion in the television population.

Gender Comparisons. An analysis of the same attributes, by sex, is in Table 4.3. The proportion of females, which ranged between 27–29 percent in the three years, is compared with the proportion of females in each of the demographic subgroups.

1. By race, the proportion of females who were black was equivalent within 1 to 4 percent to the proportion of females who were white in each season. Within each race, one sees the same three-to-one margin of males over females.

2. By age, women were younger. They dominated the under-20 age group and were over represented in the 20–34 age group. These two emphases have been consistent all three years, and the overrepresentation in the youngest age group substantially increased in the most recent season analyzed. Women were underrepresented in the two age groupings of 35–49 and 50–64.

TABLE 4.3
**Sex of TV Characters by Selected Role
Characteristics (percent female)**

		1975–76 (%)	1976–77 (%)	1977–78 (%)
I.	Total sample	27	29	29
	A. Race			
	Black	27	27	34
	White	28	31	31
	B. Age			
	≲ 20	51	60	79
	20–34	41	43	43
	35–49	22	19	20
	50–64	14	18	15
	65+	21	43	32
	C. Lawbreakers	12	28	10
	D. Job			
	Professional	33	23	30
	Manager	7	10	15
	Service	8	12	19
	All others	37	41	25
	E. Role			
	Regular	29	31	30
	Guest	24	27	29
	F. Program type			
	Sitcoms	36	35	37
	Crime	23	26	29
	Family drama	33	45	41
	Saturday live	22	35	29
	Saturday cartoons	17	18	19
	Adventure	—	15	28

3. Women were less likely to be law breakers. Only in the second season analyzed, did they achieve parity with men on this attribute.

4. Females who have jobs on television have tended to be represented in the extremes of the job classifications. They were in professional positions in all three seasons in a magnitude only marginally different than their proportion in the TV population; they tended to be excluded from middle-level positions, as either managers or service workers; they appeared regularly in all other job types. The trend over the three seasons has been for increasing appearances in managerial and service roles; in 1977–78, their proportion in those two job categories more than doubled what it had been two seasons earlier. A distinct trend toward heterogeneity among women's TV occupations can be identified in these data.

5. Women's roles as regularly appearing characters have not changed in proportion over the three seasons, and that proportion reflects their overall TV presence.

6. Larger proportions of women appeared in situation comedies and family dramas. They were specifically underrepresented in Saturday morning cartoons and have been so all three seasons. Adventure shows now present females in a normative proportion.

Age Comparisons The interactions of the age of the characters with a subset of demographic and role characteristics are in Table 4.4. The most general findings from this table are as follows:

TABLE 4.4
Age of TV Characters by Other Demographic
and Role Characteristics

			1975–76 (%)	1976–77 (%)	1977–78 (%)
I.	Total sample of characters	< 20	11	14	20
		20–34	31	33	32
		35–49	37	39	32
		50–64	17	11	14
		65+	4	3	2
	A. Sex F/	< 20	14	17	26
		20–34	45	47	45
		35–49	30	26	21
		50+	11	11	8
	M/	< 20	10	11	17
		20–34	25	26	27
		35–49	40	47	37
		50+	25	16	19
	B. Race B/	< 20	23	27	38
		20–34	35	31	33
		35–49	31	37	24
		50+	11	5	6
	W/	< 20	10	11	18
		20–34	29	33	33
		35–49	38	41	33
		50+	23	16	17
	C. Jobs Professional/	< 20	2	5	2
		20–34	39	31	39
		35–49	35	49	37
		50+	24	15	23
	Manual/	< 20	0	1	1
		20–34	15	12	14
		35–49	49	65	52
		50+	36	22	33
	Service/	< 20	0	6	9
		20–34	33	30	40
		35–49	48	47	40
		50+	20	17	12
	D. Role Regular/	< 20	20	21	28
		20–34	33	33	31
		35–49	32	32	27
		50+	15	14	14
	Guest/	< 20	6	7	12
		20–34	29	32	34
		35–49	41	46	37
		50+	25	15	17

1. The under-20 age group increasingly overrepresented females. The 20–34 group has not varied by sex over the three years, but was nearly twice the proportion of females as males; the opposite is so for those 35–49, with the addition that this age group has shown a substantial decrease in terms of female representation. The 50-and-over group has been heavily male in each season. Mature and aging women were infrequent in television series roles.

2. By race, the under-20 age group has been disproportionately black, and in the 1977–78 season the proportion of blacks under 20 constituted their primary age category. The intermediate age categories have not varied greatly by race across the three years, except that mature and elderly blacks have decreased as a proportion of that race. Few senior black citizens are to be seen, and there are fewer mature and aging white citizens than in the first season examined.

3. In the portrayal of age by occupation categories, the 20–34 age group is most likely to be seen in professional and service roles, whereas the 50-and-over group reflects its largest proportions in managerial roles. Those 35–49 are the major proportion of the employed in all of television's major occupational categories.

4. The under-20 group has been two to three times more likely to have regular roles on a weekly series than guest roles. In the first season the over-50 group was twice as likely to have guest roles than regular roles, but for the last two years the proportions over 50 appearing in regular roles and guest roles have been the same, with the full decrease occurring in the guest role situation.

5. The final age analysis dealt with age distribution across program types (omitted from Table 4.4 to save space but available from the authors). The under-20 age group was seen primarily on Saturday noncartoons, distinctly more often than in any other program type. Characters that young are also seen frequently in family drama shows and in Saturday cartoons and, in the 1977–78 season, on adventure shows. That age group is not visible on crime shows. The 20–34-year-old age group is seen primarily on situation comedies and crime shows, but in a proportion equivalent to their overall presence in the TV population. They are seen least often on Saturday programs. The 35–49-year-old age group is most visible on crime shows and to some extent on Saturday cartoons, although the latter proportion dropped substantially in the 1977–78 season. For the remaining age groups, distribution within program types was not particularly discrepant from their overall distribution. The elderly are not concentrated in any type of programming.

DISCUSSION

The population of fictional characters on television did not correspond to the population of real people. It never has nor need it do so. The population of fictional people for dramatic presentations is chosen more for its peculiarities than its regularities. Such characters are identified because they stand out rather than because they are usual. Yet this type of analysis can help determine whether some subgroups of people are associated with peculiarities that might be considered negative. Do consistent and persistent presentations of less desirable or homogeneous attributes continue—in the face of claims that they do not or in the face of protests that they should not?

Some themes are derivable from the present content analysis. Women continue to be an important minority in television fiction although outnumbered three to one. They are primarily young and overrepresented in lower-level jobs, although a trend of greater occupational variation is occurring. They continue to be overrepresented in situation comedies and in family dramas; but there is now a stronger tendency for them to be included more regularly in both crime and adventure programs than in previous seasons. Although much of this portrayal of women replicates and continues the trend of earlier studies, there is evidence of greater diversity and heterogeneity in female portrayals in certain important characteristics.

Portrayals of racial minorities continue to be of special interest. Spanish-Americans still do not exist in sufficient frequency to enable an intensive quantitative analysis, nor does any other ethnic subgroup. The quantitative presentation of blacks has been level now for close to a decade and at a parity with their counterpart proportion in the real world, that might be sufficient to silence critics. On the other hand, a disproportionate number of black characters are confined to a handful of shows which strongly emphasize black family and black neighborhood situations. Furthermore, it is the young, preadult black who is primarily accessible through television. The industry may reason that, if it is necessary to present blacks on television, then the most acceptable way to do it may be to portray black youngsters rather than what may be more threatening, black adults. Indeed, a substantial number of blacks is to be seen but if you don't choose to watch shows in which there are whole families of blacks, you are unlikely to see them in most other shows. Other than situation comedies, only Saturday cartoons featured blacks in a representative proportion. Thus, two types of comedy are the primary TV vehicle for this minority.

As for characterizations of the different age groups, young people are disproportionately female and black. And older women are far less likely to be seen than older men, directly contradictory to actuarial data. Virtually no old black people are to be seen in fictional television series. Young people are most likely to be seen on family drama shows and Saturday shows; those in their 20s through their 40s are most likely to be found on crime shows, the elderly are equally unlikely to be seen anywhere.

These data do not permit an assumption that the proportion or even the sheer frequency of presentation of any particular character type corresponds to the power of that image's impact. The question remains open as to whether child viewers or any viewers learn from consistent and rigid character portrayals. It is unclear, for example, whether children are more influenced by the overall TV portrait of some type of person, or more susceptible to some notable exceptions to typecasting. Perhaps regular viewing of programs which do not stereotype women to the same extent, e.g., "Maude," offsets the viewing of several shows which perpetuate the stereotyping of women.

Clearly, these are mixed messages, whether women or minorities or the aged are in the messages. If you are an advocate for the industry, the data support certain contentions of more roles, larger roles, etc. If you are a critic of the industry, the data equally support describing many industry statements as cavalier. That argument cannot be resolved from these data, but the data do provide systematic evidence as to the basic nature of these portrayals.

The television population is not static on all dimensions. There is growth, movement, and changing characterizations as the industry attempts to maintain its overall audience and as the separate networks try to carve out larger audience shares for themselves. Perhaps it is cyclical—an emphasis now on youth and later on maturity; an emphasis now on expanding roles for women and later regression to more stereotyped presentations. Clearly, the trend must be plotted if we are to understand the nature of the possible learning experiences which can follow from such presentations. Whether youngsters do develop expectations, aspirations, and values from these portrayals is now being examined at numerous research sites. These data should contribute to forming and testing hypotheses in such studies.

II

THE SEXES
ON TELEVISION

5

SEX DIFFERENCES
IN GIVING ORDERS, MAKING PLANS,
AND NEEDING SUPPORT ON TELEVISION

LAURA HENDERSON
BRADLEY S. GREENBERG
CHARLES K. ATKIN

The abundant recent analyses of television content portraying men and women have tended to focus on a small set of relatively static characteristics. They have emphasized head counts, demography, jobs, and physical and personality traits. The portrait that emerges is a consistent one. Head count studies show that males outnumber females by a margin of nearly three to one (Turow, 1974; Courtney and Whipple, 1974). In terms of demography, the average television female has been a young, white, married mother (Downing 1974; Dominick and Rauch, 1972), although the last two characteristics may be changing somewhat with the recent emergence of the "jiggle" shows.[1] The jobs that women have are few, and even those are restricted in terms of variety (Miller and Reeves, 1976; Katzman, 1972). Physically, women are usually tall, thin, attractive, well-dressed, and less physically active (Long and Simon, 1974). Personality assessments have usually been trait-based; in those coder assessments, women show up as more dependent, more submissive, weaker, less intelligent, more emotional, and more peaceable (Tedesco, 1974; Busby, 1974).

Fewer studies have focused on behavioral sequences of males and females. Turow (1974) examined episodes in which characters advised or ordered others and found that men prevailed in 70 percent of the

---

[1]"Jiggle" shows feature unmarried females, for whom a major activity is cavorting on the screen in a tight top or bathing suit, with minimum or absent undergarments. These same shows have been labeled "b and b shows" (*boobs and butts*) and "t and a shows." (Definition supplied on request, if needed.)

advising and ordering episodes, which was proportionate to their presence on the screen. Sternglanz and Serbin (1974) directed their attention to the consequences of a wide range of behaviors in TV cartoons. By coding behavioral consequences as positive, negative, or neutral, they determined that male behavioral outcomes were more often positive than otherwise, and female behavioral outcomes were more often neutral or negative. They interpreted the latter to mean "that in general their (female) behavior had no environmental consequences." Their research showed that females also exhibited more deference behavior.

The focus on behaviors and their outcomes is important to this paper and more generally because both are central factors within social learning theories. Bandura (1977) argues that much of behavior is learned by observing how others are reinforced for their acts. Thus, watching the behavior of men and women on television may well indicate which behaviors are sex-appropriate; watching reinforcement contingencies for those same behaviors should serve to identify the relative desirability of performing those behaviors. Mischel (1966), in a specific social learning interpretation of sex-typed behaviors, proposes that boys and girls learn the behavioral repertoires of both sexes. While learning, however, they also learn to label the appropriateness of behaviors for their respective sex due to "the difference in outcome as a function of the performer's sex."

Thus, a content analysis of major interpersonal behaviors, as they are portrayed on television, together with the outcomes of those behaviors, should provide a basis for subsequent social learning research on viewer's tendencies to acquire and model sex-role information from television programming. With this rationale, and the evidence of previous content analyses, a subset of three categories of behavior often displayed on television and culturally sex-typed, was chosen: dominance-deference behaviors, nurturant-succorant behaviors, and independent-dependent behaviors.

Dominance-deference. Based on work by Turow (1974) and Sternglanz and Serbin (1974), the dominance-deference dimension can be articulated as, "Who gives what types of orders to whom, with what outcome?" The analytic scheme, to be dealt with in the methods section, examined ordergiving as embedded either in an authority relationship (superior to subordinate) or in a peer relationship. Furthermore, deference in this context implies that the order will be further explained or justified. These notions, when overlaid on the background of prior content analyses demonstrating sex-type stereotyping on television, suggest these hypotheses:

H1: Male TV characters will originate more authority orders proportionately than female TV characters.[2]

H2: Peer orders will occur equivalently among the sexes.

H3: Female TV characters will explain or justify more of their orders than
male TV characters.

Another component in this behavioral sequence deals with the
order receivers. Turow (1974) looked only at cross-sex orders and
Sternglanz and Serbin (1974) examined dominance and deference as
separate behaviors. Here, the interaction between dominant (ordergivers) and deferent (order-receivers) characters is examined and permits
the extension of the traditional roles to these hypotheses:

H4: Male TV characters will give orders to male characters proportionately
more often than female characters will give orders to male characters.

H5: Female characters will be the receivers of orders proportionately more
often than male characters.

The further interest in the outcome of this dominant-deferent sequence creates a need to determine whether the orders given were followed. Again, the general stereotyping on television would suggest:

H6: Orders given by male characters will be followed proportionately more
often than orders given by females.

Nurturance-exigence. Television stories are cast in the context of certain individuals needing help and others providing it. This
support behavior sequence can be further differentiated in terms of the
situations in which assistance is needed, i.e., primarily in those of physical or emotional distress. This distress type differentiation permits a
greater parallelism with traditional role expectations of men and women. Deaux (1976) reviewed male and female personality traits and
found that women consistently were considered more emotional and
men more active or physical. Others (Donelson, 1975; Broverman *et al.*,
1972) discuss the cultural stereotype of women as "warm." Prior content
analyses support these depictions. Long and Simon (1974) found women
to have more socioemotional family roles. Busby (1974) reports that
women are portrayed as more emotional and fragile; men, more adventurous and sturdy. These antecedent studies suggest that, in terms of
needing support,

---

[2]The proportions reference in each hypothesis is based on the fact that men
outnumber women in television about three to one. Thus, tests of behavioral differences
should take that initial disparity into account. Here, the concern is whether the behavior
occurs disproportionately to the representation of the sex in the TV character population.
For example, if 70 percent of a given behavior occurs among men, and they constitute 70
percent of the TV characters, then men, although dominating in the behavior, are not
doing it beyond chance expectations.

H7: Male TV characters will display a need for physical support or succorance proportionately more often than female TV characters.
H8: Female TV characters will display a need for emotional support or
succorance proportionately more often than male TV characters.
H9: Female TV characters will request support proportionately more often
than male TV characters.

This behavioral sequence also has an outcome—whether the person in need of nurturance receives it, thus positively reinforcing the
expression of need. The traditional portrayal of women being nurtured
and men struggling more autonomously suggests this hypothesis:

H10: Female TV characters in need of support will receive it proportionately more often than male TV characters in need of support.

Independence-dependence. In prior content analyses, this
characteristic has uniformly been examined as a personality trait, not as
a behavior (Busby, 1974; Tedesco, 1974). Sternglanz and Serbin (1974),
however, examined "achievement-construction" in terms of planning
and carrying out one's plans, and stating desires to overcome obstacles
and to surpass one's self and others. From this was derived the less
complex behavior of plan-making as reflective of an individual's attempt
at demonstrating at least one major component of independence. Coupling the content-analytic evidence that male TV characters are judged
as more independent, with Mischel's (1966) non-TV evidence that girls
are more dependent, it can be posited that:

H11: Male TV characters will make proportionately more plans than female
TV characters.

For this dimension, the behavioral outcome consists of the success
or nonsuccess of those plans. To the extent that females on television are
portrayed in traditional role behaviors:

H12: Male TV characters will make proportionately more plans that are
successful than will female TV characters.

METHODS

Sample

The data for analysis came from one composte week of fictional television series on the three commercial networks. The original
composite week, created in the fall of 1975, was supplemented by mid-
season replacement series. In all, the sample week contained 79 program
episodes, or 59.5 television hours. Data were generated for all program
characters with speaking parts; the shows contained 1212 speaking
characters of whom 885 (73 percent) were male and 327 (27 per cent),
female.

Content Categories

Ordergiving. The conceptual attribute of dominance-deference was explicitly examined in terms of giving orders. *Ordergiving* occurred when "the character gives a directive for others to do, say or think something." From this, two order types were coded: *authority* orders and *peer* orders. The former occurred if the basis for issuance of the order stemmed from the giver's occupational position (boss), social agency role (police, doctor, nurse), or status as parent. If a character were acting as a delegate of any of these role positions, only then could that character also give authority orders. Peer orders occurred if the giver and receiver were peers or equals, e.g., husband-wife, brother-sister, coworkers.[3]

For each of these two types of orders, a further notation was made if the order was explained, i.e., if the giver included a justification for the order being followed. This justification had to occur immediately before or after the order given. An example of an authority-explained order (from teacher to student), "Be quiet, Jane. You're disturbing the other students." A peer-explained order (from wife to husband), "Come back. It's too cold to go outside without a sweather."

In addition to these order types, coders noted the sex of the receiver of the orders, and whether the order was followed (executed as given).

Needing Support. The conceptual behavior sequence of nurturance was examined in terms of whether a character needed support, and, if so, the type of support needed. A character needed support if he/she were identified as in danger or in distress. Excluded were routine requests for assistance, e.g., time of day, or social courtesies, e.g., holding a car door open for an able person in a nonstressful situation.

Three types of needs for *physical support* were coded:

1. External, in which a character is in danger of being killed, injured, or beaten by someone else, or from natural dangers;

2. Internal, in which the character is suffering from disease, illness, or other internally originated malady;

3. Physical confinement, in which the character is jailed, trapped, or otherwise involuntarily held against his/her will.

Three types of *emotional support* needs were coded:

1. Ego support, in which the character professes a personal problem

---

[3]The original scheme included a category for "threat orders," which was dropped because of its infrequent occurrence.

with which she/he is unable to cope, and for which the origin is internal, e.g., "I can't get along with my boss and I don't know what to do about it;"

2. Psychological support, in which the character's problems stem from the actions of others, but without an expressed inability to cope, e.g., "My daughter, Beth, has run off with her teaching assistant;"

3. Concern for others, in which the character needs support for his/her attempt to help some third party, e.g., "I'm worried about Debbie's habits."

For this behavior sequence, coders also recorded whether the character in need of support did or did not request it, whether it was or was not given, and the gender of the support givers.

Plan-making. The conceptual attribute of independence-dependence was explicitly examined in this study as the making of plans. A *plan* was defined: "A description of a method for achieving a goal . . . not merely an intent to do something . . . the statement of a method for doing something . . . explicit in statement or action."

Originally, a set of different plan types was created. Since there were low frequencies for most plan types, the final decision was to sum all plans, regardless of type, into a single index of number of plans made.

The other variables in this behavior sequence were the gender of the plan executor and the outcome of the plan, successful or failing.

Coding Procedures and Reliabilities

The training of coders proceeded as follows: Conceptual definitions and then operational definitions were discussed; use of the coding form was explained; practice sessions with videotape segments commenced, followed by analysis of coding problems. This sequence was repeated several times over two weeks, with four undergraduate students working in pairs during the training period. After training, the coders continued to work in pairs but coded independently.

The coding of behaviors and behavioral sequences was done in tape segments as a convenient and uniform unit of analysis. The videotape counter was set to zero and stopped at 50 cycles; 50 cycles was approximately two minutes of content; codable information was entered on coding forms as it was identified; then the machine was restarted and a new segment was viewed and analyzed. Behaviors that continued across tape segments were counted once.

Approximately half of all shows were coded by two independent coders. To compute reliability, the number of behaviors in each content category identified for a given character by one coder was correlated (Pearson product-moment correlation) with the number of behaviors for that character recorded by a second coder. The order-giving category contained nine variables, with an average reliability of .82; the index of all orders had a reliability coefficient of .95. The need-for-support category contained 17 variables with an average reliability of .66. Physical support needs had a reliability coefficient of .81; emotional support and its components were less reliable (.60) but were retained because of their theoretic interest. The plans category had the poorest reliability, averaging .57 across seven variables; overall plan-making, however, had a reliability coefficient of .74, and that variable will be emphasized in the analyses.

Data Treatment

The formal hypotheses, as stated, were tested by determining whether the total enactments of a given behavior by one sex was or was not proportionate to the presence of that sex in the population of TV characters. That population was 73 percent male and 27 percent female; these proportions were then the standard against which each coded behavior was assessed, by means of the z-statistic (Hays, 1963). For example, the hypothesis that physical support needs would be disproportionately found among males would be tested by statistically comparing the proportion of physical support needs that did occur among TV males with the proportion of males in the TV character population.

Among the subset of characters who performed one or more instances of a given behavior, a second analysis was done to determine whether that behavior was exhibited at a higher rate by one gender. The mean rates of occurrence of the behaviors between genders were assessed by t-tests. This analysis offers indirect evidence for evaluating the hypotheses.

The former analysis tests the enactments of these behaviors relative to the presence of each sex in the TV population; the latter tests the absolute magnitude of the acts performed by each sex.

Both analyses were performed across the entire sample of TV content. In addition, gender differences were examined within three major TV program types: situation comedies, crime-adventure, and Saturday morning shows. Analysis of these dominant program types is exploratory but identifies deviations and similarities from the more general results.

RESULTS

Results will be presented successively for each of the three major behavioral sequences—ordergiving, need for support, and plan-making. Within those three sections, evidence will be presented for differences among program types.

Ordergiving

It was hypothesized that males would generate more authority orders (H1), that peer orders would occur equivalently by gender (H2), and that females would originate more explained orders (H3). Table 5.1 contains the pertinent findings. For all order types, whether authority or peer originated, whether explained or not, males generated significantly more—both proportionately and per capita. Males, who comprised 73 percent of the characters, were responsible for 80 percent of the orders. And, in a striking disparity among those characters who gave one or more orders, males emitted three to every one by a female ordergiver.

Thus, although only one of these three hypotheses was supported, the television behavioral sequence for ordergiving was identified as very consistently sex-typed.

H4 posited that males would receive orders from males more often than females. This occurred to the extent that 82 percent of all orders originated by males were received by males; male ordergivers directed three times as many orders to males as females did to males. H5 posited that females would be order receivers more so than males. This did not occur. Of all orders received, from both female and male ordergivers, males received 75 percent. Thus, order reception by gender was not significantly disproportionate to the presence of males and females in the TV character population.

The final hypothesis for ordergiving (H6) stipulated that orders from males would be more followed than orders originating from

TABLE 5.1
Giving Orders by Gender of TV Characters

	Females	Males	t	z^*
	$(n = 294)$	$(n = 395)$		
I. Order types				
A. Authority orders	.27	1.33	$< .001$	$< .001$M
B. Peer orders	.92	2.12	$< .001$	$< .05$M
C. Authority explained	.06	.28	$< .001$	$< .01$M
D. Peer explained	.20	.57	$< .001$	$< .01$M
E. ALL ORDERS	1.45	4.29	$< .001$	$< .001$M
II. Order receivers				
A. Females	.41	.94	$< .001$	n.s.
B. Males	.91	2.99	$< .001$	$< .001$M
III. Orders followed				
A. Followed	.94	3.17	$< .001$	$< .001$M
B. Not followed	.53	1.21	$< .001$	n.s.

*For all tables, if the subscript for the p value is M, the proportion of this behavior performed by males exceeded their proportionate representation in the TV character population; if the subscript is F, the proportion of this behavior performed by females exceeded their proportionate representation in the TV character population.

females. Strong support is found in Table 5.1. Eighty-two percent of all orders followed came from males, and the per capita rate was nearly 3.5 to 1 for male over female ordergivers. Orders not followed occurred equivalently for the two sexes.

Program Type Differences. Table 5.2 provides comparable information for three program types: situation comedies, crime/adventure shows, and Saturday morning programs. Given the consistency of results across order types in Table 5.1, Table 5.2 presents the single summary measure of all orders.

The three program types provide clear evidence of differential ordering behaviors by the sexes. In situation comedies, and only in that type of program, females originated more orders proportionately than males, and more of those orders were received by females. Males were receivers of orders and orders were followed equivalently from both genders. But more orders originating from females were not followed.

In crime/adventure programs, males dominated in ordergiving, order-receiving and orders followed both proportionately and in rates among ordergivers. This program genre was distinctly male.

On Saturday morning shows, males dominated in proportionate ordergiving, order receipt, orders followed, and orders not followed, although the per capita rates were not different among ordergivers.

Thus, the most rounded participation of females in the ordergiving behavior sequence was in situation comedies, their lowest yield was in

TABLE 5.2
Giving Orders by Gender by TV Program Type

	Females	Males	t	z
I. Situation comedies	(n = 32)	(n = 73)		
A. All orders	4.09	3.56	n.s.	> .01F
B. Female receivers	1.88	.96	n.s.	> .001F
Male receivers	1.97	2.23	n.s.	n.s.
C. Orders followed	2.53	2.58	n.s.	n.s.
D. Orders not followed	1.63	1.07	n.s.	< .01F
II. Crime/Adventure	(n = 34)	(n = 152)		
A. All orders	2.77	4.62	< .05	< .001M
B. Female receivers	.53	.97	< .05	< .001M
Male receivers	2.00	3.44	< .05	< .001M
C. Orders followed	1.91	3.43	< .05	< .001M
D. Orders not followed	.91	1.32	n.s.	< .001M
III Saturday a.m.	(n = 25)	(n = 106)		
A. All orders	3.72	4.35	n.s.	< .001M
B. Female receivers	.36	.61	n.s.	< .01M
Male receivers	2.64	3.11	n.s.	< .001M
C. Orders followed	2.56	3.23	n.s.	< .001M
D. Orders not followed	1.16	1.18	n.s.	< .01M

crime-adventure shows, and their performance on Saturday morning tended to male predominance.

Need for Support

Table 5.3 presents the results about the different types of support needs of television characters, and related information. The two major hypotheses were that males would be portrayed disproportionately in physical support need situations (H7), and that women would be portrayed in parallel fashion in emotional support need situations (H8). The data in Table 5.3 support both propositions. For physical support needs, whether physical internal, physical external, or physical confinement needs, males were more likely to be shown in those circumstances, in terms of both the proportions of acts committed and the rate of acts. For emotional support needs—ego support, concern for others, and psychological support—females were disproportionately reflected in the television content with no differences in the raw rates among those expressing some need. Overall, females, who constituted 27 percent of the TV characters, displayed 40 percent of the emotional support needs.

Furthermore, the context of support needs as evidenced in Table 5.3 supports the expectations that females would be more likely to request support (H9) and be given it (H10). The data also show that both female and male support givers were more likely to direct their support to females in need.

Program Type Differences. Table 5.4 presents parallel data for support needs by program type. For this behavioral sequence, there is more symmetry across program types than differences. First, regard-

TABLE 5.3
Support Needs by Gender of TV Characters

	Females	Males	t	z
	($n = 291$)	($n = 337$)		
I. Physical support types				
A. Physical internal	.21	.62	$< .001$	$< .01$M
B. Physical external	.25	.85	$< .001$	$< .001$M
C. Physical confinement	.10	.28	$< .001$	$< .05$M
D. All physical types	.56	1.75	$< .001$	$< .001$M
II. Emotional support types				
A. Ego support	.68	.70	n.s.	$< .001$F
B. Concern for others	.34	.27	n.s.	$< .001$F
C. Psychological support	.58	.75	n.s.	$< .01$F
D. All emotional types	1.60	1.72	n.s.	$< .001$F
III. A. Support requested	1.20	1.35	n.s.	$< .001$F
B. Support not requested	.67	1.66	$< .001$	$< .01$M
IV. A. Support given	1.16	1.52	$< .05$	$< .001$F
B. Support not given	.70	1.44	$< .001$	n.s.
V. A. Female givers	.39	.44	n.s.	$< .001$F
B. Male givers	1.14	1.50	$< .05$	$< .001$F

TABLE 5.4
Support by Gender by TV Program Type

	Females	Males		
I. Situation comedies	(n = 38)	(n = 70)	t	z
A. All physical support types	.13	.83	< .01	< .05M
B. All emotional support types	3.55	2.83	n.s.	< .001F
C. Support Requested	2.42	1.84	n.s.	< .001F
D. Support given	2.42	1.70	n.s.	< .001F
E. Female support givers	1.21	.47	< .01	< .001F
F. Male support givers	1.79	1.97	n.s.	< .05F
II. Crime/Adventure	(n = 40)	(n = 125)		
A. All physical support types	1.30	1.82	n.s.	< .01M
B. All emotional support types	2.70	1.27	< .01	< .001F
C. Support requested	1.85	1.16	< .05	< .05F
D. Support given	1.98	1.37	< .05	n.s.
E. Female support givers	.48	.38	n.s.	n.s.
F. Male support givers	2.35	1.44	< .05	< .01F
III. Saturday a.m.	(n = 28)	(n = 111)		
A. All physical support types	2.21	2.48	n.s.	< .01M
B. All emotional support types	1.64	1.26	n.s.	n.s.
C. Support requested	1.93	1.04	< .05	n.s.
D. Support given	1.68	1.58	n.s.	< .05M
E. Female support givers	.29	.41	n.s.	< .05M
F. Male support givers	1.75	1.20	n.s.	n.s.

less of program type, physical support is significantly more likely to be needed by males than females; emotional support is significantly more likely to be needed by females on situation comedies and crime-adventure shows, and the trend is the same on Saturday morning shows. Furthermore, on situation comedy and crime/adventure shows, females in need of support are more likely to ask for it and to receive it, from both sexes. On Saturday shows, there are anomalous differences with regard to the giving and granting of requests for support, with the low frequency of females a contributing factor.

Plan-making

H11 hypothesized that males would make more plans than females, as a measure of the concept of independence. Table 5.5 presents support for this hypothesis. Proportionately more plans (82 percent) were made by males, and this was so whether the plans were intended for males or for females. H12 posited that more of the male plans would be successful, and this was also supported by the data in Table 5.5; note, however, that proportionately more male plans also were unsuccessful. The average rates of plan-making and outcomes did not differ.

The data also show that plan executors typically corresponded by sex to the plan-maker. Plans made by females were more typically executed by females, plans made by males were more typically carried out by males.

TABLE 5.5
Plan-making by Gender of TV Characters

	Females	Males	t	z
I. Plan-making	$(n = 44)$	$(n = 167)$		
A. All plans	1.41	1.64	n.s.	< .01M
B. For females	.14	.20	n.s.	< .05M
C. For males	.66	.80	n.s.	< .01M
II. ˉPlan executors				
A. Females	.50	.04	< .001	< .001F
B. Males	.32	1.08	< .001	< .001M
III. Plan outcomes				
A. Success	.73	.89	n.s.	< .01M
B. Failure	.59	.65	n.s.	< .05M

Program Type Differences. Table 5.6 provides comparable information by program type, although the original low frequency of female plan-makers, when further subdivided in this manner, results in quite low cell sizes for that gender. For that reason and because of the initial lesser reliability in coding this behavior, the findings are more tentative. In situation comedies, plan-making occurred equivalently overall, although plans for males were created disproportionately by

TABLE 5.6
Plan-making by Gender by TV Program Type

	Females	Males	t	z
I. Situation comedies	$(n = 17)$	$(n = 39)$		
A. All plan-making	1.06	1.33	< .05	n.s.
B. Plans for females	.12	.21	n.s.	n.s.
C. Plans for males	.35	.56	n.s.	< .01M
D. Female executors	.53	.03	< .01	< .001F
E. Male executors	.12	.85	< .001	< .01M
F. Successful plans	.59	.74	n.s.	n.s.
G. Failures	.24	.39	n.s.	n.s.
II. Crime/Adventure	$(n = 7)$	$(n = 53)$		
A. All plan-making	1.43	1.76	n.s.	< .001M
B. Plans for females	.43	.25	n.s.	n.s.
C. Plans for males	.86	1.09	n.s.	< .001M
D. Female executors	.57	.06	n.s.	< .05F
E. Male executors	.29	1.26	< .05	< .001M
F. Successful plans	.57	1.00	n.s.	< .01M
G. Failures	.86	.70	n.s.ᵣ	< .05M
III. Saturday a.m.	$(n = 10)$	$(n = 53)$		
A. All plan-making	1.90	1.83	n.s.	< .01M
B. Plans for females	.00	.11	< .05	< .05M
C. Plans for males	.90	.81	n.s.	n.s.
D. Female executors	.40	.02	n.s.	< .01F
E. Male executors	.70	1.15	n.s.	< .01M
F. Successful plans	1.00	.85	n.s.	n.s.
G. Failures	1.00	.83	n.s.	n.s.

males. Plan outcomes were not different by sex, although the plan-maker remained the same sex as the plan executor.

In crime/adventure shows, males made more plans proportionately overall and for other males than did females, and more of those male plans were both successful and unsuccessful. On Saturday morning shows, more plan-making was done by males especially for females, with no difference in plan outcomes between the genders.

Thus, males were most likely to dominate the behavior sequence of plan-making on crime/adventure shows, did so to a somewhat lesser extent on Saturday morning, and performed equivalently on situation comedies.

DISCUSSION

These results contribute to the accumulating evidence regarding the potential for sex-role learning from television in two particular ways: (1) they examine a subset of behavioral sequences, including the outcomes of those behaviors, rather than more static descriptions of manifest demographic or physical characteristics or judged personality traits; (2) they demonstrate that the general tendency to lump all of television together to create an "average" picture may mask significant deviations within television content in its portrayal of men and women.

As for dominance and deference behaviors, examined here in terms of ordergiving, the "average" depiction is one in which men are far more likely to give orders to other men, both as superior to subordinate and peer to peer. Further, as reinforcement to this behavior, those male-originated orders are more likely to be followed. This is especially accurate in describing crime and adventure series and basically correct for Saturday morning shows. The viewer of situation comedies, however, is more likely to be exposed to this behavioral sequence in the form of women giving the orders disproportionately to other women. And the orders originated by women are less likely to be followed, yielding less reinforcement for such behavior by females.

On the nurturance and exigence dimension, more sensitive understanding of content comes less from program types than from a basic distinction among the kinds of needs TV characters have. The behaviors observed indicate substantial need for physical assistance by males and a disproportionate need for emotional assistance by females. Females are more likely to request aid; males are more likely not to. Then, the outcome is more likely to reinforce the female in need; she is given nurturance for her plight.

With regard to behaviors related to independence, the uniform pattern identified was for males to make plans for both sexes, and for those plans to both succeed and fail at a greater rate for males. The infrequent occurrence of manifest plan-making makes this a more tenuous finding.

Some cautions are necessary. First, this analysis comes from a single season, and it is necessary to determine whether there are substantial year-to-year variations. In subsequent seasons, presented in Chapter 6 the new shows began featuring females more prominently (although not in greater frequency) and how those behavioral sequences emerge will be determined. Studies, done earlier, in several different seasons, do not indicate sharp differences among more static attributes examined over time. Second, the findings are cast principally in terms of whether these behaviors occur more than would be expected from the sheer numbers of each gender. The initial difference of three males for each female means that virtually every behavior occurs in an absolute sense more often among males. Researchers in social learning have not previously examined whether viewers are sensitive to disproportionate displays of behaviors in a fashion parallel to sheer frequency of behaviors. Thus, the process of predicting the impact of these portrayals increases in complexity. Mischel (1966) writes, the "manner in which the model's behavior is presented with respect to the frequency, rate, and clarity of presentation critically affects the extent to which the modeled behaviors are acquired." Thus, the question of women doing something more often than would be expected may not reach an adequate frequency for acquisition of the behavior. What that critical mass or frequency is remains indeterminate.

A related issue is the viewer's attachment to specific television characters. Here, dealing across all characters, one ignores the likelihood that certain characters, especially attractive to viewers for various reasons, may have an inordinate capacity to induce modeling or social learning. Females who are attached to an unusually dominant and independent female, e.g., "Maude," may focus on her behavioral pattern and ignore a host of others. We have no evidence to permit an estimation of the difference in learning that could originate from "critical instances" of television exposure, i.e., viewing a small set of favorite "regulars" or such specials as "Jane Pittman," in contrast to viewing a subset of the entire panorama of females available. Is the glut of consistent behaviors that are sex-typed more dominant in social learning acquisitions than idiosyncratic and intensive deviations, or selective attention to a favored subgroup of characters?

If reinforced behaviors are more likely to be acquired and performed, then both boys and girls should wish to give orders and make plans, for the orders will be followed and more of the plans successful, in general, at least when males originate them. This partly accounts for recent findings that girls will make more crossover sex preferences of TV characters than boys (Miller and Reeves, 1976).

It is men who do these things more regularly with greater success. Does the same logic apply to nurturance behavior? Females needing help, especially for emotional distress, are likely to receive assistance, after they request it; men, needing help for physical distress, are less likely to request aid and less likely to receive it. This appears to be a more complex sequence, with the further contingency involved of asking for help. Yet, it is possible to argue that the most desirable role in this behavioral sequence is not the receiver of needed assistance, but the provider of it; the primary nurturing on television is done *by* men *of* women. For every act of nurturance by a female of either a male or female in distress, there were more than three acts of nurturance by males. Thus, the social learning lesson may be that it's all right for women to express needs for support; a man is likely to respond to those needs, once requested.

Content analysis is a precursor to specific examination of social learning issues. These findings have demonstrated a homogeneity in certain behaviors of sex-role models and their reinforcement. The critical tests of these ideas must come from empirically determining whether, and how much, television content contributes to sex-role learning of behaviors.

6

TRENDS IN SEX-ROLE PORTRAYALS ON TELEVISION

BRADLEY S. GREENBERG
MARCIA RICHARDS
LAURA HENDERSON

Chapter 5 demonstrates that sex-role stereotyping is woven more deeply into the television programming fabric than merely an abundance of male characters over female characters, or young, nubile females over older, less jiggly ones. The interpersonal interactions of men and women are boxed into demonstrable patterns of dominance, nurturing, and independence for men, and complementary patterns of deference, receiving succorance, and dependence for women. What has been identified for a single season merits examination in additional time periods.

The single year of sex-role findings just presented gives us a baseline from which subsequent comparison can be made. If, in response to self-imposed or external pressures, the networks promise new conceptions of women or new female role models on television, then one can check up on those promises. At least, one can examine whether specific role models or the entire population of female television characters is exhibiting similar or deviant patterns of order-giving behaviors, support-needing behaviors, etc.

The substance of the findings in the last chapter requires replication. They are static information; they have no prior history, nor any future, but merely describe the state of affairs for a single composite week. In fact, the composite week could be suspect if, for uncontrollable reasons, the collection of 80 or so episodes were quite aberrant from a more "normal" collection. Hardly likely, but yet another reason for wanting more information on the same issues. It's better science to have more support.

Conceptually, the desire for trend information also is linked to the notion that the dominance/deference dimension and the nurturance-giving/succorance-seeking dimension were generated as fundamental reflections of societal sexism. As one moves from those higher-order concepts to such operational levels as ordergiving, support types, or success/failure rates, risks are involved. The operation may not be sensitive enough to detect sex-role differences, or they may be too infrequent to pursue, or they may not be central to the overarching concepts of interest. The first-year findings identified a subset of variables which did yield consistent differences, those which are too small to be of further concern, and those which appear to validate the hypothetical dimensions with which we started. Replicating the conceptual scheme, albeit on content from different seasons, can serve to strengthen the model being used to analyze and understand sex-role behaviors.

This last point leads to a reminder that the content portrayal information is a starting point, not an end result. Identifying how men and women differ on television—here particularly in terms of their interpersonal interactions—serves as a prelude to determining what kind of carryover there may be from television to real life. Our interest in cataloging the culture and civilization of fictional television content is not to be confused with our interest in which of television's norms, values, and themes are learned, modeled, and simulated by viewers. Trend studies serve well those subsequent research goals; to the extent that specific sex-role behavioral differences are perpetuated not only across programming within a season, but also across multiple seasons, one can better place bets as to what is being learned from exposure to television.

Therefore, the project replicated its examination of sex-role portrayals for two additional sample weeks, one in the fall of 1976–77, and the final one in the fall of 1977–78.

METHODS

The analysis of the portrayal of sex roles on television for the second and third years of this project was designed to be as parallel as possible to that done for the first year. The primary outcome sought was the examination of trends and only through relatively strict replication would that purpose be served.

It is important to note some attributes of the overall sample of shows and characters. Each season contained from 60 to 70 television hours, encompassing 80 to 90 different episodes of fictional television series. This analysis was primarily concerned with the interactions of males and females. Important both for description and analysis is the relative distribution of the two sexes. In each season we dealt with the behaviors of more than 1000 speaking television characters; nonspeaking characters were omitted from all analyses in this book. In the first season (1975–76), the males in the sample constituted 73 percent of the eligible population of television charactars; in year 2 (1976–77), and year 3 (1977–78), the proportion of males obtained was 71 percent. Thus one interesting observation is the consistency in the absolute and relative levels of prominence of males over females.

Content Categories

The first-year project developed three conceptual categories: *order-giving,* an operational category used to assess dominance/deference; *support needs* operationally used to estimate nurturance giving/getting; and *plans,* a variable designed to estimate independence/dependence. The categories of orders and supports were continued with minor changes in the second and third years of data analysis. The concept and measurement of plans was dropped completely after the first year; the low incidence of occurrence of planmaking among females did not permit most of the desired analyses. In the first year studied, we could find only 44 females who had made any kind of specific plan in the entire sample week. Thus the examination of the comparative independence of men and the large-scale inactivity of women as plan-makers was not carried any further. Here let us briefly re-describe the two remaining sex-role activities for which three years of trend data will be presented.

Ordergiving. Essentially, ordergiving consisted of examining this behavior sequence: "Who, by sex, gave what type of order to whom, by sex, and was the order carried out or not?" Examined were *authority* orders, those which were likely to be complied with because of occupational superiority, parental deference, or origin with a representative of a particular preeminent social agency or institution, e.g., a police officer, a teacher, or a doctor. Then there were *simple* orders, which occurred among equals or peers. Originally we had successfully differentiated those orders which could be clearly understood as threats from these two. The low frequency of threats found, however, led to its deletion. These two basic order types, authority and simple, were further subdivided into those situations in which they were explained or not explained. *Explanation* consisted of the ordergiver's including some justification or reason for following the order. Thus the basic analysis of ordergiving dealt with the extent to which men and women gave and received simple and authority-originated orders, with and without reasons for executing them, and whether or not those orders were followed.

Needing Support. The coding of support types did not differ among the three seasons analyzed in terms of the basic variables. Essentially this behavior sequence was to be analyzed: "If a character is identified as in need of some type of support, what kind of support was needed and by whom, by sex? By sex, who requested support, who was given support, and who were the givers of that support?"

Need for support existed if it was reliably assessed that a television character was in danger or distress. That general description obtained its substance from the specification of support types that would aid coder identification of danger and distress situations.

The first differentiation was between physical and emotional needs situations. Need types and definitions conform to those presented in Chapter 5. Here a brief reminder of each of those types will facilitate interpreting the present results. Three types of physical support needs were examined:

1. *Physical external support* need in which the television character is in danger of being injured or killed; the origin of the threat is external to the character;

2. *Physical internal support* need, where the television character is suffering from disease, illness, or some other internally originated ailment; the physical distress comes from within the character;

3. *Physical confinement,* where the character's activities have been restrained by another character, e.g., the individual is in jail, trapped, or otherwise held against his will; the confinement is involuntary.

Three types of emotional support needs were coded in all three seasons:

1. *Ego support.* Here the television character identifies a personal problem he/she is unable to cope with and for which the character estimates that others will dislike him or hold him in less esteem; the origin of emotional discomfort comes from within the character;

2. *Concern for others.* The character seeks support for a friend, relative, or associate from a third party. The focus is that support is needed by someone else in trouble.

3. *Psychological support.* Here the television character is in distress because of the actions of others but does not express a lack of self-confidence nor an inability to cope. But a need for support is expressed.

In addition to these need support types, coders also examined whether the television characters in need of support did or did not ask for help in resolving that need, identified whether television characters in need were given support independently of whether they requested it, and who provided that particular support.

Coding Procedures

One significant procedural change occurred between the first and subsequent years in these analyses. During year one, coders recorded data in 2-minute time segments. The principal deficiency of this procedure was that the arbitrary time stopping often interrupted codeable behavior sequences. This was changed to a method in which "scenes" became the coding unit. A *scene* was defined as a series of acts continuous in time and space, not broken or interrupted by the addition or departures of characters or by a change in setting. Thus if the characters and the location remained the same, the scene was the same. One exception supplemented this basic definition: a television commercial was considered to mark the end of a given scene, even if the characters and setting were identical before and after the commercial break. The scene, a nonarbitrary time unit, served the same purpose as timed segments. It organized the coding process whenever a scene ended, the coders were able to turn off the videotape equipment and record the extent to which codeable acts had occurred.

Coding procedures for year 1 and year 2 were identical. After intensive training programs, independent coding was done by individual coders. The reliability obtained with this procedure varied extensively across variables and attributes, but was at more than minimal levels. In year 3 we sought to improve this process further and instituted pair coding. A team of coders viewed each show together and produced one set of data. Reliability scores were calculated between this pair and a second pair of coders examining the same content, as well as between members of each pair. Between pairs reliabilities ranged from .65 to .75 on the orders dimension and from .54 to .89 on the supports dimension. Between members of a pair, reliability scores nearly always exceeded .9 on both dimensions. The higher reliability between members of a pair was to some extent induced because members of a pair deliberately and/or inadvertently cue each other when a codable act appears. Coders working on the same program even independently of each other are more likely to arrive at the same number of codable acts than individuals working separately. Beginning with the same set of codable acts substantially reduces error in reliability.

Analysis

Analyses for all three years were the same. Indexes for the orders and supports variables were constructed as identified in Chapter 5 in this book.

All analyses focused on two questions of primary interest. Each question pertains to a different sex-based referent group. First, the results identify whether the proportion of sex role acts in the orders and supports dimensions are comparable to, or deviant from, the proportions of male and female characters in the television population. That is, for example, the question of whether the total proportion of authority orders originating with male television characters is significantly different from the proportion of males in the population of television characters. The second main analysis deals with the absolute rate of sex-role behaviors by gender. This answers the question, "Do men or women express a greater need for physical support, in the sex role dimension of support needs?" The former analysis examines sex-role behaviors relative to the presence of each sex in the television population; the second analysis tests the absolute magnitude of these behaviors performed by each gender. Both analytic modes were carried out for the entire sample of television shows in each season. In addition, we present findings which further clarify and portray sex-role behaviors on television by subdividing the full complex of programming into two major program types—situation comedies and crime/adventure shows—and three time blocks—Saturday morning; 8–9 p.m.; 9–11 p.m.

RESULTS

The findings for all three sample weeks are presented successively for the two behavioral sequences examined in all three seasons—giving orders and expressing need for support. Within each, findings will be presented first for all the fictional shows, and subsequently for those same shows subdivided into some basic program types and by time of broadcast. These results also provide an opportunity for replicated tests of hypotheses created in Chapter 5. In this presentation of results, the narrative will focus on apparent trends; the hypotheses will be specifically examined in the final section of this chapter.

Ordergiving

Table 6.1 summarizes the major findings for all the order-giving variables for the three seasons. In the tables, we have identified differences between males and females and only those differences which are statistically significant are reported in the tables as M > F or F > M. Such a notation indicates a statistically significant difference at least at the .05 probability level. The actual means and statistical results can be found in Henderson (1978) and Richards (1980).

Let us then proceed in Table 6.1 to determine what kind of sex-role differences appeared in terms of ordergiving variables. The results indicate that men gave more orders on the average than did females in each of the three seasons for all four order types summed together. Furthermore, the total number of orders of all types given by males was proportionately larger than that given by females, also in each of the three seasons. This is a large and most consistent finding.

The source of the greater prevalence of ordergiving by males was predominantly that of authority orders. The findings show that both the rate and proportion of authority orders and the subcategory of authority orders explained was consistently male-dominated in all 12 comparisons possible in Table 6.1. In the first and second seasons studied, males also dominated in peer ordergiving; in the third, there was no greater giving and/or explaining of orders by peers among males than among females.

Thus, males give more orders on television fictional series than do females, but the most regular context of that ordergiving is from a male authority figure. Among peers, orders were as likely to originate with females as with males in the most recent television season; the general trend, however, was for males to supercede females in peer situations.

Turning next to the examination of order-receivers, Table 6.1 in-

TABLE 6.1
Orders by Sex in All Shows

		Years		
		1	*2*	*3*
I. All orders	Rate	M > F	M > F	M > F
	Proportion	M > F	M > F	M > F
A. Authority orders	Rate	M > F	M > F	M > F
	Proportion	M > F	M > F	M > F
B. Authority orders explained	Rate	M > F	M > F	M > F
	Proportion	M > F	M > F	M > F
C. Peer orders	Rate	M > F	n.s.	n.s.
	Proportion	M > F	M > F	n.s.
D. Peer orders explained	Rate	M > F	M > F	n.s.
	Proportion	M > F	M > F	n.s.
II. Order receivers A. Females	Rate	M > F	n.s.	n.s.
	Proportion	n.s.	F > M	n.s.
B. Males	Rate	M > F	M > F	M > F
	Proportion	M > F	M > F	M > F
III. Orders followed A. Yes	Rate	M > F	M > F	M > F
	Proportion	M > F	M > F	M > F
B. No	Rate	M > F	n.s.	n.s.
	Proportion	n.s.	n.s.	n.s.
C. Unknown	Rate	*	M > F	M > F
	Proportion	*	M > F	M > F

*Not determined in Year 1

dicates that there is little consistency across the three sets of data in terms of whether females are more likely to receive orders from one sex or the other. In firm contrast, it is demonstrated that males receive more orders from other males both on an absolute and proportional basis, and did so in each of the three seasons with the same consistency. Females get their orders equivalently from men and women; men get their orders from other men.

We explored, also, the extent to which orders were followed and whether the following of orders was related to the sex of the individual ordergiver. These results, too, are in Table 6.1. Male-originated orders were followed more frequently and disproportionately more often than were orders originating with females in each of the three years. Not following orders was not related to sex; orders originating with men and women had the same likelihood of going unfollowed. Finally, in the second and third years, we further analyzed whether orders whose fate was unknown differed in terms of their sex origin. Consistently, orders from males were more likely to have unknown fates than orders from females. Having orders followed was sex-role related and oriented to orders originating with males; orders of unknown fates originated more with males; orders definitely not followed started equivalently with both sexes.

Program Type Differences

Table 6.2 provides comparable information for two program types, situation comedies and crime/adventure shows. In this text, we also discuss Saturday cartoon programming, but we have not tabled this since the analysis was done for only the most recent season studied. In Table 6.2 we reduced the number of results presented by omitting the categories of explained orders. The relatively low frequency of occurrence warranted this attempt to modify the data presentation. Let us turn first to the findings for situation comedies, in the left half of Table 6.2. Here the predominant trend is for there to be no significant differences in the rates of ordergiving, order-receipt, or order-following between men and women. In essence, the average number of occurrences of ordergiving variables is the same for men as for women. Some things do occur in situation comedies disproportionately between the sexes. Most notable of these is the greater proportion of peer orders given by females than by males in all three seasons, and the parallel finding of disproportionate order-receiving by females from other females in all three seasons. Thus, in situation comedies, one of the two most frequent program types presented on television, there is parity between the sexes in the rates with which they engage in order-giving behaviors. For orders occurring among people very similar to each

TABLE 6.2

Orders by Sex in Situation Comedies and Crime/Adventure Shows

	Years:	Situation Comedies			Crime/Adventure Shows		
		1	2	3	1	2	3
I. All orders	Rate	n.s.	n.s.	n.s.	M > F	M > F	M > F
	Proportion	F > M	F > M	n.s.	M > F	M > F	M > F
Authority	Rate	n.s.	n.s.	M > F	M > F	M > F	M > F
	Proportion	n.s.	M > F	M > F	M > F	M > F	M > F
Peer	Rate	n.s.	n.s.	n.s.	n.s.	n.s.	n.s.
	Proportion	F > M	F > M	F > M	M > F	M > F	M > F
II. Order receivers							
Female	Rate	n.s.	n.s.	F > M	M > F	n.s.	M > F
	Proportion	F > M	F > M	F > M	M > F	M > F	M > F
Male	Rate	n.s.	n.s.	M > F	M > F	M > F	n.s.
	Proportion	n.s.	n.s.	M > F	M > F	M > F	M > F
III. Orders followed							
Yes	Rate	n.s.	n.s.	n.s.	M > F	M > F	M > F
	Proportion	n.s.	n.s.	n.s.	M > F	M > F	M > F
No	Rate	n.s.	n.s.	n.s.	n.s.	n.s.	M > F
	Proportion	F > M	n.s.	n.s.	M > F	M > F	M > F

other, among peers, there is more order-giving and order-getting activity among women than among men. And more recently, it seems that authority order distinctions between the sexes are becoming more regular in situation-comedies; men are exceeding women in that behavior.

Crime/adventure shows are not only a mirror image of the sex-role differences just identified for situation comedies, but also constitute a program type in which there is virtually no equity between the sexes. In the right half of Table 6.2 which presents the crime/adventure show findings, male dominance exceeds any of our other analyses. Males give more orders overall, more authority orders, and more peer orders. They do so in terms of relative rates and also disproportionately to the representation of their sex in the population of TV characters. Both female order-receivers and male order-receivers get their orders from males in crime/adventure shows. They do so in each season and in 11 of the 12 possible comparisons of that behavior. The trend with regard to the orders being followed is the same; more orders originating with males are followed than those which originate with females, and more orders originating with males also go unfollowed. In crime/adventure shows, the male predominates in all aspects of ordering, in terms of giving orders of all types, in terms of being the origin of orders for both females and males, and in having orders both followed and unfollowed.

On Saturday cartoon shows, examined for sex-role differences only for year three, we found that male cartoon characters exceeded female cartoon characters in terms of giving each of the different order types—authority and peer, explained and unexplained—disproportionately more than females. Females were as likely to have received their orders from males as from females, but the male orientation to other males as receivers continued. Furthermore, orders originating with males were disproportionately likely to be followed on the cartoons; orders that went unfollowed were not different by sex.

Broadcast Time Differences

There was a further interest in whether men and women behaved differently toward each other during different broadcast time periods. The most typical division of broadcast time for network series includes the breakdown: Saturday morning, daytime, early evening (8–9 p.m.), and later evening (9–11 p.m.). We have three of these time periods, excluding daytime programming. The major results and trends are in Table 6.3. Looking first at the results for Saturday morning, which here include both the cartoon and noncartoon series, order types show a distinct male bias, primarily in terms of disproportionate presentation of both authority and peer orders originating with male television charac-

TABLE 6.3
Orders by Sex by Broadcast Time Period

		Saturday Morning			8–9 p.m.			9–11 p.m.		
Years:		1	2	3	1	2	3	1	2	3
I. All orders	Rate	n.s.	n.s.	n.s.	n.s.	n.s.	n.s.	M > F	M > F	M > F
	Proportion	M > F	M > F	M > F	M > F	n.s.	M > F	M > F	M > F	M > F
Authority	Rate	M > F	M > F	n.s.	n.s.	n.s.	M > F	M > F	M > F	M > F
	Proportion	M > F	M > F	M > F	M > F	n.s.	M > F	M > F	M > F	M > F
Peer	Rate	n.s.	n.s.	n.s.	n.s.	n.s.	n.s.	M > F	n.s.	n.s.
	Proportion	M > F	M > F	M > F	n.s.	n.s.	n.s.	M > F	M > F	n.s.
II. Order receivers										
Females	Rate	n.s.	n.s.	n.s.	n.s.	F > M	n.s.	M > F	n.s.	n.s.
	Proportion	M > F	n.s.	n.s.	n.s.	F > M	F > M	n.s.	M > F	n.s.
Males	Rate	n.s.	n.s.	n.s.	n.s.	M > F	M > F	M > F	M > F	M > F
	Proportion	M > F	M > F	M > F	M > F	M > F	M > F	M > F	M > F	M > F
III. Orders followed										
Yes	Rate	n.s.	n.s.	n.s.	n.s.	n.s.	n.s.	M > F	M > F	M > F
	Proportion	M > F	M > F	M > F	M > F	n.s.	M > F	M > F	M > F	M > F
No	Rate	n.s.	n.s.	n.s.	n.s.	n.s.	n.s.	M > F	n.s.	n.s.
	Proportion	M > F	n.s.	n.s.	n.s.	n.s.	n.s.	n.s.	n.s.	n.s.

ters. The rates are more similar except for authority orders where the tendency is for both the rate and the proportion of authority orders to be unusually large for males. Let us examine order types during the other broadcast time periods before looking at the other ordergiving variables. The middle segment of Table 6.3 indicates what happens in terms of order types from 8–9 p.m. on network television. Then, there is greater equity between the sexes. There is a pattern of no differences between the sexes in terms of ordergiving. The only exception to this is that males still reflect a pattern within authority orders that has been distinctively evident in the earlier presentation of results. This tendency is weaker in this time slot than in the other time slots. Turning finally to the righthand segment of Table 6.3 and examining the sex-role results for 9–11 p.m., male preeminence again asserts itself. In terms of both overall rate of ordergiving and proportion of ordergiving, especially within the authority order typology, the male excels without exception. It is in this time period that many of the crime/adventure series are broadcast as well as other hero type programming. Thus, there is some redundancy between the findings for this time period and the findings for certain program types presented earlier. What this segment of Table 6.3 demonstrates is a distinct male superiority in later prime-time periods and on Saturday morning, with somewhat greater parity between the sexes from 8–9 p.m.

Order-receiving is in the lower half of Table 6.3. On Saturday morning, males disproportionately receive orders from other males. That is the only identifiable sex role difference. From 8–9 p.m., however, females are more likely to receive orders from other females; even more consistently, males receive orders from other males in all three seasons. So this early evening time period does segment the sexes, with female receivers oriented to female order-givers and male receivers oriented to male order-givers. This stops at 9 p.m. where the trend for the final two prime-time hours is for a clear distinction for male order-receivers and little distinction among female order-receivers. In all possible comparisons of both rate of reception and proportion of orders received, males get their orders from males. Females no longer are getting their orders from females. At best there is no difference in terms of where females get them, and in some comparisons they are also more likely to get them from males in the later evening programs.

The final segment of Table 6.3 deals with whether orders are followed or not, differentially by sex in the three broadcast periods. On Saturday morning, male-originated orders are more likely followed; from 8–9 p.m. there is some evidence of a disproportionate male bias toward orders followed. After 9 p.m. it is found each time that male orders are more likely to be followed than female orders, with no sex differences in terms of orders not followed.

The broadcast time period analysis demonstrates male superiority after 9 p.m., little sex difference from 8–9 p.m., and some steady trends for male dominance in Saturday morning programming.

Support Needs

The second major category of sex-role behavior examined in all three seasons was that of the support systems established among male and female television characters. We looked at types of support with specific breakdowns for various physical support types and emotional support types. Furthermore, we examined whether support was requested, whether it was given, and the sex of the individual television character providing the support.

The findings for this set of variables begin in Table 6.4 with information about support types across all the shows in each of the three seasons. Among physical support types individually and collectively, males needed these support types significantly more so than did females on both the measures of rate and proportionality. For the specific support types, the overall findings held for external and internal physical support but not so consistently for physical confinement. In the two more recent seasons, need for physical support in physically confining situations was equivalent among men and women television characters. Nevertheless, the overall rates for physical support needs show a clear superiority of male needs in this area.

Table 6.4 demonstrates the opposite pattern for emotional support

TABLE 6.4
Support Types by Sex in All Shows

			Years		
			1	*2*	*3*
I.	Physical support types				
	A. Internal	Rate	M > F	n.s.	M > F
		Proportion	M > F	M > F	M > F
	B. External	Rate	M > F	M > F	M > F
		Proportion	M > F	M > F	M > F
	C. Confinement	Rate	M > F	n.s.	n.s.
		Proportion	M > F	n.s.	n.s.
	D. All physical	Rate	M > F	M > F	M > F
		Proportion	M > F	M > F	M > F
II.	Emotional support types				
	A. Ego support	Rate	n.s.	n.s.	n.s.
		Proportion	F > M	n.s.	n.s.
	B. Concern for	Rate	n.s.	F > M	n.s.
	others	Proportion	F > M	F > M	n.s.
	C. Psychological	Rate	n.s.	n.s.	F > M
	support	Proportion	F > M	F > M	F > M
	D. All emotional	Rate	n.s.	n.s.	F > M
		Proportion	F > M	F > M	F > M

needs. If not so consistently in terms of the rate measure, then clearly women needed each of the several emotional support types disproportionately more than men in most of the possible comparisons, and clearly so in the summative index of emotional supports. Women needed ego support, psychological support, and support in connection with their concern for others significantly more than did the male television characters. This orientation of men to physical needs and women to emotional needs continues a stereotypic pattern identified earlier in other media forms as well as television.

Continuing with the trend analysis for support variables across all shows, Table 6.5 delves further into the characteristic situations of support requests and support provisions found in these samples of television shows. The findings demonstrate certain consistencies:

1. Women are more likely to request support than are men.

2. Men are significantly more likely not to request support in situations in which they might do so. This holds for their average rate of not requesting support as well as the overall proportion of these nonrequests.

3. Support was given disproportionately to the females in all three seasons, and given to females at a higher rate than males in two of the three seasons.

4. The reverse was true with respect to those situations in which support was not given. Males did not receive support disproportionately to females in all three seasons, and this was at a significantly higher rate of nonsupport in two of those three instances.

5. There was a trend for both male and female givers of support to focus that support on female recipients.

TABLE 6.5
Support Requests and Responses by Sex in All Shows

				Years	
			1	*2*	*3*
A.	Support requested	Rate	n.s.	F > M	F > M
		Proportion	F > M	F > M	F > M
B.	Support not requested	Rate	M > F	n.s.	M > F
		Proportion	M > F	M > F	M > F
C.	Support given	Rate	M > F	F > M	F > M
		Proportion	F > M	F > M	F > M
D.	Support not given	Rate	M > F	n.s.	M > F
		Proportion	M > F	M > F	M > F
E.	Female givers	Rate	n.s.	F > M	n.s.
		Proportion	F > M	F > M	n.s.
F.	Male givers	Rate	M > F	n.s.	n.s.
		Proportion	F > M	n.s.	F > M

Program Type Differences. Table 6.6 summarizes findings about the sex-role behavior of support systems within the two major program types analyzed, situation comedies and crime/adventure shows. In this presentation we have reduced the data to the overall summative indexes of physical and emotional support types. The situation comedy

TABLE 6.6
Support Needs by Sex in Situation Comedies and Crime/Adventure Shows

		Situation Comedies			Crime/Adventure		
	Years	1	2	3	1	2	3
A. Physical support types	Rate	M > F	n.s.	n.s.	n.s.	M > F	n.s.
	Proportion	M > F	n.s.	n.s.	M > F	M > F	n.s.
B. Emotional support types	Rate	n.s.	n.s.	n.s.	F > M	n.s.	n.s.
	Proportion	F > M	F > M	F > M	F > M	n.s.	F > M
C. Support requested	Rate	n.s.	n.s.	F > M	F > M	n.s.	n.s.
	Proportion	F > M	F > M	F > M	F > M	n.s.	F > M
Support not requested	Rate	n.s.	n.s.	n.s.	n.s.	n.s.	n.s.
	Proportion	n.s.	n.s.	n.s.	n.s.	M > F	n.s.
D. Support given	Rate	n.s.	n.s.	F > M	F > M	n.s.	n.s.
	Proportion	F > M	F > M	F > M	n.s.	n.s.	n.s.
Support not given	Rate	n.s.	n.s.	n.s.	n.s.	n.s.	n.s.
	Proportion	n.s.	n.s.	n.s.	n.s.	n.s.	n.s.
E. Female givers	Rate	F > M	n.s.	F > M	n.s.	n.s.	n.s.
	Proportion	F > M	F > M	F > M	n.s.	n.s.	n.s.
Male givers	Rate	n.s.	n.s.	n.s.	F > M	n.s.	n.s.
	Proportion	F > M	n.s.	n.s.	F > M	n.s.	n.s.

results are reflected in the left half of Table 6.6 and the crime/adventure results in the righthand portion.

The tendency for greater male physical support needs found in both program types in the first season was found a second time in the crime/adventure programs in year two, but in neither program type was there a significant sex difference in year three. In contrast, the identified disproportionate need for emotional support among females was found in all three seasons in situation comedies and in two of the three seasons of crime/adventure programs. The same tendency existed in both program types for requests for support; females requested support in proportions significantly larger than males. From that point on, with respect to the other support variables, the pattern in crime/adventure programs showed no particular sex differences. In situation comedies, however, two other consistent findings in Table 6.6 should be identified. For one, support was given disproportionately to females who had requested it, in greater numbers than their representation in the television population would have required. Second, females gave support to other females significantly more often than men provided that support system; males gave support equivalently to male and female television characters in situation comedies.

On Saturday cartoons in Year 3, the stronger male persisted. He needed more physical supports, was less likely to ask for help, and was less likely to be given it. Females were given aid at a significantly higher rate.

Program type is not so sharp a differentiator of support behaviors as it was with the order variables presented earlier. In fact, where differences were found in each of these program types, they tended to corroborate rather than contrast with each other. Women needed more emotional support in different program types and requested it more.

Broadcast Time Differences. Table 6.7 identifies the support systems portrayed by the sexes on Saturday morning, from 8–9 p.m., and from 9–11 p.m. Beginning with the Saturday morning results, men needed physical support more often in this genre of programming than did women. Proportionately, men needed more of the several physical support types in all three seasons. As for emotional support needs, there were no systematic differences. The same may be said for the extent to which support was requested by either of the sexes. Very consistently, however, men were less likely than women to request support in the Saturday morning shows. The concept of the self-sufficient male predominated in sex-role portrayals at that time period. On Saturday morning, support was given to men and women equivalently; support was not given disproportionately to men, strengthening the attribute of self-sufficiency.

TABLE 6.7

Support Needs by Sex by Broadcast Time

	Years	Saturday Morning			8–9 p.m.			9–11 p.m.		
		1	2	3	1	2	3	1	2	3
A. Physical support types	Rate	n.s.	n.s.	M > F	M > F	n.s.	n.s.	M > F	n.s.	M > F
	Proportion	M > F	M > F	M > F	M > F	M > F	n.s.	M > F	n.s.	n.s.
B. Emotional support types	Rate	n.s.	n.s.	F > M	n.s.	n.s.	n.s.	n.s.	F > M	F > M
	Proportion	n.s.	M > F	n.s.	F > M	n.s.	F > M	F > M	F > M	F > M
C. Support requested	Rate	F > M	n.s.	n.s.	n.s.	F > M	n.s.	n.s.	F > M	n.s.
	Proportion	n.s.	n.s.	n.s.	F > M	F > M	F > M	F > M	F > M	F > M
Support not requested	Rate	M > F	M > F	M > F	n.s.	n.s.	n.s.	M > F	n.s.	n.s.
	Proportion	M > F	M > F	M > F	n.s.	M > F	n.s.	n.s.	n.s.	n.s.
D. Support given	Rate	n.s.	n.s.	n.s.	n.s.	F > M	n.s.	M > F	F > M	F > M
	Proportion	M > F	n.s.	n.s.	F > M	F > M	n.s.	F > M	F > M	F > M
Support not given	Rate	n.s.	M > F	M > F	n.s.	n.s.	n.s.	M > F	n.s.	M > F
	Proportion	M > F	M > F	M > F	n.s.	n.s.	F > M	F > M	F > M	n.s.
E. Female givers	Rate	n.s.	n.s.	n.s.	F > M	F > M	n.s.	n.s.	n.s.	n.s.
	Proportion	M > F	n.s.	n.s.	n.s.	F > M	n.s.	F > M	n.s.	F > M
Male givers	Rate	n.s.	n.s.	n.s.	n.s.	n.s.	n.s.	M > F	n.s.	n.s.
	Proportion	n.s.	n.s.	n.s.	n.s.	n.s.	n.s.	F > M	F > M	F > M

In the early evening prime-time hour, three general statements can be made:

 1. The tendency for men to need more in the way of physical support than women persisted through the first two seasons analyzed but not into the third.

 2. Women were disproportionately likely to need emotional support, to request it, to be given it, and to be given it by other women.

 3. Other than needing physical support, men were not different from women.

In sum, in the 8–9 p.m. time period, women tended to be most active in these support system variables, although the quality of their activity corresponded to preexisting stereotypes of women, in the kinds of support they needed and the frequency with which they would ask and get it.

Finally, the 9–11 p.m. time period did not look distinctly different from that of 8–9 p.m. Sex-role differences in terms of physical support needs favored men; sex-role differences in terms of emotional support needs favored women disproportionately. Women were more likely to request support than were men, and they were more likely to receive it. Further, female support givers gave support primarily to females. From 9–11 p.m., males also disproportionately gave support to females.

The broadcast time analysis indicates that Saturday morning is the most male-dominated in terms of the greater occurrence of male behaviors in the support sequence examined. It is males doing more of certain behaviors than females across a number of different characteristics. By contrast, prime-time programming is more likely to identify female-dominated sex-role behaviors; those female-dominated behaviors, however, are quite stereotypic.

DISCUSSION

Three years of findings on the same basic questions give us an unusual opportunity to reexamine our original hypotheses and to identify the kinds of support there may be from multiple tests of the questions asked. It seems most appropriate to begin discussing these results from that viewpoint.

One set of hypotheses originated with the issue of what kinds of dominance and deference might differentiate male and female characterizations on commercial television programs. We articulated this dimension as, "Who gives what types of orders to whom with what outcome?" We looked at ordergiving as imbedded in either an authority relationship (superior to subordinate) or a peer relationship. One hypothesis specified that male television characters would originate more authority orders than female television characters. There was substantial support for the proposition in all three seasons, differences that were consistently statistically significant. Furthermore, that finding held up within our program type breakdown for those hero type shows grouped as crime/adventure shows. The hypothesis was not supported for situation comedies. That same hypothesis was consistently supported in two significant time periods—throughout all the Saturday morning shows and all the later evening prime-time shows, from 9–11 p.m. There was less support for that proposition in the evening hour, 8–9 p.m.; that inconsistency fluctuated between male dominance and no sex dominance. In no time did females exhibit any superiority in authority order creation.

We were ambiguous with regard to peer orders. Our original hypothesis projected that they would occur equivalently for the sexes; that essentially is what was obtained across all the shows. It is, however, more enlightening to look at what was found with peer orders in different types of programs. Contrasting results in situation comedies and crime/adventure shows generated the lack of difference across all shows. In situation comedies, females originated significantly more peer orders in proportion to their representation in the television character population than did males. The reverse was true for crime/adventure shows; males consistently originated more orders both relatively and proportionately. These more subtle findings by program type were not conveyed in the broadcast time analysis. In that subdivision, there was either equivalence between males and females in peer ordergiving or, in some few instances, males exceeded females in this activity.

We further hypothesized that female characters would explain or justify more of their orders than male characters. This was not so for peer orders; there was a tendency for males to explain more often than females. It was specifically not so for authority orders. The justification or explanation of authority orders by males exceeded that of females in both rate and proportion for all three seasons. Whereas we had conceived that explaining or justifying orders would be more of a deferential behavior, it was regularly performed more often by males. Perhaps the behavior of explaining an order is still a dominance trait. If so, it will be necessary to look at other attributes that would indicate deference more precisely.

Another hypothesis examined for this content dimension specified that male characters would more often give orders to male characters than females would give them to male characters. A parallel hypothesis was that female characters would receive orders proportionately more often than male characters. What we found consistently was a male-giving, male-getting syndrome in all three seasons. This was exemplified most steadily in crime/adventure shows and in all three broadcast time periods. In contrast, from the all-shows data, one could not make a reasonable conclusion about whether females were receiving their orders more from one sex than another. On situation comedies, we found systematic female-female interaction in ordergiving and getting, which was reversed on crime/adventure shows. On the latter, male dominance again exerted itself; females disproportionately received more of their orders from men and did so at a significantly greater rate than they received them from women. Dominance in order reception persists with male superiority in most television content, except for the situation comedy. Only there does the woman appear not only in greater equity with men but in actual superiority to men in this interaction form.

A final hypothesis on the orders dimension dealt with the success of ordergiving, whether the orders given were followed or not followed. Across all shows, orders originating with men were followed at a significantly higher rate and proportion than orders originating with women. This overall finding was consistently so with crime/adventure shows and from 9–11 p.m.; within situation comedies, however, the success of orders was not related to the sex of the ordergiver. So again the interaction of the broadcast of situation comedies in the early evening and the greater prevalence of women in those comedies is juxtaposed with finding greater equity between the sexes only in that special category of programming. Finally, orders not followed were no more associated with one sex or the other. That might itself be an interesting finding because it signifies that orders followed more often originate with men, whereas orders unfollowed originate equally with men and women. Therefore one might argue that men are more regularly shown as winners, whereas women are shown as losers at least as often as are men for these particular behaviors.

The second major dimension for hypothesis testing was that of nurturance giving and receiving. When placed in distress situations, how are men and woman portrayed? The stereotype of sex-role behavior we were working with suggested that women would be more emotional, more fragile and more likely to be portrayed in situations of psychoemotional distress. The same literature suggested that the media typically depict men as active, physical and adventurous. One major hypothesis we worked with was that male television characters in need would be more likely to need physical support or nurturance than female television characters. The findings clearly confirmed that expectation. The primary physical support types identified as most characteristic of males were the needs for both internal and external support, when a character is in physical jeopardy suffering from some internally originated illness. Physical support was more likely to be associated with males than with females across all shows, specifically on crime/adventure shows and most often on Saturday morning and late evening shows.

The parallel hypothesis argues that female television characters more often would display a need for emotional support. This orientation of women to emotional distress situations was confirmed on a proportionate basis. The rates of expressed emotional support needs did not vary by sex, but consistently the proportion of emotional support needs displayed by females significantly exceeded that of males. It did so whether the emotional support dealt with an ego need, a concern for others, or a general need for psychological support. This greater need for emotional support by women occurred in situation comedies and in crime/adventure programs; it occurred consistently across all the evening hour programs examined.

A further hypothesis argued that female television characters would ask for support more often. Again, the anticipated depiction of the male as more autonomous and more independent partly structured that expectation. And the data confirmed that expectation in two ways. In each of the three seasons, the proportion of support requests originating with females exceeded that of males. Furthermore, it did so in all major types of commercial programs and in all the evening hours. Only the Saturday morning shows tended to show no sex differences for support requests. The second way in which this hypothesis was supported was that males exceeded females in not requesting support. Although males were often shown needing some kind of support, they asked for it at a lower rate and in lesser proportion than would have been expected from them. It is worth adding that males most often demonstrated this trait of not asking for help on Saturday morning shows, when the audience may be most vulnerable to sex-role stereotyping. On Saturday morning, men in stress worked it out more often on their own than did female characters seen then.

Following the same logic, we posited that support was more often being given to females than to males. With one exception, this was the case across all shows and it was particularly so in situation comedies more than in crime/adventure shows. It was also evident in evening programming that women wanting assistance would be given it more often. We examined the extent to which support not given was related to the sex of the nonrecipient. Results were the same; more males than females were not given support although they were in situations which would have warranted the giving of support.

Finally, although not a formal hypothesis, we looked at the extent to which the givers of support were more likely to orient their giving to one sex or another. In general, the expectation was that nurturance would be characterized by males giving support more often to females than to other males. Whatever tendency there was suggested that givers of both sexes disproportionately extended support to female recipients. This happened as much for female givers as for male givers and for female givers was most likely to be found in situation comedies.

Thus the idea that women were more likely to be nurtured manifested itself in several significant ways: they asked for more support; they were given more support; and both male and female givers directed their support to female recipients. In contrast, the behaviors of males manifested itself not so much in what they did but in what they did not do; they did not ask for support so often and support was not given to them; they were able to function without having been nurtured to nearly the same extent as their female counterparts.

In looking through the tabulated findings, we are impressed more by the perseverance of evidence than by either anomalies or inconsistencies. If one wants to see women in other than a dominated or nurturance-receiving role, the best bet is to watch women on situation comedies. They'll still be there in those roles, but there will be female counterparts exhibiting complementary behaviors. The greater variance of female role characterizations on situation comedies tends to balance some of the stereotypic presences. On the other hand, if you wish to see women dominated and strongly nurtured, then tune to crime/adventure programs and/or confine your viewing to the final two hours of prime-time programming. Sex-role stereotyping does not appear to have undergone any deliberate, accidental, or even random changes in the three years reflected in these data. Rather, we seem to have a reaffirmation of findings scattered throughout the literature from smaller samples, different seasons, and different media.

In Chapter 5, we cautioned against making judgments from analyzing data from that one season. As we entered subsequent seasons, the new shows were being promoted as featuring females more prominently. Perhaps there was greater prominence but little difference appears in the behavioral interactions among men and women. On the other hand, the data contained in reports such as this, where all males and females have been combined, does not take into account individual differences which might be identified among television characters. It does not separate characters with major roles from others and determine whether major female characters have different sex-role behaviors than nonmajor female characters, or how those major/minor distinctions relate to the sex of the character. We would not expect to find much that is different from this current set of findings, but that approach has not yet been used.

Apparently, for script writers and producers, women may have equity with men in comic situations; indeed, they may even acquire dominance in comic situations. Women will, however, still find themselves in emotional trouble more often, seeking help and getting help, and they'll not find themselves any more successful in their order-giving postures.

We can suggest another extension of this type of study. That would be not to treat all characters as equals in positing possible social outcomes of this kind of content for viewers. We might wish to identify the dozen or so male and female characters especially liked by a broad viewing group, for example, 9–12-year-old children. Then we would propose isolating the typical behavior patterns of those characters, most likely using multiple episodes of the series in which they appear and doing the same kind of analyses performed here. That would provide evidence about the role models most likely to be emulated by such a viewing group. It would also serve to focus on the more intense portrayals of each sex for young viewing groups. There is ample evidence now that young girls make significantly more crossover sex preferences for television characters than young male viewers. Perhaps not finding role models who correspond to their expectations or to information received from other sources leads to that choice pattern. At the same time it would be as useful to determine whether there are very popular male leading characters who do not consistently engage in male-typed sex-role behaviors and to assess their role-modeling propensities. We recommend moving from this content paradigm toward those alternative research directions.

7
SEX-TYPING OF COMMON BEHAVIORS ON TELEVISION

Laura Henderson
Bradley S. Greenberg

Sex-role typing is persistent and consistent in fictional television series during both prime time and Saturday morning. There are more men then women in major roles on television (Busby, 1974; Miller and Reeves, 1976); men are heroes, women are more apt to be helpless, and they differ considerably across a variety of social and emotional characteristics (Tedesco, 1976; Busby, 1974; Long and Simon, 1976). A further question is how far television also sex-types the everyday, common behaviors of the men and women it displays. Are men more likely to eat, drink, and be merry, while women sit, sew, and chat? Do men generally tend to job-related activities, and women care for children and groom themselves?

This study had two general objectives. First, it determined how broad a set of common, everyday behaviors television portrays. Second, it examined to what extent the performance of those behaviors is sex-typed, i.e., displayed disproportionately by one sex. The first question required stipulating common kinds of behaviors which could be observed and analyzed in television content. A set of general behavioral categories was conceived, and discrete behaviors within each category were the focus of a content analysis of prime-time and Saturday morning television. Most general categories of prominent TV behaviors were selected for which no sex-typing allegation has been made.

Twenty-one general categories were developed to encompass a broad perspective of the activities of a normal person's day. Each is presented and illustrated here:

General Category	Sample Behavior
Housework	Washing clothes
Food preparation	Cooking
Games	Playing cards
Yard work	Mowing the lawn
Media use	Watching TV
Sewing	Sewing
Entertainment	Singing
Writing	Writing letters
Driving	Driving a car
Riding	Passenger in truck
Operate machinery	Operating a tractor
Phone use for business	Calls for business
Personal phone use	Calls for personal reasons
Office work	Filing papers, meeting clients
Athletics	Playing tennis
Shopping	Buying groceries
Child care	Diapering a baby
Personal grooming	Combing hair
Drinking, smoking	Offering alcohol
Social courtesies	Opening the door for someone

From traditional stereotypes of what men and women do differently emerge the basic assumptions that women are more associated with homebound activities and men with out-of-home roles. Assuming that television presentations would more likely reinforce than deviate from those stereotyping propositions, it was specifically hypothesized that

I. *Women would do more of these things:*
Housework; food preparation; sewing; entertainment; riding; using the phone for personal reasons; shopping; caring for children; and caring for their bodies.

II. *Men would do more of these things:*
Consume food; drink and smoke; do yard work; drive, operate machinery; use the phone for business reasons; be sports participants; and extend social courtesies.

No hypotheses existed for the remaining categories of playing games, office work, using the media, and writing.

METHODS

Coding was completed on 158 videotapes of network programs aired during two sampled weeks in the fall of 1975–76 and of 1976–77. There were 115 prime-time evening programs and 43 from Saturday morning. Coders analyzed 117.5 hours of television. Coding was done for each character with a speaking part, each specific behavior that occurred within a category was coded. Coders were assigned singly to each show (six coders over two years) rather than in teams because the content of interest consisted entirely of physical, manifest behaviors. Coder training focused on the differentiation of discrete instances of the listed behaviors; coders were instructed that a change of scene defined an instance, unless it were obviously a continuation of the same act. Thus acts continuing across scenes, e.g., driving, were coded once within a scene, reoccurring acts were coded once if the act continued without a scene change, e.g., getting in and out of the water while scuba-diving. A *scene change* consisted of the introduction of any new characters within the setting, or the placement of the same characters in a different setting. This coding procedure does not account for duration or sequencing of behavioral acts, only their simple frequency.

Two kinds of changes were made in the original coding list as the coding progressed. Certain miscellaneous behaviors occurred frequently enough to be transferred to an existing or new category. Others of low occurrence were collapsed, e.g., team and individual sports. The analyses were conducted on additive indexes; i.e., the number of occurrences of a given behavior were summed, and the several behaviors reflected in a general category were summed. The end product was a set of general category indexes, summed across individual instances of multiple behavioral components.

Five categories of behaviors were deleted from further presentation because they occurred less than 50 times each among 2300 TV characters in the two-season sample of shows. They were yard work (45 times), shopping (30), child care (11), office work (35), and sewing (11). Further, the category "operating machinery" contained such a diverse set of specific examples that only the portion of acts reflecting the use of firearms was indexed.

The two seasons of data were combined here in order to work with a larger and presumably more reliable data base than either season alone would afford; text comparisons between the two seasons will be offered where appropriate.

RESULTS

Table 7.1 contains the overall frequencies and rates of behavior for each index, for the two samples of content. Let us briefly describe what kinds of things happen more or less often on television, and then look for sex differences in these occurrences.

TABLE 7.1
Frequencies and Rates of Common TV Behaviors
(117.5 hr)

	f	rate
Behavior indexes		
1. Driving	652	5.55
2. Media use	603	5.13
3. Personal grooming	447	3.80
4. Eating	426	3.63
5. Riding	415	3.53
6. Business phone calls	345	2.94
7. Entertaining	339	2.89
8. Drinking, smoking	230	1.96
9. Food preparation	165	1.40
10. Playing games	160	1.36
11. Writing	130	1.11
12. Using firearms	120	1.02
13. Social courtesies	101	.86
14. Personal phone calls	86	.73
15. Athletics	84	.71
16. Indoor housework	60	.51

Following the outlined procedures, the coders identified more than 4500 codeable acts. Two indexes—driving and media use—were portrayed more than five times each program hour; three others—personal grooming, eating and riding—occurred more than three times per hour; three others—entertaining, making business phone calls, and the combination of drinking and smoking—were found two to three times per hour. The remaining seven indexes consisted of behaviors found from .5 to 1.4 times per hour.

Altogether, the coders sought 94 discrete behaviors; 53 occurred less than 10 times each, including such activities as infant care, operating factory machinery, personal typing, etc.

The top five indices accounted for 48 percent of all the codeable behaviors. Whether one examined the entire set of indexes, or only those in the top half of the frequency table, it is reasonable to conclude that television characters do a relatively small number of categorical behaviors to accompany the development of story plots. A dozen indexes accounted for all behavioral indexes found more than once per television hour.

Within the indexes of largest magnitude are some findings of special interest. For example, the high rate of media use consisted largely of print media use, i.e., reading things; watching television, listening to radio, etc., altogether accounted for just 10 percent of the media use behaviors. The disparity in driving and riding rates reflects considerable display of drivers without riders; the disparate rates for eating and food preparation indicate that most food consumed is prepared off camera.

And the phone is used far more often for business than for personal purposes.

Table 7.1 combined two sample weeks from two different seasons. Inspection of the data within each season revealed more consistency than inconsistency across seasons. Ordering the 16 indexes by size for each season and correlating the two listings yielded a correlation of .75. The second season had far more displays of personal grooming and driving and substantially fewer portrayals of riding, writing, and media use than did the first. Thus, although the relative magnitude of these behavioral indexes is very consistent across seasons, one may anticipate large numerical differences from one sample of content to another.

Table 7.2 is a breakdown of this information by the sex of the characters performing the behaviors. This analysis must take into account the skewed distribution of males and females available on television to perform the behaviors. Of the total of 2322 characters with speaking roles, 28 percent were females; 72 percent were males. Codeable behaviors were observed in 1679 of these characters, with exactly the same sex distribution. The chance expectation for any category of behaviors would be that females would account for 28 percent of them, and males the remainder. Thus, the appropriate statistical procedure

TABLE 7.2
Sex Differences in the Performance of
Common Behaviors on TV
(% Performed by Females)

		(p)
Behavior Indexes		
1. Driving	17.3**	< .001
2. Media use	28.7	n.s.
3. Personal grooming	27.5	n.s.
4. Eating	27.2	n.s.
5. Riding	25.0	n.s.
6. Business phone calls	22.0**	< .05
7. Entertaining	38.0*	< .001
8. Drinking, smoking	20.0**	< .01
9. Food preparation	48.4*	< .001
10. Playing games	29.3	n.s.
11. Writing	30.0	n.s.
12. Using firearms	10.0**	< .001
13. Social courtesies	22.7	n.s.
14. Personal phone calls	27.9	n.s.
15. Athletics	19.0**	< .05
16. Indoor housework	43.3*	< .01
(All Acts)	(26.3)	

*This identifies behaviors disproportionately performed by females.
**This identifies behaviors disproportionately performed by males.
    The p-value reflects the results of a statistical analysis (z) testing the difference between the proportion of behaviors performed by females and the proportion of females (.2769 in the sample of TV characters). (McNemar, 1955.)

must be to compare the observed proportion of acts by females for each behavioral index with the expected proportion of 28 percent. Table 7.2 reflects this procedure.

In no comparisons were females doing a majority of any indexed behavior. Females were, however, portrayed doing disproportionately more

> Entertaining others, by singing or playing a musical instrument
> Preparing and serving food
> Performing indoor housework

Females were displayed doing disproportionately less:

> Driving
> Participating in sports
> Using firearms
> Conducting business on the phone
> Drinking and smoking

All these differences were as anticipated in the set of hypotheses, and they conform to the baseline expectation that women would be homebound and men typically more active in out-of-home settings. Expectations that women would do more personal grooming, riding, and personal phone calls were not supported; expectations that men would do more eating and display more social courtesies were not supported.

Each year's data were inspected separately to determine whether these combined results were internally consistent. For four of the eight significant categories—driving, entertaining, food preparation, and the use of firearms—each year's data provided significant results. For the other four, the results were significant in the more recent season, but not in the first season's sample of content. For three other categories which were inconclusive overall—media usage, personal grooming, and personal phone use—men performed more of the behavior in one sample, and women performed more in the second content sample. Thus, wherever consistent differences were found, they were in the predicted direction, and the more recent season yielded an even larger set of predictable stereotypical behaviors.

DISCUSSION

Perhaps it is not surprising to find sex-typing of common behaviors on television shows. After all, sex-typing of character attributes, interactive behaviors, social roles, and occupation roles have already been demonstrated. In one way, then, the results merely add a new content area which confirms prior studies of the sexes on television.

However, the basic results have additional implications of considerable interest that will be made manifest.

First, the stereotyping depicted is not present in all content areas in which it might be anticipated. Here, 8 of 13 expected differences were obtained; for five others where traditional stereotyping might be expected, it was absent. Second, the stereotyped set of common behaviors is two-faced: for five of the obtained differences, men were more commonly portrayed; for three, women. Social learning theories typically base their expectations on the impact of repeated presentation of various stimuli, and not on the *absence* of such presentations. Therefore, men are stereotyped at least as much if not more than women, if one focuses on sheer magnitude of occurrences. This, however, raises an interesting theoretical issue: how much impact accrues from absence as well as from prominence. If some behaviors are almost exclusively portrayed by men, does that imply that women do not or cannot do those behaviors? Third, and not unrelated to the point just discussed, most of the behaviors discarded from the original coding list would have reflected female activity had they been observed, e.g., sewing, shopping, child care. By contrast, only one male-oriented behavior was deleted.

Finally, only one of the five most commonly occurring behaviors showed sex-typing. In fact, the set of indexed behaviors that showed no sex-typing encompasses 54 percent of all coded acts; the set of behaviors that showed male-prominent sex-typing accounted for 33 percent; the set that displayed female-prominent sex-typing accounted for only 13 percent. Therefore, if one focuses solely on magnitude of presentation, as many discrete everyday acts did not show sex-typing as did; where there was sex-typing, it was most heavily male behaviors. This formulation sharpens the issue of who it is that is being more heavily stereotyped. Clearly, males are far more present on television, and their overall presence contributes to their greater share of sex-typed behavioral activity. These same behaviors among females are stereotyped primarily so far as one can argue that the relative absence of their performance contributes to stereotyping.

There remains the argument that sheer frequency of instances is not an adequate assessment of content; it contains no qualitative dimensions and treats all instances as nominally equivalent. One can move from this approach to the development of additional content indicators, such as intensity, strength, and duration of behavior, if these are believed to be critical in anticipating potential social effects from media content. These data identify certain manifest behaviors that viewers could be expected to associate more readily with one sex than another partly on the basis of their television experiences.

III

SOCIAL BEHAVIORS ON TELEVISION

8

ANTISOCIAL AND PROSOCIAL BEHAVIORS ON TELEVISION

Bradley S. Greenberg
Nadyne Edison
Felipe Korzenny
Carlos Fernandez-Collado
Charles K. Atkin

Violence on television! The phrase has become the battle cry of the PTA and the AMA; it has been the wailing wall of the networks in their pleas against censorship; and it has been the star of repetitious Senate hearings. No other communication research issue has been studied so often, nor by so diverse a collection of social scientists, therapists, physicians, and lay groups. More federal dollars have supported research on the effects of televised violence than on any other topic which bears on the social effects of the commerical media. It is the best-known question asked about television, and is likely to be the one about which most people have an opinion.

Yet it all hinges on the answer to an earlier question—just how much and what kinds of violence are available to be seen? That is a critical question, and certainly George Gerbner and his colleagues at the University of Pennsylvania have been answering it now for more than a decade with great precision, care, and comprehensiveness. If you want to know about physical violence, its incidence, its characteristics, and its participants, the documented evidence collected at Pennsylvania provides a superior data base. Our interest here went further, in one respect, and less so, in another. It seemed apparent to us that the research energy directed at physical violence on television was at the expense of other negative social behaviors also available on television. So we became involved with a broader set of antisocial behaviors, with physical violence but one of several. We also wanted to look at lying, cheating, stealing, insulting, etc. At about this same time, Liebert and his colleagues began issuing reports about prosocial content and prosocial learning from television, i.e., how much television program content contained messages quite opposite from those of violence. That interest was in content which depicted scenes and contained discussions of helping behaviors, the expression of concern and sympathy for others, sharing, cooperating, etc. It seemed appropriate, then, to begin to bring together these conceptually similar issues and to study them as concurrently as possible. What is the full range of antisocial behaviors on television, in addition to physical violence? What is the parallel sorting out of prosocial activities? Who does which ones of them? This, then, extends research interests from one explicit social behavior (physical violence) to a more comprehensive set within the same dimension (antisocial acts) and joins to it the opposing pole of the social behaviors dimension (prosocial acts). Although it is presumptuous to talk of these as polar opposites, it provides a convenient framework for an initial set of thoughts and an initial set of data. The shortcoming is that there will be less detailed information about any individual behaviors than when fewer such behaviors are systematically examined. Here, resources were put into broadening the issues studied, rather than into the depth of individual issues.

Now let us review the major strands of research which provided the basis for this study.

Antisocial Content

George Gerbner and his colleagues at the Annenberg School of Communication of the University of Pennsylvania have completed annual studies of television's *violent* content since 1967 (Gerbner *et al.*, 1979). They have identified violence as:

> The overt expression of physical force (with or without weapon) against self or other, compelling action against one's will on pain of being hurt or killed, or actually hurting or killing. Must be plausible and credible; no idle threats, verbal abuse, or comic gestures with no credible violent consequences. May be intentional or accidental; violent accidents, catastrophes, acts of nature are included. (Gerbner, 1974, section C)

Gerbner's content analysis project used three basic measures in order to assess amount of violence: prevalence, rate, and role. *Prevalence refers to the proportion of TV hours or programs that contain any violence. Rate* is the proportion of violent episodes per TV hour or program. Various *roles* include the percentage of victims, of violent characters, of killers, and of killed characters in a season's sample of shows. Gerbner's group considered more than a dozen qualitative measures, in order to categorize violent actions:

1. Tone, e.g., humorous, serious;
2. Time, e.g., past, present, future;
3. Place of violent action, e.g., United States or other country;
4. Setting, e.g., urban, rural, and social class of characters;
5. Presence and reaction of witnesses;
6. Context, e.g., interpersonal, small group, large groups, or act of nature, etc.;
7. Human or nonhuman participants;
8. Familiarity of the violent opponents;
9. Presence, behavior, and role in violence of agents of the law;
10. Means used to commit the violent action, e.g., hand gun, explosive, knife, etc.;
11. Physical consequences shown in scene, e.g., portrayal of pain, suffering, expression of physical damage;
12. Recovery or nonrecovery of the victim;
13. A body count and the count of injured parties;
14. Duration of the violent act.

Other major content indicators used have been "risk ratios" expressed as the number of "victims divided by the violents (those who commit violent acts) or violents by victims within the same groups and percents of characters involved in any violence plus percents involved in killing" (Gerbner, 1976, p. 20).

For our purposes, the trends identified are of most import. Gerbner and his colleagues had just reported on their ninth yearly violent content study when this chapter was written (Gerbner, *et al.,* 1979). The 1978 Violence Index for all programs had taken a sizable jump over 1977. The index was a composite of several measures, including program rates and hourly rates of violence incidents, and proportions of characters involved in violence and killing. Over the years, the index shows no consistent pattern. In 1967–68, the index stood at 190, dropped each year through 1973 when it hit its low of 160. Then it increased to 183, fell marginally to 177, hit its high of 204 in 1976, dropped to 166, and regained its 183 level in 1978. Since we use an hourly rate of violence in our own findings section, let us identify here the major trends across that set of nine studies, principally in terms of hourly rates of violent acts.

The first report and each one thereafter identified weekend-daytime (children's) programming as the most prone to contain violence. The per hour rate was 22.3 incidents in 1967–68, the first year reported. It dropped to a low of 12.2 in 1974–75, jumped to 22.4 in 1976, dropped to 15.6 in 1977, and zoomed to 25.0 in 1978. This time period looked like a roller coaster when graphed. By contrast, the first prime-time rate reported was 5.2 acts per hour and with periodic minor rises and falls, reached its high of 6.1 in 1976, and was 4.5 in 1978.

Violence in different program types is also of interest. Cartoons and movies have been more violent than prime-time series. Among those series, however, action programs and "serious tone" programs top the violence indexes, trailed substantially by situation comedies and shows new to a given season.

The networks also fluctuate among themselves as leaders in this content area. In 1977, NBC was the runaway leader from 8–9 p.m.; in 1978, ABC was far in front. In 1977, NBC led modestly in the 9–11 p.m. time slot; in 1978, that network far outstripped the others.

The same reports consistently show that certain groups of television characters are more likely to be the victims of violence than others. These include women of all ages, nonwhites, foreigners, and both upper- and lower-class people, but not middle-class ones.

In recent years, the Pennsylvania researchers have established a linkage between heavy TV viewing and those viewers' conceptions of their personal security. From a variety of indicators of people's anxieties, the analysts conclude, ". . . heavy viewers' expressions of fear and personal mistrust, assumptions about the chances of encountering violence, and images of police activities can be traced in part to television portrayals . . . one correlate of television viewing is a heightened and unequal sense of danger and risk in a mean and selfish world" (Gerbner, *et al.,* 1979).

The Pennsylvania research scheme has been important in both its conception and execution, and it served as a starting point for our development of content-analytic categories and procedures. But our main question was different. We wanted to examine a fuller range of negative social behaviors available from television. A variety of noxious behaviors other than violence is available on television. Theft, for example, need not necessarily be violent, and yet is disruptive of society. Deceit and lying are unsatisfactory social behaviors. Further, they are both easier to imitate and model for young viewers, and more relevant to current social concern with so-called white-collar crimes. Verbal aggression is unpleasant and potentially injurious to an individual's self-concept. And verbal aggression is a far more frequent and likely behavior than physical aggression. Thus, the present focus began with a more expanded set of social behaviors, as a base for tracing some of television's potential impact.

Antisocial behavior was conceptualized here as that which is psychologically or physically injurious to another person or persons whether intended or not, and whether successful or not.

The subset of negative behaviors studied was those considered as modelable by social learning theorists and child psychologists. Within the broad label of antisocial behaviors, we included physical aggression, verbal aggression, theft, and deceit. The last three have not been studied in past attempts to analyze negative behaviors.

Physical aggression is the behavioral category with the oldest tradition in content analysis, perhaps because of its visual accessibility. It has consistently been shown in laboratory experiments to be susceptible of modeling effects (Bandura, 1965, 1973; Hicks, 1965, 1968; Collins, 1970; Stein and Friedrich, 1972; Steuer, Applefield, and Smith, 1977; Ellis and Sekyra, 1972). Gerbner and his collaborators have been concerned largely with the use of hand guns and other firearms, explosives, clubs and other hitting instruments, knives and other slashing or stabbing instruments, ropes, chains, and other lashing instruments, and attacks with fists or feet (Gerbner, 1974). Our categorization of physically aggressive acts subsumed all of these and also accounted for physical control or restraint of others, e.g., grabbing, shoving, pushing, holding; physical invasion of privacy, such as entering private property without permission; and elaborated fighting, in which the sequences of individual aggressive acts are indistinguishable, for example, a bar fight involving 10 people concurrently.

This set of physically aggressive acts includes several antisocial behaviors not generally included in previous content analyses. The distinctiveness of this analysis is better differentiated by the systematic examination of the antisocial acts as verbal aggression, deceit, and theft.

The conceptualization of *verbal aggression* has been guided by the work of Buss and Durkee (1963) and Gottschalk, Gleser, and Springer (1963). Although little attention has been paid in the past to imitation effects, one study underlines the importance of tapping this type of behavior. Wotring and Greenberg (1973) conducted two experiments with adolescent boys in order to test the effects of televised verbal and physical aggression on the boys' own level of verbal and physical aggression. They found a tendency for televised physical aggression to increase the level of verbal aggression. The rationale underlying that study was that socialization stimuli condition both physical and verbal aggression simultaneously by generalization. Vicarious stimulation, by television, for example, was hypothesized to affect behavior in a similar fashion. To provide a broader base for examining the effects of verbal televised aggression on the verbal aggression of youngsters, this study made a major effort to quantify the availability of verbal aggression on TV. It included the specific examination of verbal *hostility*, verbal *rejection* of others, and verbal *threats*.

Finally, acts of *deceit* and *theft*, although sometimes more subtle behaviors, are also disruptive of society and readily available on television. Lying or cheating and stealing have been considered as antisocial behaviors that may be modeled by children. "Modeling experiments clearly demonstrate that dishonest models can increase deception in children" (Burton, 1976, p. 183). Stein (1967), Ross (1971), Rosenkoetter (1973), and Wolf and Cheyne (1972) have also demonstrated the imitability of these types of behaviors.

Prosocial Content

The determination of what constitutes prosocial behavior comes from a body of psychological literature which examines the learning of behaviors of positive types. Broadly speaking, *prosocial behavior* can be defined as that set of behaviors which is generally accepted by society as constructive, appropriate, and legal. Behaviors such as altruism, expressing concern for others, self-control, and generosity fit this depiction. Learning these types of behaviors by children follows the same process as the acquisition of antisocial behaviors. Observational learning theory has been tested in a number of studies dealing with the learning of prosocial types of behaviors. These studies have supported the contention that observation of models will enhance children's altruistic and cooperative behaviors (Krebs, 1970; Bryan and London, 1970; Midlarsky, 1968). It has also been demonstrated that learning prosocial behavior can occur after witnessing a televised model eliciting that type of behavior. A series of studies conducted on charitable behavior determined that children who saw a charitable model on television were more likely to share than those who witnessed a noncharitable model (Bryan and Walbek, 1970a, 1970b). Cooperation has also been elicited more from children who witness a televised model performing in that manner.

Stein and Friedrich (1972) also demonstrated the learning of prosocial behaviors in a natural setting. Children (ages three to five) were exposed to aggressive programming ("Batman" and "Superman" cartoons), prosocial programming ("Mister Rogers") or neutral programming (children working on a farm). The children's behavior was observed two weeks before viewing, four weeks during viewing, and two weeks after viewing. Two types of behavior were noted: *self-control,* which included obeying rules, persisting in a task, and delaying gratification; and *interpersonal prosocial behavior,* which included cooperating, nurturing, and expressing feelings. Results indicated that the self-control category was enhanced by the prosocial programs and inhibited by the antisocial programs, and that children in low socioeconomic classes, who were exposed to prosocial programming, increased in their positive interpersonal behaviors.

Liebert has done extensive work in the area of content analyzing prosocial behaviors on television. He and his associates analyzed 72

Saturday morning programs for prosocial content (Poulos, Harvey, and Liebert, 1976). The prosocial categories were altruism, sympathy, explaining feelings, reparation for bad behavior, control of aggression, and resistance to temptation. Altruism occurred with the greatest frequency, six acts in every half-hour of programming. Acts of sympathy and explaining feelings occurred at slightly more than two per half-hour. The remaining prosocial behaviors occurred very infrequently, with control of aggression least frequent, occurring less than once per hour.

Comparing cartoons with live Saturday morning shows, cartoons averaged slightly higher in altruistic acts. For the other prosocial categories, the mean number of acts was greater for live shows. Further, coders compared two samples of programs to determine consistency in programming from one week to the next. Correlations between the two weeks were .56 for altruism, .82 for sympathy and explaining feelings, and .61 for resistance to temptation. Coders found little relationship between the two weeks of programming for reparation for bad behavior (.28) and control of aggression (.01).

These prosocial categories used by Stein and Friedrich and also by Liebert and his associates comprise our base of prosocial variables. The predominant prosocial behaviors to be analyzed in this study encompass altruism, showing affection, expression of feelings and concern for self and others, reparation for bad behavior, self-control, and controlling others' antisocial behaviors.

Before examining the effects of television programming on young people, one must determine what actually is being portrayed on television. This first step is content analysis. In developing a content-analytic scheme, one must use a theoretical perspective to orient the necessary components of the analytic system. The content-analysis procedures outlined here expand the work of Gerbner and Liebert by (1) increasing the range of antisocial behaviors to include other physically aggressive acts, verbal aggression, deception, and theft; (2) measuring both pro- and antisocial behaviors in one system, and (3) doing so for multiple samples.

METHODS AND PROCEDURES

Here, we present the methods used in our three-year analysis of these social behaviors. This section describes the basic content categories for antisocial and prosocial behaviors, the coder training program, coder reliability estimation procedures, and the samples of television content.

Samples of Television Shows

One episode of all prime-time (8–11 p.m.) and Saturday morning fictional television series was videotaped for analysis in each season. The taping commenced in early October of each year and concluded when one episode of each series had been taped. This continued over a four-week period, due to preemptions, schedule changes, and cancellations.

The distribution of shows and hours of television time for the three years was as follows:

By Network	ABC	CBS	NBC		
1975–76					
Shows	26	34	31		
Hours	20.5	23.5	23.5		
1976–77					
Shows	23	28	26		
Hours	19	18.5	20.5		
1977–78					
Shows	22	32	26		
Hours	18	23	22		

By Program Type	Sat. Cartoon	Sat. Non-Cartoon	Sit. Com.	Family Drama	Action Crime*
1975–76					
Shows	16	8	26	7	30
Hours	9	4.5	13	7	30
1976–77					
Shows	10	8	29	2	22
Hours	7.5	5.5	14.5	2	22.5
1977–78					
Shows	14	5	28	6	15
Hours	11.5	3	15	6	15

By Time Period	Sat. a.m.	8–9	9–11		
1975–76					
Shows	24	36	32		
Hours	13.5	26	29		
1976–77					
Shows	18	26	32		
Hours	13	17.5	27.5		
1977–78					
Shows	19	29	32		
Hours	14.5	22	26.5		

*During year 3, another program type was created—Action/noncrime—to encompass the several shows that in that season were not focused on police/detective series, e.g., "Grizzly Adams," "James at Fifteen." These are excluded from this analysis.

Content Variables: Antisocial Acts

Antisocial behavior is behavior which is physically or psychologically injurious to another person, often intended to be so, but sometimes not so intended, often, but not necessarily succeeding. A subset of behaviors, both physical and verbal, was chosen because those behaviors are generally viewed as negative or undesirable interpersonal acts within a particular social system by members of that society.

Four specific categories of acts were operationally defined within this rubric. They were acts of: (1) *physical aggression,* (2) *verbal aggression,* (3) *deceit,* (4) *theft.*

Physical aggression refers to any overt behavior intended to frighten, injure, or damage oneself, another individual, an animal, or property. Common and tolerated physically aggressive behaviors, i.e., contact sports, hunting and fishing for game animals, butchering of domestic animals, and legal demolition of property, are not considered as physically aggressive behaviors. Physical aggression in year 1 included the following subcategories: abridgment of privacy, bombing, burning, defacing property, hitting empty-handed, hitting with an object, physically threatening someone, shooting, stabbing, constraint of others, and extended fighting. Since many of these subcategories did not occur with much frequency or independently, the system was revised and new subcategories developed. The content categories common to all three years were: assaults with and without an object, detention, abridgment of privacy or security, physical threat, shooting, and extended fighting.

Assault without an object is an act of physical aggression by an agent who attacks a human or nonhuman target, with any body part, but without weapons or any other objects. Inluded are biting, kicking, shoving, pushing, grabbing, jerking, hitting, pinching, strangling, scratching, etc.

Assault with an object is an act of physical aggression with the assistance of a weapon, or object, which may be large or small, conventional or unconventional. Shooting a gun is not included here. Instances of assault with an object include: use of large machinery to inflict injuries or illegal destruction of properties; stabbing; the use of any object in an aggressive fashion against human or nonhuman targets.

This subcategory subsumes five subcategories from year 1: bombing, burning, defacing property, hitting with an object, and stabbing.

Detention is a physically aggressive act consisting of keeping some target, human or nonhuman in captivity. An animal in a circus and a bird in its cage are not considered here as acts of detention. Cartoon humanized characters or robots which are forced into captivity are considered to be detained involuntarily. Acts of detention include kidnapping, incarcerating, tying up, binding, confining to a room, caging, surrounding, and any other means of restricting free movement that cannot be considered assault. Grabbing somebody's arm is not detention in this scheme since it is considered to be assault without an object. When, however, a person is kidnapped, and in the course of the kidnapping the person is hit, grabbed, or jerked, then two acts were coded; one of detention, and one of assault without an object. When a person is ordered to obey because a weapon is pointed at him or her, the act was considered physical threat, not detention. This subcategory contained what was coded in year 1 as constraint of others.

Abridgment of privacy is an act of physical aggression consisting of the violation of the space rights of a person. Instances of abridgement of privacy are Peeping Tom behavior and entering private property without permission.

Physical threat consists of endangering the well-being of a target person. Instances of physical threat are pointing a gun, physically menacing someone, and holding a knife against a person.

Shooting is the behavior of firing any firearm against a person target. The firearm may be a cannon, a pistol, a rifle, a bazooka, and machine gun, etc. This act of physical assault with an object was coded separately from other assault-with-object situations.

Extended fighting consists of inseparable or indistinguishable acts of assault with or without an object or firearm. It is a long series of such acts in which the agent becomes the target and vice versa in rapid movement.

Verbal aggression involves sending noxious symbolic messages. The message may take the form of rejection, verbal threat, or hostility. A noxious message is *rejection* when it contains criticism, insults, cursing, or a negative affective reaction, e.g., negative evaluations of a person or objects the person relates to, such as, "Your work is terrible." *Verbal threats* are warning of intentions to cause noxious, undesirable outcomes for a person, e.g., "If you don't give me your money, I'll kill you." *Hostile* acts were all nonthreatening or nonrejecting acts of verbal aggression conveyed by yelling, screaming, or shouting, e.g., a wife shouting angrily to her husband, "Wash the dishes now!"

Deceit is conceptualized as the intentional misleading of someone for purposes that are detrimental to an individual, group, or institution. Deception includes instances of fraud, cheating, lying and assuming the identity of another person. *Fraud* is deception for purposes of unlawful gain. *Cheating* is deception for unfair gain, usually occurring in competitive or test situations. *Lying* consists of conveying a false impression or incorrect information in cases other than fraud or cheating. *Assuming the identity* of another person consists of purposely conveying the impression that one person is another. Cases of undercover agents and secret police are included. Examples of deceit would be a businessperson who files an income tax report without reporting all taxable income (fraud): and a taxi driver who sees an accident but tells the police that she/he didn't (nonfraudulent lying).

Theft is the intentional and deliberate taking of another person's or institution's property without right or permission. Instances of theft are exemplified by *shoplifting*, e.g., a man in a grocery store puts a package of cigarettes in his pocket, then leaves without paying for them; *burglary*, e.g., a woman enters a house through a window and steals jewelry; *larceny*, e.g., a boy walks into the locker room at school and removes a watch from an open locker; *robbery*, e.g., a person waits in an alley and robs a passerby; and *extortion*, e.g., a woman is forced to pay money to keep her husband from learning of her extramarital affair. Theft was originally subdivided into two main categories: theft with and without confrontation. Examples of theft with confrontation are robbery and extortion. Theft without confrontation can be exemplified by shoplifting, burglary, and larceny. Subsequently, these two were collapsed.

Content Variables: Prosocial Acts

Prosocial behaviors are those deemed appropriate, redeeming, and legal by society. Essentially, they are affiliative interpersonal acts, as characterized by the present analysis. Eight types of prosocial behaviors were analyzed in the first year content analysis: (1) altruism, (2) showing affection, (3) explaining feelings of self, (4) explaining feelings of others, (5) reparation for bad behavior, (6) delaying gratification/task persistence, (7) controlling others' antisocial behaviors, (8) self-control. It was determined in the first content analysis that only the first four types of prosocial behaviors occurred with sufficient frequency. Thus, for the second and third years, only the first four behaviors were categorized.

Altruism consists of sharing, helping, and cooperating among humans or animals when engaged in nonillicit acts. *Sharing* was defined as the spontaneous gift or loan of one's own possessions or anything one has to legitimately offer to another person. For example, a child shares half her lunch with a friend who lost his. *Helping* was defined as giving aid to another so that the other can move toward his/her goal. It included physical assistance, instructions, helping with a task, giving advice, giving requested or needed information. For example, two people are sailing and one falls overboard; the other person rescues him from the water. *Cooperating* was defined as the working together by two or more individuals to achieve interdependent goals. For example, two people putting up a camp tent.

Only altruistic behaviors aimed toward prosocial goals were coded as altruism. Thus, if someone aided or helped in an illegal act it was not coded as altruism.

Showing affection refers to the overt display or offer of positive emotions towards humans or animals. It can be either verbal, e.g., "I love you," or physical, e.g., hugging, kissing, holding hands.

Explaining feelings was a category that was subdivided into (1) explaining feelings of self, (2) explaining feelings of others, (3) sympathy or expressing concern for others. Here, we combined the last two subcategories.

Explaining feelings of self consists of verbal statements explaining the feelings, thinking, or actions of self which attempt to affect positive outcomes. This includes attempts to increase others' understanding of self's feelings, to resolve strife, to smooth out difficulties, or to alleviate tension experienced by the self. An example of explaining feelings of self was a wife explaining to her husband why she has been unhappy with their marriage. She explains why she is upset and how she feels. Sympathy for self, i.e., self-pity, was not coded.

Explaining feelings of others consists of verbal statements which explain the feelings, thinking, or actions of others which attempt to effect positive outcomes. This includes attempts to increase the understanding of others, resolve strife, smooth out difficulties, or reassure others. Statements which explain feelings of others may be directed at the recipient or expressed in conversations with others about the recipient. For example, a father explains to his son the problems his mother has been having at work and why she has been edgy.

Sympathy or expressing concern for others is a verbal or behavioral expression of concern for others and their problems. Verbal expression may be directed directly to the recipient or in conversation with others about the recipient. Behavioral expression of sympathy may be displayed by putting an arm around someone. An example of sympathy is one friend telling another that she knows times have been rough, but she's sure everything will work out.

Coding Procedures

This section details the training and coding procedures of the pro- and antisocial behaviors discussed in the preceding section. The training process was as nearly identical each season as possible. The same trainers were used each year, sometimes supplemented by members of the previous season's coding teams.

Coder Training for Categorizing Behaviors

From five to eight undergraduates at Michigan State University were used as coders of the pro/antisocial content behaviors. All coders had to understand and agree upon the conceptualizations of the behaviors. They also had to use the same criteria for determining the presence of the behaviors and they had clearly to differentiate one behavior from another. The process that took place was one of negotiation of meaning and consensual establishment of a coding symbol system. The coders had to be able to conceive of the behaviors in the abstract and yet recognize them in concrete examples. To facilitate these goals, an intensive training program was developed and carried out.

The training program involved working with the coders for about 50 hours. One week before the beginning of training, all coders were given training manuals. The coders were asked to study and familiarize themselves with the variables and the special and conditional definitions for the behaviors.

The first step in actual training was to introduce each behavior, e.g., altruism, to the group of coders. The group and the researchers discussed the conceptualization of the variable. Discussion continued until it was clear to the researchers that all coders understood and agreed upon the operational meanings of the variables. At times, modifications in the conceptualizations were made during the discussion.

Next, discussion on the special conditions for each variable took place. The coders had to understand the different circumstances in which the variable might be present. For example, discussion took place as to why helping a friend rob a bank would not be coded as altruism. It was explained that since this behavior was an illicit act, it would not be in accord with the conceptualization. This process of discussion and negotiation of the conceptualizations and conditions of the behavior took several hours for each category of behavior coded. Practice coding then began with tapes of shows. Each time the behavior under discussion was thought to be elicited, the coders independently coded it. Discussion then took place to determine whether there were any discrepancies among the coders. When all coders understood and agreed on the meaning and the criteria of the behavior, within acceptable reliability standards, a new variable was introduced and the same process was repeated.

Once all the pro/antisocial content behaviors had been studied and discussed, there was practice coding for the full set of acts. The coders independently coded the first ten minutes of a show and then compared their observations. Problems or disagreements identified now were discussed until there was consensual agreement. Three days were devoted to practice coding of TV show segments. A training tape, illustrating each of the coded behaviors was produced during year 1 and used in subsequent-year training sessions.

Reliability

When actual coding of the shows began all coders were paired. The purpose of this was insuring that all coders were as similar to each other as possible. Ten shows were pair coded. Reliabilities were obtained several times during coding. Reliabilities were estimated for what a given act was, i.e., does an observed act fit into any of the pro- or antisocial content categories, and which one does it fit? When reliabilities reached an acceptable level (.7–.8), individual coding of shows began.

Analyses

Having followed these procedures as closely as possible, we believe we can present reliable and concurrently valid estimates of trends in the incidence of a variety of antisocial behaviors for each of the three years. The subtypes of antisocial behaviors are quite physical, visual and pronounced, as defined here. They have more of those overt qualities than the set of prosocial behaviors, where greater interpretation of verbal content is required. We consider the attempt to define and itemize the prosocial behavior at a more exploratory stage, both conceptually and methodologically. Thus, we present the results slightly differently for the two sets of social behaviors. First, the results describe the year-by-year trends in antisocial content. Second, we present a composite compilation of the prosocial behavior across the first and third years in which those data were collected. Subsequently, we should like to examine specific trends for prosocial acts, as for antisocial acts, but do not believe we are prepared to be quite that precise at this time.

Further, during the course of these analyses of anti- and prosocial behaviors, we had the opportunity to explore certain other content aspects; although we shall report on these at a later time, it is worth identifying here just what it was that we thought warranted preliminary examination. For one, initial attempts were made to cope with ascertaining the motives and consequences of the coded acts. Each year, we varied slightly in our approach to this issue, and we have three quite different sets of data from these examinations. Needless to say, when we are able to add important information about the motives and consequences of the discrete acts of social behavior, then a more comprehensive context will exist for understanding those acts. We also explored the problem of assessing the "intensity" of the individual acts of social behavior, e.g., determining whether two fist fights, which would nominally be coded in the same way, could also be differentiated along some dynamic dimensions in terms of the degree of intensity in each. Or whether two altruistic acts could be similarly differentiated. It seemed to us that content analysis of such behaviors ought to be moving beyond the simplistic nominal counting of incidence, and to be adding some measurable qualitative information. Although partial results could be presented for each of these, that extension would go beyond our central focus here. Therefore, the results section will focus on the primary issues—the incidence of antisocial and prosocial behaviors—and their location in time and context on the television spectrum.

RESULTS

We begin by describing acts of antisocial behavior that were identified and coded in the three seasons in which these data were collected. Table 8.1 identifies the frequency of acts in the four antisocial categories studied and also presents the percentages of each type of act for each season. Several important findings can be derived from this basic table. First, our interest in examining verbal aggression as an antisocial act is supported. It was the single largest act category in all three seasons, and in two of those seasons it constituted a majority of all the antisocial acts identified. Situations in which people are verbally hostile,

TABLE 8.1
Incidence of Antisocial Acts in Three Seasons

	Year 1*		Year 2		Year 3	
I. Physical Aggression	*f*	%	*f*	%	*f*	%
a. Assault with no object	466	(15.7)	248	(10.8)	370	(13.6)
b. Assault with object	111	(3.7)	159	(6.9)	177	(6.5)
c. Physical threat	180	(6.1)	233	(10.1)	135	(5.0)
d. Shooting	106	(3.6)	75	(3.2)	74	(2.7)
e. Other**	128	(4.3)	171	(7.4)	130	(4.8)
II. Verbal Aggrssion	1629	(55.0)	1099	(47.6)	1464	(54.0)
III. Theft	61	(2.1)	72	(3.1)	44	(1.6)
IV. Deceit	283	(9.5)	251	(10.9)	319	(11.8)
Total	2964		2308		2713	
Hours Analyzed	(68.5)		(58)		(63)	

*Year 1 was the 1975–76 season; year 2, 1976–77; year 3 1977–78.
**Other* included extended fighting scenes; abridgment of privacy, e.g., breaking into an occupied business or home; and detention, e.g., kidnapping.

insulting, and rejecting of others is a major activity on television and occurred more than a thousand times in each of the three sample weeks. Its large prominence warrants intensive investigation as a form of behavior that may be modeled by consistent viewers. Our interest in expanding antisocial activity from physical violence into other areas is supported further by the results obtained from looking for the behavior of deceit. Acts of lying and cheating constituted an average of more than 10 percent of all of the antisocial acts. The occurrence of deceitful behaviors was exceeded in frequency only by the incidence of verbal aggression and by one of the physical assault behaviors. It occurs often enough for followup research on its potential impact.

Turning now to the frequency of physically aggressive acts, the original subset is here presented in five subcategories: assault with no object, assault with an object, physical threats, specific instances of shooting at others, and a catchall miscellaneous category into which we have collapsed the other individually coded acts of physical aggression. The most frequent act of aggression is assault with no object, encompassing 11 percent to 16 percent of the antisocial acts in the three seasons. Second in terms of occurrence to this particular form of physical aggression are two others: assault with an object and the physical threat of violence. Each of these could be expected to account for about 6 percent of all antisocial acts. Our final discrete category of physical aggression was shooting, and it maintained an incidence that accounted for about 3 percent of all these acts. No other discrete subcategory maintained that high an incidence and that was the basis for collapsing them into the "other" category.

This table also shows that acts of theft were low in overall magnitude, inclusive of about 2 percent of all the antisocial acts.

In sum then, the predominant form of antisocial behavior on commercial television has been verbal aggression. The totality of all types of physical aggression (31–38 percent) is not far behind that of verbal aggression. Most frequent is that of two people fighting, hitting, or slapping. In addition, there is a substantial amount of hitting others with something and an equivalent amount of physical threat presented to television characters. Further, acts of deceit are plentiful for observers.

Because the frequencies based in Table 8.1 come from somewhat different total numbers of hours of television in each season sampled, Table 8.2 converts those frequencies to an hourly rate of antisocial behavior. In doing that, we have summed the discrete types of physical aggression, and present the hourly rates for the three major categories of antisocial behavior which occur frequently enough to warrant further

TABLE 8.2
Hourly Rate of Antisocial Acts

	Year 1	Year 2	Year 3
I. Physical Aggression	14.47	15.22	14.06
II. Verbal Aggression	23.78	18.90	23.23
III. Deceit	4.13	4.21	5.06
Overall	42.38	38.33	42.36

analysis and breakdown—physical aggression, verbal aggression, and deceit. From Table 8.2, the reader first might note the overall hourly rate of antisocial acts as about 40 acts per hours across these three major subcategories of antisocial behavior. Although there was a 10 percent drop in that rate during year 2, the overall consistency is perhaps more impressive than some moderate deviations. The typical hour of television will contain 14 acts of physical aggression, more than 20 instances of verbal aggression, and a handful of acts of deceit. The only substantial difference in these data sets was a decrease in frequency of identified acts of verbal aggression in the second year, the same year in which there was a slight increase in the hourly rate of physical aggression. Again it seems that the consistency and the relative prevalence of these types of acts are more striking than deviations.

The remainder of the analysis of these antisocial acts will consist of subdividing this overall rate of occurrence by what we consider to be some critically interesting characteristics. We wish to determine whether there are substantial differences in the occurrence of these acts and the kinds of acts that occur by the time of day when the telecasting occurs, by the program type in which they occur, and by the network presenting the programs.

Table 8.3 begins this analysis by identifying the relative rate of occurrence of antisocial acts in three distinct time periods. We are interested in how much of this occurs on Saturday morning, when programming is designed to attract substantial child audiences. We are also interested in the prime-time hours, 8 p.m.–11 p.m., but wished to differentiate the first of these, 8–9 p.m. from the last two, 9–11 p.m. About four years ago, the first hour of the prime-time evening programming was designated as the "Family Viewing Hour." Although that label has been removed technically from any necessary obligation on the part of the networks, each of them has independently promised to provide programming in that time period which is primarily suited to general family viewing. One can test that promise by comparing content found during that hour with content found later in the evening. The original effort for the family hour was to be a reduction in both violence and sex-oriented

TABLE 8.3
Hourly Rate of Antisocial Acts by Time Period

	Year 1	Year 2	Year 3
I. Physical Aggression			
Sat. a.m.	22.9	25.2	21.2
8–9 p.m.	8.8	9.3	11.9
9–11 p.m.	15.6	14.4	11.9
II. Verbal Aggression			
Sat. a.m.	23.1	16.7	16.6
8–9 p.m.	25.7	20.3	23.0
9–11 p.m.	22.4	19.2	27.1
III. Deceit			
Sat. a.m.	5.6	5.4	4.1
8–9 p.m.	4.3	3.9	4.9
9–11 p.m.	3.3	4.1	5.7
IV. Overall			
Sat a.m.	51.6	47.3	41.9
8–9 p.m.	38.8	33.5	39.8
9–11 p.m.	41.3	37.7	44.7

presentations during that time slot. We focus here on the violence aspects. The issue of the portrayal or discussion of intimate sexual behavior is found in Chapter 9.

Begin then by looking at the occurrence of acts of physical aggression during these three time periods. It is apparent in Table 8.3 that Saturday morning has been and continues to be the time frame most prone to the portrayal of acts of physical aggression. In all three seasons there were more than 20 such acts per hour; for no other time period was there nearly so much physical aggression. The 8–9 p.m. period appears to have increased slightly in physical aggression during each of the three years studied and the hourly rate from 9–11 p.m. has decreased during each of the three years. This offsetting pattern has resulted in equivalent amounts of physical aggression all evening long, at just about 12 acts per hour or roughly half the rate of occurrence of acts of physical aggression found on Saturday morning. It is promising to see the reduction in late evening acts of violence, and one could argue that the change from 8–9 p.m. in a upward direction has not been as large as the decrease in the latter time period. However, that increase between 8–9 p.m. has resulted in 40 percent more acts of physical aggression in the year 3 sample than in the year 1 sample. During the same years, the consistently higher rates on Saturday morning show marginal fluctuation.

Acts of verbal aggression on Saturday morning decreased between the first and second year and remained at the lower level in Year 3. Acts of verbal aggression from 9–11 p.m. are substantially more frequent in Year 3 than in the first two years. Although all three time periods have relatively the same rate in the first year, verbal aggression was minimal on Saturday morning in Year 3 and maximum in the late evening hours.

The rate of occurrence of deceit showed marginal fluctuation either across seasons or by time periods. The pattern, however, appears to be similar to that obtained for verbal aggression, more deceit late at night in year 3 as compared with year 1.

If one combines all the categories of antisocial acts, then one finds marginal differences between the time periods in the most recent year analyzed. Although the first and second year showed Saturday morning to be the clear leader across these categories of antisocial acts, by the third season, Saturday morning was not very different than the family hour and both were less antisocial than late evening programming. But one must bear in mind that such an overall measure masks substantial differences in the different kinds of antisocial acts. For example, although on an overall basis, Saturday morning is not very different from the family hour, the more detailed data show that Saturday morning was twice as physically aggressive as any other time period, but less verbally aggressive. Clearly for the younger audience there is a tendency to present more physical action which tends to be translated by script writers into physical aggression. There is less verbal activity presented for an impatient age group on Saturday morning.

Table 8.4 presents information about five different types of programs; situation comedies, family drama, e.g. "The Waltons," action/crime, Saturday cartoons, and Saturday noncartoons. In the third year, we subdivided the action/crime category and created a grouping known as *action/noncrime*. These included such programs as "Grizzly Adams" and "James at Fifteen." In order to maintain a similar base in all three seasons of data, we present here only the action/crime category results.

Looking first at instances of physical aggression, it is apparent that the Saturday morning glut of violence is found primarily in the cartoons. If one's Saturday morning viewing were focused on the noncartoon programs, the incidence of physically aggressive acts would be half that of the cartoons. After cartoons, the crime series show most acts of physical aggression, averaging about 18 such acts per hour in comparison with about 25 acts per hour in the Saturday cartoons. One should note, however, that the rate of occurrence of physical aggression in Saturday cartoons has decreased consistently from year 1 to year 3. The program type likely to contain the fewest acts of physical aggression is that of family drama, which in the last two seasons contained fewer than a handful each hour. Situation comedies are also likely to be relatively low in the hourly incidence of physical aggression.

By contrast, the situation comedies have been the runaway leaders in terms of verbal aggression. In two seasons, the average exceeded 30

TABLE 8.4
Hourly Rate of Antisocial Acts by Program Type

	Year 1	Year 2	Year 3
I. Physical Aggression			
Sitcoms	7.1	5.6	8.9
Family drama	8.9	3.0	3.5
Action/Crime	17.4	19.6	17.8
Sat. cartoons	28.8	25.0	23.8
Sat. noncartoons	11.1	15.1	11.3
II. Verbal Aggression			
Sitcoms	34.5	25.5	39.7
Family drama	16.7	10.0	13.3
Action/Crime	22.0	19.3	24.5
Sat. cartoons	23.7	13.2	16.7
Sat. noncartoons	22.0	21.5	16.0
III. Deceit			
Sitcoms	3.3	5.1	6.7
Family drama	2.3	3.0	2.2
Action/Crime	4.8	4.2	6.0
Sat. cartoons	7.3	6.1	4.3
Sat. noncartoons	2.2	3.8	3.3
IV. Overall			
Sitcoms	44.9	36.2	55.3
Family drama	27.9	33.6	19.0
Action/Crime	44.2	43.1	48.3
Sat. cartoons	59.8	44.3	44.8
Sat. Noncartoons	35.3	40.4	30.6

acts per hour and in the most recent year studied contained nearly 40 interactions per hour that were insulting, rejecting, or verbally hostile to other people. The bulk of the interactions on situation comedies were classified as instances of verbal aggression. Family dramas again were least prone to contain verbal aggression and were a genre by themselves in their comparative lack of incidence of this activity. Action/crime shows, Saturday cartoons, and Saturday noncartoons were very similar in year 1 but have shown more fluctuation in the two more recent years. In year 3, verbal aggression was more plentiful on action/crime programs than in either of the Saturday show types.

Program types differ dramatically in their composition of antisocial acts. Whereas there is very little violence on situation comedies, there is an abundance of verbal aggression. The rates of physical and verbal aggression are about equivalent on action/crime shows and that is a rate of occurrence of nearly 20 acts of each kind per hour. Saturday cartoons are more plentiful in physical aggression than in verbal aggression but both levels are high. Family dramas contain the least of both of these major types of antisocial acts.

The occurrence of deceit by program type is relatively small by comparison and quite similar amounts occur across program types.

Some trends are worth noting. Deceit in situation comedies has increased steadily from the first to the second to the third year and its occurrence on Saturday cartoons has decreased steadily in the same three samples. Here, too, the family drama shows the lowest level and is low on an absolute basis.

Again the overall summary of rate of occurrence by program type in Table 8.4 perhaps masks more than it reveals. During the first year, there were 60 instances of antisocial acts on Saturday cartoons in each hour telecast. This dropped to a 44 hourly rate in year 2 and remained there in the third season. Situation comedies, second in the first year, decreased in the second year. They abruptly shifted upward in year 3, so much so that situation comedies provided the largest overall rate of antisocial acts, averaging 55 per hour. Action/crime was the most stable program type in all three years ranging from 43 to 48 acts. Family drama has consistently been the lowest provider of antisocial acts beginning in year 1 but even that low level was decreased by one-third in the most recent year. Using this expanded set of content behaviors, there is a large amount of antisocial behavior in most of these program types but it is differentially distributed across program types. Although one can point to a lack of physical violence in situation comedies, perhaps one should be equally concerned about the very high rate of verbal aggression in that same program type.

Table 8.5 compares networks in terms of their relative productivity of these behaviors. For physical aggression, a shift occurred from ABC's preeminence in the first year to NBC's leadership in physical violence during years 2 and 3, on the basis of this hourly rate measure. Perhaps

TABLE 8.5
Hourly Rate of Antisocial Acts by Network

	Year 1	Year 2	Year 3
I. Physical Aggression			
ABC	20.5	15.9	13.9
CBS	13.5	9.5	12.3
NBC	10.2	19.4	16.0
II. Verbal Aggression			
ABC	25.2	18.1	21.1
CBS	23.8	18.2	25.7
NBC	23.3	20.2	22.4
III. Deceit			
ABC	4.7	3.9	6.4
CBS	4.6	4.6	4.4
NBC	3.3	4.1	4.6
IV. Overall			
ABC	50.4	37.9	41.4
CBS	41.9	42.3	42.4
NBC	36.8	43.7	43.0

most interesting is that there were sharp differences between networks within a season and differences within a network across seasons. Take the NBC data as an example. In the first year, there were an average of 10 physical aggressions per hour, half the rate of the ABC shows. By the second year, the NBC rate nearly doubled while both ABC and CBS were providing one-third fewer acts of physical aggression. By year 3 ABC's rate continued to decline, now joined by a decline at NBC and an increase in CBS shows. One may point out that program content is susceptible to change, but we cannot assess whether the change is accidental or deliberate.

In terms of verbal aggression within each year there were relatively minor and insignificant differences among the three networks. For verbal aggression ABC was slightly higher in year 1, NBC was slightly higher in year 2, but CBS became the leader in the third year sample. Similar minor changes were found for acts of deceit.

Here the overall rates are intriguing. The trend has been for a leveling of differences among networks. In the first year studied, the ABC rate of antisocial behavior was sharply different from the other two networks and the CBS lead over NBC was also nontrivial. In the second year, CBS and NBC were virtually identical and ABC trailed by a marginal figure. In the third year, the three networks were not significantly different from one another in their overall rate, each exceeding 40 antisocial acts per hour. Further, the composition of those antisocial act rates was not very different among the three networks.

The final analysis of antisocial acts scrutinizes the characteristics of the givers (agents) and receivers (targets) of these acts. We can focus on a small set of demographic characteristics of the participants, i.e., sex, race, and age, and on an equivalent-sized set of role characteristics, i.e., whether the character was a regular or a nonregular performer in the series, whether the character was cast in either a hero or villain role, excluding those falling in between, and whether the role within this particular episode was of major, intermediate, or minor importance.

Although we computed the data separately on whether the individual was a target or agent of a given antisocial act, Table 8.6 presents the findings only for the agents, because the same findings emerged whether the individual was agent or target, unless noted otherwise.

Males are consistently more active committers of antisocial acts than females for all three of the antisocial act categories, but the only substantial difference is in terms of their rate of using physical aggression. The average male rate of physically aggressive acts was more than twice that of females whether the male was the giver or receiver of the act. By race, the differences are trivial; whites and blacks were equally likely either to commit or to receive each of the kinds of antisocial behavior. By age, there are interesting differences between both age

TABLE 8.6
Rate of Antisocial Acts
by Demographic and Program Role Characteristics of Agents*

		(n)	Physical Aggression	Verbal Aggression	Deceit
Sex:	Male	(1653)	.82	1.35	.23
	Female	(625)	.34	1.11	.17
Race:	White	(1752)	.63	1.27	.21
	Black	(213)	.59	1.46	.23
Age:	Under 20	(254)	.55	1.05	.22
	20–34	(669)	.67	1.12	.20
	35–49	(830)	.74	1.41	.24
	50 plus	(382)	.35	1.54	.16
Role:	Regular	(963)	.80	1.79	.33
	Nonregular	(1371)	.65	.94	.14
	Major	(654)	1.72	2.82	.60
	Intermediate	(543)	.60	1.33	.15
	Minor	(1133)	.20	.37	.04
	Hero	(1984)	.50	1.20	.20
	Villain	(265)	2.08	1.94	.38

*Data from years 1 and 2 are combined.

groups and act type. Physical aggression increases steadily from the youngest age group to those in their 30s and 40s and then declines markedly among those who are 50 or older. Physical antisocial acts are largely committed by young and middle-aged adults, a behavior denied the older groups. Verbal aggression on the other hand increases steadily with age and is at its maximum in the oldest age group. These age findings pertain to the agents more so than to the receivers. In terms of receiving acts of physical aggression, all age groups receive these acts equivalently except for the oldest age group which receives far fewer of them. The receipt of verbal aggression is similar across all age groups.

Turning next to the program role characteristics, regular characters have a higher rate of antisocial acts of each type. This is most pronounced in verbal aggressiveness. A similar but more emphatic pattern is found when the characters are subdivided in terms of the importance of their role in the particular episode examined. Those judged to be major characters predominated as agents for all three types of antisocial acts. The findings with regard to the targets of these acts were very similar, again most of the activities occurred from, and to, major characters and not by those in intermediate or minor roles.

The final program role characteristic was the heroism or villainy of the character. Table 8.6 shows that the villains were four times as likely to commit acts of physical aggression and also were more active in verbal aggression and deceit. These same villains were foremost in the parallel analysis of targets of these behaviors; these acts were primarily directed at villains as well as being originated by them. For example, villains were the targets of an average of 1.25 physically aggressive acts in comparison to .44 acts directed at heroes or heroines.

From this limited set of characteristics, one can begin to isolate the major sources and receivers of antisocial acts on television. Males are far more active than females, as they tend to be on most other behavioral dimensions. Young people and middle-aged adults tend to be most active, with those who are aging less likely to be physically active but equally or more likely to be more verbally aggressive. These antisocial behaviors are committed by major program characters rather than minor ones and tend to be heavily concentrated among those who are more easily labeled villains or lawbreakers.

Prosocial Behaviors. The exploratory analysis of prosocial acts follows the same format as that for antisocial acts. Table 8.7 identifies the frequency of each kind of prosocial act coded, the percentage each subcategory contributed to the whole, and the hourly rate of each type of act. No single category predominated to the same extent that verbal aggression predominated among types of antisocial behaviors. The most frequently occurring prosocial behaviors were altruistic acts— sharing, helping, and cooperating with others. For the composite data presented, acts of altruism occurred 14.3 times per television hour. Second were acts in which an individual explained how he or she felt about something. Acts of affection and the explanation of the feelings of others, including expressions of concern and sympathy, each accounted for about one-fifth of the prosocial acts identified. Perhaps most interesting in this initial presentation is that the sum total of prosocial acts, 42.7 per hour, is quite comparable to what was identified a few pages ago as the overall rate of antisocial acts per hour. They are nearly identical. Therefore, if one were to place all the antisocial behaviors on one side of the viewing scale and all the prosocial behaviors on the other side, using hourly rate as the measuring unit, the scales would balance. That overall balance, however, disguises differences in the composition of the antiso-

TABLE 8.7
Incidence and Hourly Rate of Prosocial Acts
(131.5 hours)

	f	Percentage	Rate
I. Altruism	1882	34	14.3
II. Affection	1079	19	8.2
III. Explaining Feelings of Others	1148	20	8.7
IV. Explaining Feelings of Self	1514	27	11.5
Overall	5623	100	42.7

cial acts and it is equally deceptive about the distribution of prosocial acts. The subanalyses which verify this assertion follow.

Table 8.8 breaks down the prosocial acts by the three time periods of Saturday morning, 8–9 p.m., and 9–11 p.m. There, it is apparent that acts of altruism are a majority in the Saturday morning shows and about half that rate in the late evening shows. In contrast, affection during all of prime time is frequent and quite infrequent on Saturday morning. Similar differences occur by time period with the other major prosocial behaviors. Overall, the lowest rate of prosocial behaviors is on Saturday morning, and the largest rate is in the family hour from 8–9 p.m. Indeed, if altruism were not so abundant on Saturday morning, then the Saturday shows would be relatively weak in their presentation of prosocial behaviors. It is worthwhile to make direct comparisons of these data with the parallel analyses of antisocial acts. Where there are 35 prosocial acts per hour on Saturday morning, we identified an average closer to 47 antisocial acts. From 8–9 p.m. the situation is reversed; there are more prosocial acts per hour (47) then antisocial acts (37). In the final time period, 9–11 p.m., the hourly rates of each are nearly the same, slightly more than 40 acts per hour.

TABLE 8.8
Hourly Rate of Prosocial Acts by Time Period

	Sat. a.m.	8–9 p.m.	9–11 p.m.
I. Altruism	19.6	15.1	11.0
II. Affection	3.8	10.0	8.9
III. Explaining Feelings of Others	7.0	10.2	8.3
IV. Explaining Feelings of Self	5.0	11.7	14.7
Overall	35.4	47.0	42.9

Turning next to the relative occurrence of prosocial acts in different program types, Table 8.9 presents the relevant findings. Altruism is maximal in both Saturday morning types and minimal in action/crime programs. Acts of affection predominate in situation comedies and in family drama and fall off sharply in the other program types. Acts of explaining the feelings of others are more often found in program types higher in verbal activity and lower in physical activity, being most prominent in situation comedies, family drama, and Saturday noncartoons. These acts are less frequent in action/crime programs and Saturday cartoons.

The overall rates of prosocial acts by program types identify the situation comedy as most prone to portray these behaviors; Saturday

TABLE 8.9
Hourly Rate of Prosocial Acts by Program Type

	Sitcoms	Family Drama	Action/ Crime	Sat. Cartoons	Sat. Non-cartoons
I. Altruism	15.6	13.9	10.6	19.3	20.2
II. Affection	16.1	10.3	5.4	2.6	7.5
III. Explaining Feelings of Others	11.9	10.8	7.9	5.9	10.2
IV. Explaining Feelings of Self	16.1	8.5	15.0	5.5	3.7
Overall	59.7	43.5	38.9	33.3	41.6

cartoons trail substantially in this incidence. A direct comparison with the program type data for antisocial behavior provides informative contrasts. The most antisocial program type corresponds to the least prosocial program type—Saturday morning cartoons. The least antisocial program types—family drama and Saturday noncartoons—correspond to two of the leading prosocial program types. Situation comedies are a remarkably active hybrid. For the most recent season analyzed, the rate of antisocial acts was more than 55 per hour in situation comedies; here, the rate of prosocial activity in the same program type is nearly 60 acts per hour. The situation comedy then is the most active program type on both ends of the dimension of evaluative social behavior. Although there are undoubtedly substantial differences between particular situation comedy series, the genre itself contains the most behaviors that are codeable on both pro- and antisocial dimensions.

Table 8.10 provides prosocial act information by network. The similarities are more impressive than the differences, with the overall rates and the individual act category rates very similar. If one compares this table with the information on antisocial activity by network, particularly for the most recent season analyzed, the same conclusion emerges. The three networks are more alike than different in their overall presentation of both prosocial and antisocial acts, and the rates per network of each of the major categories of behaviors are also more alike than different.

TABLE 8.10
Hourly Rate of Prosocial Acts by Network

	ABC	CBS	NBC
I. Altruism	16.7	13.5	14.3
II. Affection	7.4	8.6	8.5
III. Explaining Feelings of others	8.6	9.3	8.1
IV. Explaining Feelings of Self	10.1	13.2	11.1
Overall	42.8	44.6	41.2

Finally Table 8.11 examines prosocial behaviors as they occur among particular demographic subgroups and program role subgroups. Acts of altruism occur equivalently among males and females, but acts of affection are more typically originated by females. They also are more typically received by females. Similarly, females tend to be more active in explaining the feelings of other people in the program episodes. No consistent differences exist by race, except that white characters more often explained their own feelings or expressed concern and sympathy for others, and whites were more often the receivers of that particular prosocial behavior. The age differences have no particular pattern.

The findings for program role characteristics are consistent. For all four prosocial categories of behavior, regular characters originated and received them more often than nonregular characters, and major characters originated and received them more often than intermediate characters who were more active than minor characters. Finally, the division of TV characters into those who were primarily heroes and those who were primarily villains indicated that the former were more likely to behave in prosocial ways.

There is a substantial amount of prosocial behavior on television. This analysis provides support for subsequent consideration of social learning of prosocial behaviors from television content, which probably should be done concurrently with the possible social learning of antisocial behaviors. Major kinds of prosocial behaviors occur with sufficient regularity to warrant maintaining the kinds of distinctions made here. It

TABLE 8.11
Rate of Prosocial Acts
by Demographic and Program Role Characteristics

		Altruism	Affection	Feelings of Others	Feelings of Self
Sex:	Male	.63	.31	.34	.45
	Female	.68	.67	.55	.56
Race:	White	.67	.44	.41	.52
	Black	.55	.42	.51	.30
Age:	Under 20	.76	.33	.37	.25
	20–34	.69	.50	.45	.50
	35–49	.62	.44	.41	.56
	50 plus	.60	.35	.45	.51
Role:	Regular	1.09	.65	.68	.68
	Nonregular	.34	.23	.20	.33
	Major	1.41	.93	.83	.75
	Intermediate	.56	.40	.49	.48
	Minor	.22	.10	.10	.16
	Hero	.70	.41	.44	.58
	Villain	.29	.27	.17	.40

is also apparent that there is a differential presentation of prosocial acts by time period and by program type but not necessarily by network. Finally, these prosocial behaviors tend to be strongly concentrated among regularly appearing major "good" characters on the shows.

DISCUSSION

This particular examination of television content suggests an expansion from what may be an overconcern with a single kind of behavior—physical violence—to a multifaceted examination of collateral social behaviors on television. To understand that violence takes place in a content mix of other antisocial behaviors which itself is surrounded by a variety of prosocial behaviors begins to yield a better mapping of the content universe. "All you ever wanted to know about television violence . . . and were not afraid to ask. . ." has been worth examining, but not if it precludes other, equally intriguing issues.

Let us for a moment focus on the quite large presentation of verbal aggression on television. It is, of course, all talk, and therefore less prone to be a public or political concern of the magnitude of physical violence. Yet, from a social learning standpoint, it is less prone to negative sanctions if imitated or modeled. It is easier to practice. We do not know, however, whether it is any easier to learn, or just how learnable it is from television characters. A child's ability to learn linguistic skills is responsive to the stages of development of his reasoning capacity, conceptual skills, and verbal fluency, among other characteristics. Further, a child's recognition of certain language offerings as insults, rejection, or hostility will be highly variable. We don't know what "meaning" those units coded as verbally aggressive acts hold for young listeners. Yet, so far as favored or liked characters engage in behaviors, verbal or otherwise, that lead to success or to victory, the likelihood that they will be emulated increases. It is reasonable to expect a young viewer to pick up expressions, forms of interaction, and language styles that are used by such characters. It may be reasonable then to expect an increasing level of verbal aggression from avid viewers of program types high in such content.

Physical violence has been the centerpiece of previous research for reasons other than those of public policy or social learning theories. It is more easily codable. It is easier to see something being done, and label it, with fewer possible alternative interpretations, than to code verbal outbursts or exchanges. Coding and counting a fist fight or a shooting is subject to fewer omissions or misidentifications than an insult or an explanation of how some other person is feeling. It may be that verbal subtleties are less likely to be emulated or recalled for that primary reason. Physical action with its strong visual accompaniment, and verbal activity, requiring more primary experiences on the part of the viewer for a comprehensive understanding, are kinds of information that may well be processed quite differently.

Then, one may question whether any kind of balance is achieved by looking concurrently at the relative loads of antisocial and prosocial behaviors. Take a program in which one finds 20 units of antisocial and 20 units of prosocial behavior. There is no presumption here that the units are in any way equivalent to one another. And it sounds suspect to suggest that 20 acts of physical aggression can be balanced in some cognitive fashion with 20 acts of altruism, with the viewer leaving the situation not noticeably different because of some presumed equality or cancelling effect. Social learning theory suggests that the viewer is likely to learn both kinds of behavior in that setting, that both would rise in the probability of their occurrence in the individual's repertoire of alternative behaviors when next the individual faces certain coping circumstances. The question remains as to how one might begin to relate or contrast an instance of fighting with an altruistic incident, let alone show-fuls of each. Then, consider two different programs, one with 30 acts of verbal aggression and 30 of altruism and affection, by contrast with a second program, with 10 acts of each. Is one to expect the same outcome? Does not sheer frequency of an activity have some impact, regardless of other parallel or opposing activities in similar magnitude?

Beyond juggling the numbers of times certain behaviors occur, analysts may wish to examine other content attributes. During the first year of this project, an effort was made to code the "intensity" of each act which occurred. Standards were created for each social behavior category, in which an act of average intensity was established and coders were required to indicate how different any subsequent coded act was from that average. We succeeded in establishing reliability for this measure and also in finding differences in intensity among program types, time periods, etc. When that measure of act intensity was incorporated into standard audience measures of viewing violent shows, it did not improve the prediction of responses. That is, the correlation between sheer exposure and pro- or antisocial behavior did not increase when the intensity measures became part of the exposure index. We have not reported on that measure in this book, although it would add an interesting element to the content analytic literature. Since the main purpose of these content analyses has been to provide a basis for better prediction of responses to content and since the measurement of intensity did not do that, it has been omitted. At the same time, the issue of wanting to estimate what happens if a show contains multiple antisocial and prosocial content examples, in contrast with a program that contains primarily antisocial content, requires more information about the content than has yet been presented by any research effort, Or the projected equality of impact of two different types of antisocial behavior, e.g., one act of hitting with the hand, vs. one act of hitting with a club, vs. three insults and two acts of deceit. The combinations are endless. Yet the logic of positing the kinds of differences that may result has yet to be developed. Adding more variables from the context of the content, such as the motives and consequences of the acts, probably yields factors that are not summative, but interactive. A model for content examination which would provide that type of dynamic quality is not yet available.

Some scenes of fighting, or loving, or shooting, excite us more than others. If that differential response is not solely a function of individual differences, and if there are content indicators to be assessed, attention should be turned to locating them. Is it the length of the incident, or the participants, or the "intensity" of the interaction, or what?

For some, using content analysis for sheer description may be sufficient, e.g., as an indicator of cultural output. Understanding the potential consequences of one variety of content, by direct comparisons to related content, has been a second goal in this study. Here, that goal has been served by identifying other major content elements which should be considered concurrently, and which may be concurrently influential in predicting those consequences.

9
SEXUAL INTIMACY ON COMMERCIAL TELEVISION DURING PRIME TIME

Bradley S. Greenberg
David Graef
Carlos Fernandez-Collado
Felipe Korzenny
Charles C. Atkin

In the spring of 1978, we published our first profile of the incidence of explicit and implied acts of, and references to, intimate sexual behaviors for a sample week of prime-time and Saturday morning television (Fernandez-Collado *et al.*, 1978). This chapter reports parallel studies of two additional sample weeks from a second television season and a summer period.

Interest in the occurrence of intimate sex behaviors and references on television stems from two principal sources. It is the primary concern or complaint now heard about television content from the viewing audience in national surveys, exceeding public concern about violence, for example (Johnson and Satow, 1978). Second, young viewers may have a strong potential for learning about sexual intimacy from such content. According to Roberts (1973), childhood and adolescence are periods of information-seeking during which the child learns what to expect from the world and what the world expects from the child. Although television inputs are one among multiple sources of information, it may be a more primary input for certain content areas, particularly those that are beyond the young viewer's immediate, personal, or likely experiences. The representation of, and reference to, intimate sex behaviors would seem to qualify as a content area of quite limited personal experience for the young viewer. Furthermore, the young viewer's greater belief in the veracity of television content and the high level of use of television for purposes of "social learning," i.e., learning about life, identify the child as particularly prone to learning from such content (Greenberg, 1974; Greenberg and Reeves, 1976).

An earlier version of this chapter was published in *Journalism Quarterly*, Vol. 57, No. 2, 1980.

In the first published work in this area, Franzblau, Sprafkin, and Rubenstein (1977) analyzed 50 hours of programming, found more physically intimate behaviors in the 8–9 p.m. time period than later in the evening, and that these most often occurred in situation comedies and variety shows. Their most frequent "intimate" behaviors were kissing, embracing, flirting, partner-seeking and nonaggressive touching. They identified no homosexual activity and only two acts of implied heterosexual intercourse. In contrast, Fernandez-Collado *et al,* (1978), in a 58-hour sample of programs in a more recent television season, found that more than twice as many acts and references occurred from 9–11 p.m. than from 8–9 p.m., that the most frequent act implied was sexual intercourse between unmarried partners (41 instances), and that acts of prostitution were frequent (28 instances).

This new investigation was prompted by the much higher incidence reported in the more recent study as well as by the need to establish more longitudinal trends, as a precursor to field and/or experimental studies examining the impact of such content.

METHODS

In the fall of 1977, and the summer of 1978, two sample weeks of prime-time fictional television series were videotaped for analysis. The former contained 48.5 hours; the latter 56 hours. Variety shows, news and public affairs programs were excluded; movies were sampled only in the summer of 1978, to enable a first examination of that content type.

Intimate sexual behavior was defined as each explicit, insinuated, or endorsed act of sexual intercourse, any type of illicit sexual behavior, or homosexuality. It included these subacts:

Rape, homosexual or heterosexual: A forced act of intercourse, usually accompanied by assault or threat;

Homosexual acts: Sexual behaviors, other than rape, between two persons of the same sex:

Intercourse between marriage partners;

Intercourse between unmarried people, but only heterosexual acts;

Prostitution: Including the portrayal of pimps and the selling of sex;

Other intimate sexual behaviors: Other sexual behaviors considered illegal or intimate sex acts that did not fit the other definitions, e.g., physical petting, the appearance of a "flasher" on one show, discussion of pornography on another.

Intensive coder training involved conceptualization of the behaviors, practice coding sessions, discussion of disagreements and errors, joint coding, and finally, systematic coding, when acceptable reliability had been obtained.

In addition to analyzing the incidence of these content categories during prime time, show types and networks were also compared. Further, by combining the two sample weeks, an adequate number of individual participants in these acts was obtained to permit a demographic analysis of the targets and agents of intimate sexual acts. Comparisons of sex, race, age, and marital status were made.

RESULTS

Table 9.1 presents the rate of occurrence of each of the coded acts of sexual intimacy for the two new sample weeks, and that obtained in the first reported analysis. The latter was recalculated to reflect only prime-time hours (8–11 p.m.), inasmuch as no such acts occurred on Saturday morning. The fall, 1977, sample also included Saturday shows, but again, zero acts were identified, and those hours were deleted from the present analysis.

First, each successive sample showed a drop in the available rate of intimate sexual references. From a high of more than two per hour in the fall, 1976, the most current sample reflected just over one per hour. Second, for all three samples, the most prevalent sexual references were to intercourse among nonmarried partners. In the two recent sample weeks, these averaged about one reference in every two hours of prime-time television. The rate of references to sexual intercourse among marriage partners never exceeded one-fourth the rate of that activity among

Table 9.1
Rate of Intimate Sexual References in Prime Time
(per hour)

	Fall 1976	Fall 1977	Summer 1978
Acts referred to			
1. Rape	.11	.00	.04
2. Homosexuality	.16	.06	.07
3. Unmarried intercourse	.91	.52	.42
4. Married intercourse	.13	.21	.07
5. Prostitution	.62	.04	.28
6. Other intimacies	.29	.52	.16
Overall rate:	2.22	1.35	1.04
Total acts	100	67	59
Total hours	45	48.5	56.5

non-married partners. In raw frequencies, the coders isolated 47, 35, and 28 references to sexual intercourse in the three sample weeks, not including rape and prostitution. The greatest variability occurred with prostitution, with the first sample week showing an especially high rate. Instances of rape and homosexuality were uniformly low, never exceeding more than a half-dozen in frequency in any of the samples.

Thus, although the higher rates of the first sample were not maintained, certain intimate sexual acts occurred regularly in the evening, and at much higher rates than reported by Franzblau and her colleagues.

Table 9.2 regroups some of the acts, adding the few instances of rape and homosexuality into the "other" acts category. In addition, the first sample week's results were excluded because they are available elsewhere; where appropriate, textual comparisons will be made. Clearly, in Table 9.2a, the rate of these acts after 9 p.m. was substantially greater than their occurrence from 8–9 p.m. In these two samples, they were three to four times as frequent after 9 p.m.; in the prior study, they were nearly 2½ times as frequent. This was particularly the case for acts of intercourse between unmarried partners, and for the substantial collection of miscellaneous acts or references to sexual intimacies. After 9 p.m., this set of acts appeared 1½ to 2 times during each hour of commercial series.

The results in Table 9.2b reflect the relative incidence of acts in major program types. Situation comedies showed the greatest flux. In the earlier study, 1.43 intimate sexual acts per hour were coded; here the rates are 2.41 and .72. Perhaps the situation comedies chosen for reruns during the summer sample week were preselected to avoid complaints about this type of content. The incidence on crime shows, by contrast, was remarkably similar in all three sample weeks, with rates of 1.61, 1.27, and 1.72 per hour successively. The act composition of those rates varied greatly, with prostitution as the keynote in two seasons (1976 and 1978) and a more miscellaneous collection in the third (1977). Table 9.2 also identifies movies as a principal vehicle for these acts, averaging more than one per hour in the single sample in which movies were coded. They contained one of the highest rates of representation of intercourse among unmarried persons (and zero instances among marriage partners).

A comparative analysis of the three commercial networks was also done. In all three seasons, NBC was the least frequent presenter of the acts coded here, although for the third sample, the differences among networks were negligible. Successively, the rates for ABC were 1.71, 1.36, and 1.11; for CBS, 1.98, 1.78, and 1.14; for NBC, 1.21, .97, and .90.

TABLE 9.2
Intimate Sexual References by Time Period and Major Program Types

Acts:	2 a. Time Periods				2 b. Program Types				
	Fall, 1977		Summer, 1978		Fall, 1977		Summer, 1978		
	8–9pm	9–11pm	8–9pm	9–11pm	Sitcoms	Crime	Sitcoms	Crime	Movies
1. Unmarried intercourse	.27	.72	.11	.59	.87	.20	.16	.36	.74
2. Married intercourse	.18	.23	.11	.05	.60	-0-	.16	-0-	-0-
3. Prostitution	.05	.04	.05	.40	.07	.07	.08	.91	.23
4. Others	.18	.98	.05	.37	.87	1.00	.32	.45	.29
Overall rate:	.68	1.97	.32	1.41	2.41	1.27	.72	1.72	1.26
Total acts	15	52	6	53	36	19	9	19	22
Total hours	22	26.5	19	37.5	15	15	12.5	11	17.5

Finally, selected demographic characteristics of the participants in these sexual instances were determined. Table 9.3 summarizes those results. Women were as likely as men to be participants, both in initiating and receiving roles. Given the lack of acts of homosexuality, it is not surprising to find roughly one man and one woman engaged in each intimate sexual act coded, although men outnumbered women among all television characters by three to one. The distribution of participants by race showed lesser participation by blacks than might have been expected. Blacks constituted 10 percent of all the TV characters, but only 5 percent of the targets and agents of these intimate sex acts. No other ethnic groups participated.

The concentration of intimate sex in the young adult and mid-adult years is also shown in Table 9.3. Fully 75 percent of all acts occurred among those 20–49 years of age, a proportion 11 percent greater than that age range's representation in the population of TV characters. Finally, the earlier findings of the disproportionate occurrence of sexual intercourse among nonmarried partners was reconfirmed in the marital status data. Exactly half the targets and agents of these acts had never been married, among those for whom there was sufficient program information to code this variable. This was 2½ to 3 times the proportion of currently married television characters identified as participants in these acts.

TABLE 9.3
Participants in Intimate Sexual References

	Agent (%) (n = 156)	Target (%) (n = 146)
1. Females	58	50
2. Blacks	5	5
Other whites	93	95
3. Age:		
< 20	9	10
20–34	42	34
35–49	34	41
50–64	15	15
65+	0	0
4. Never married	50	50
First marriage	16	22
Widowed	7	7
Divorced	3	6

DISCUSSION

The portrayal of intimate sexual acts on commercial prime-time television appears to have certain noteworthy continuities and discontinuities. Among the former, it can be demonstrated that these acts are not infrequent, occurring once or more an hour. They are particularly prevalent after 9 p.m. The modal act referred to is that of heterosexual intercourse, and it occurs predominantly among unmarried people. Sexual deviation is very rarely suggested. Those conclusions emerge from three independent studies. Irregularities do occur in the types of programs most likely to provide these portrayals, and in the regularity of occurrence of some of them, e.g., prostitution. Notably, there was a distinct downward slope in the overall rate of occurrence. For that trend, these data cannot differentiate such alternative causes as a true and valid decline from insufficient sample sizes for this type of content phenomenon. For subsequent research, we would argue the latter, that there may be sufficient instability in the presentation of this type of content from week to week that the one-week sampling method should be supplemented by additional weeks. Where one is analyzing TV content behaviors, e.g., physical aggression, verbal aggression, sex-role behaviors, that occur in hundreds of instances each week, the one-week sample has been demonstrated to be adequate. Where a total yield of sex acts from a week of prime-time television does not exceed 100 instances, elaborated analyses may not be as reliable. Therefore, before concluding that sex on television has decreased substantially, it might be well to sample and analyze a half-dozen weeks of content throughout a television season.

Further investigation should elaborate on the dimension of explicitness or implicitness of these content instances. Most of these sex acts were not portrayed; they were discussed, alluded to, or implied. Since the primary reason for this content analysis is the subsequent determination of whether social learning accrues from this available content information, particularly among young viewers, one would anticipate that the more explicit the reference, the more likely it would be understood. Perhaps before, or at least concurrent with, any study of children's social learning about sexual intimacy from television, those children should be tested in terms of their cognitive understanding about the content of these acts. Shown a man and woman in bed together, with suggestive verbal interaction, accompanied by initial embracing and the inevitable fade-out, what does the viewer think is happening, or about to happen? Given the verbal exchange between prostitute and "john," what does a young viewer think is happening? One anticipates large differences in understanding among different age groups, and substantial variability within younger age groups. Identifying the cognitive responses to these content instances is itself a portion of social learning, but they also serve as likely antecedents for other impacts, e.g., evaluation of the portrayals, sexual anticipations, and fantasies.

Additional content attributes of these acts and references should be examined from the perspective of possible social learning. For example, whether the participants are favorite characters with whom the children identify may be more critical than if the acts are being portrayed by unknowns. The consequences of the acts, as well as their motivations, should provide important contextual information for predicting outcomes for the viewer; rewarded, enjoyable acts are more likely to be responded to favorably.

The question of just how many acts provide a critical mass has yet to be considered, let alone answered. If something happens once an hour, or once every two hours, is that sufficient for social impact? Does it build up over weeks and years to stimulate a certain perspective about sexual intimacy? Rates presented in hourly terms mask the sheer frequency of observation available over long periods of time; the longitudinal issues require even more elaborate research efforts.

10

TRENDS IN USE OF ALCOHOL
AND OTHER SUBSTANCES ON TELEVISION

BRADLEY S. GREENBERG
CARLOS FERNANDEZ-COLLADO
DAVID GRAEF
FELIPE KORZENNY
CHARLES K. ATKIN

Concern about the portrayal of alcohol and other drugs on television shows is tied to the expectation that these portrayals are frequent and typically favorable. If that is so, then the further expectation is that viewers will respond to such displays of alcohol in terms of their attitudes and possibly their drinking habits as well.

More specific concern about television's depiction of alcohol and other drugs focuses on the potential social learning which might occur among young viewers. Young viewers are expected to be particularly vulnerable because childhood and adolescence are periods of information-seeking during which the child learns what to expect from the world and what the world expects from the child. Children derive information from many sources, but television in particular provides graphic and dramatic exposure to worldly behaviors which go substantially beyond the child's immediate experiences. And television presents attitudes and values which may differ from those of family and peers (Roberts and Schramm, 1971; Roberts, 1973). There also is substantial evidence that observation of social models, specifically including television models, may account for a significant segment of the information that is communicated to young people (Bandura and Walters, 1963; Flanders, 1968; Hartup and Coates, 1970).

Lyle and Hoffman (1972) found that first graders spent about 24

The original version of this article was published in *Journal of Drug Education,* Vol. 9 No. 3, 1979, Baywood Publishing Co., Inc.

hours each week watching television, sixth graders about 30 hours, and tenth graders about 28 hours. More current national audience data from Neilsen indicate that all age groups have expanded their viewing time since the early 1970s. Thus the potential for learning from television exists in terms of time spent with the medium, and the young viewer's use of TV for social information.

This rationale is built on the premise that alcohol is available on a widespread basis during television's prime hours, inside the programs, exclusive of commercials. Yet, evidence on this issue is scanty and less than systematic. This chapter reports on a content analysis of the usage of alcohol, tobacco, and illicit drugs during two recent television seasons, 1976–77 and 1977–78.

In a long review of mass media content dealing with alcohol and other drugs, Winick and Winick (1976) asserted, "During the last few years, there has been a decline in the presentation of casual social drinking on television, along with the larger culture's growing sensitivity to the problems posed by alcoholism." They provide no data to support either assertion, and the present review of the few empirical studies available on television's alcohol content does not support the first proposition.

In 1973, Hanneman and McEwen analyzed television content for 80 program hours in March and for 21 hours in November. The hours were "essentially prime time." They recorded references to, and the use of, alcohol, tobacco, and both licit and illicit drugs in entertainment programs. They found 105 alcohol instances in the first time period and 32 in the second, or an average depiction of 1.3 to 1.5 incidents per program hour; all other substances analyzed were neglible by comparison. The incidents were fairly evenly divided between situation comedy/variety shows and dramatic shows, and actual usage exceeded references (McEwen and Hanneman, 1974; Hanneman and McEwen, 1976).

In 1975, Garlington (1977) coded alcohol use in five episodes of each of 14 different soap operas. He found alcohol being used an average of three times in each segment, with the segments running about 21 minutes for each half-hour show, given commercial inclusions. Drinking took place in drinking scenes, rather than as background or by reference to drinking; the home setting predominated, and the modal drink was straight liquor.

In the spring of 1975 and again that December, the *Christian Science Monitor* reported its own study findings. The December study (Dillin, 1975) analyzed 66 hours between 8 and 11 p.m. and said that little difference had been found between this study and the one the previous spring. One incident of alcohol usage was found for each 17 minutes of program time, or about three incidents per hour in the evening.

The sparse data available dispute the Winick and Winick contention. But the several studies represent different sampling frames for programs and airtimes, as well as different seasons. And the Winicks may have believed that these reported levels were lower than what was available before 1973, the first season for which some empirical evidence was reported. The present study updates the available data on this issue and provides the first set of data which is comparable for more than a single television season. Although focusing on alcohol, it also presents information on tobacco and illicit drug portrayals.

METHODS

In each of two seasons—1976–77 and 1977–78—a composite week of the three commercial networks' programming was videotaped off the air. The week included one episode of each prime-time and Saturday morning fictional series. Each season, approximately 60 hours were taped, representing about 80 different shows. The taping was normally completed over a three-week period, to accommodate preemptions and other alterations of the regularly scheduled series.

Content Analysis

As part of a more comprehensive coding of specific behaviors and character interactions during the shows, a special effort was made to identify and code all instances of specific substance use. *Substance use* was defined as that set of behaviors which included each incident of the consumption of, attempt to consume, inducement to consume, and making laudatory remarks about the consumption of alcohol, tobacco, and illegal drugs. It also included the sale of illegal drugs, such as marijuana, heroin, and LSD. In addition, demographic information was collected for each TV character who participated in these behaviors, e.g., sex, age, and race, enabling a portion of this analysis to identify selected characteristics of television's substance users.

Coders underwent about 40 hours of training, a portion of which was devoted to the subset of behaviors analyzed here. Given the manifest nature of the substance usage behaviors, reliability in identifying substance usage was consistently high. Coders had the videotapes available and could examine the material as often as necessary to make their coding judgments.

RESULTS

The first analysis describes the overall substance usage rates for the two seasons; the second breaks down usage rates by time and type of programming and by network; the final analysis describes attributes of substance users on commercial television.

Table 10.1 presents the overall incidence of substance acts for each of the sample weeks, for alcohol, tobacco, and illegal drugs. In both seasons, alcohol predominated, accounting for more than two-thirds of all the coded substance acts. More than two acts of alcohol use were found per hour in each season, with the 1977–78 sample week averaging 2.66 alcohol acts per hour of fictional television programming. This was an increase of nearly one more alcohol act every two hours. Tobacco usage averages under an incident per hour; illicit drug use is also at that level.[1]

TABLE 10.1
Frequency and Rate of Substance Use

	1976–77			1977–78		
	f	%	Hourly*	f	%	Hourly
1. Alcohol	128	70	2.19	168	67	2.66
2. Tobacco	41	23	.70	31	12	.48
3. Illegal drugs	13	7	.22	52	21	.83
	182	100	3.11	251	100	3.97

*In 1976–77, there were 58.5 hours; in 1977–78, 63 hours.

Whereas a viewer had to watch television for two hours to observe someone smoke a cigar, cigarrette, or pipe, and more than one hour for illegal drug usage to occur, that same viewer could observe alcohol being offered and/or consumed every 21 minutes in the second year's sample of shows, exactly the rate Garlington (1977) identified in his study of soap operas. The trend between seasons suggests an increase in alcohol use portrayals.

Table 10.2 extends the analysis of alcohol use on television by examining its use by time period, by program type, and by network. There were clear and consistent differences in the analysis by time period. The three time periods used represent Saturday morning programming of

[1]In the 1977–78 data, one episode of "All in the Family" accounted for 18 of the drug acts.

TABLE 10.2
Usage Rate of Alcohol in Fictional TV Series

	1976–77	1977–78
I. Overall per hour rate	2.19	2.66
II. Rate by time period		
a. Saturday a.m.	-0-	.08
b. 8–9 p.m.	1.78	1.64
c. 9–11 p.m.	3.36	4.92
III. Rate by program type		
a. Family drama	2.50	2.00
b. Situation/comedy	1.40	4.72
c. Crime	3.78	4.60
d. Action/adventure	2.74	1.20
e. Saturday noncartoons	-0-	-0-
f. Saturday cartoons	.12	.08
IV. Rate by network		
a. ABC	1.80	3.22
b. CBS	2.70	2.98
c. NBC	2.04	1.86

cartoons and noncartoons, especially for child audiences; 8–9 p.m., formerly known as the *family viewing hour*, but now a period during which the networks claim to be providing programs for a general family audience; and 9–11 p.m., the key prime time designated for more mature programming. In each of the two season's samples, significant differences ($p < .001$) occurred across these three time periods. Alcohol use on Saturday morning programs was nil; it occurred somewhat more than 1½ times per hour during the 8–9 p.m. time slot; from 9–11 p.m., it exceeded three instances per hour in the first season analyzed, and bordered on five instances per hour in the second season. Whatever trend appears for an increase in alcohol display in fictional television programming was entirely accounted for during the 9–11 p.m. time period, a jump of more than 1½ instances per hour in the 1977–78 data.

The program type data were consistent across seasons for some types and not for others. Significant differences occurred across program types within each season ($p < .001$). Both types of Saturday shows—cartoons and live character programs—contained trivial incidences. Crime shows in both seasons displayed about four instances of alcohol use per hour and family dramas contained about two per hour. Situation comedies, relatively low in incidence during the first season analyzed, showed a striking rise to first position during the second season, with 4.72 acts per hour, making them equivalent to crime shows—which had the highest incidence during the first season.

By network, CBS shows typically contained somewhat more frequent instances during the first season, but ABC reached the CBS level during the second year analyzed. If anything, NBC was the least frequent purveyor of alcohol acts during the 1977–78 season, based on this sample of programs. However, the differences among networks within a season, or for the same network between seasons were not statistically significant.

Similar analyses were performed for the tobacco and drug acts. The low frequencies involved do not warrant full presentation of those two substances. Rather, Table 10.3 combines all three substances into a single index to permit an examination of trends for the substances as a group.[2] The overall substance use rate increased from just over three instances per hour during the 1976–77 shows to almost four instances per hour in the 1977–78 shows analyzed. The sharp distinction among time periods identified in the alcohol usage table is even more apparent in Table 10.3. The Saturday shows did not average one act among these substances in an hour; from 8–9 p.m., the viewer could anticipate two to three acts per hour; and from 9–11 p.m., the viewer could receive five to six acts per hour.

By program type, both types of Saturday shows remain quite sterile in terms of showing drinking, smoking, or drug acts. Crime shows were the most frequently consistent purveyor of all three categories of acts, with situation comedies showing the most inconsistency. Family dramas and action/adventure shows were likely to be in the one to two acts per hour range. Again, the differences among program types were statistically significant in each season ($p < .001$).

TABLE 10.3
Usage Rate of Three Substances* in Fictional TV Series

	1976–77	1977–78
I. Overall per hour rate	3.11	3.97
II. Rate by time period		
a. Saturday a.m.	.32	.42
b. 8–9 p.m.	2.00	3.62
c. 9–11 p.m.	4.98	6.18
III. Rate by program type		
a. Family drama	3.50	2.16
b. Situation/comedy	1.52	7.86
c. Crime	5.84	6.32
d. Action/adventure	3.50	1.50
e. Saturday noncartoons	-0-	.32
f. Saturday cartoons	.62	.44
IV. Rate by network		
a. ABC	2.42	3.82
b. CBS	3.86	5.40
c. NBC	3.06	2.56

*The three substances were alcohol, tobacco, and illegal drugs.

[2]Tables for tobacco and drugs separately are available from the authors.

The network differences are not consistent, although the trend was for NBC to display the fewest of all three substance acts.

The frequency of occurrence of alcohol acts was sufficiently large to permit an analysis of the demographic attributes of the television characters who engaged in those acts. The original analysis separated agents or proferrors of alcohol from targets or recipients of alcohol. The results were identical, no matter who was being analyzed. Table 10.4 presents the information for the agents.[3] The data reflect proportions who were users, the proportions of acts each user group committed, and the average number of instances for each user category. For example, 65 percent of the users were males (they constituted 71 percent of the television character population), who committed 68 percent of the alcohol acte, with an average number of acts quite similar to that of females. Thus, one can conclude that males and females participated in alcohol acts in proportions and quantities similar to their representation in the population of television characters.

By race, blacks (who were 9 percent of the TV population) were 6 percent of the users, committed 6 percent of the acts, and did not differ substantially in total average acts of alcohol usage from white characters.

By age groupings, those under 20 (20 percent of the TV population) were less likely to be users, and committed fewer acts both proportionately and on the average than any of the other age groupings. Of

TABLE 10.4
Attributes of Alcohol Users on TV

	% of users (n = 78)	% of acts (n = 154)	x̄ acts
I. Sex			
Males	65	68	2.04
Females	35	32	1.85
II. Race			
Black	6	6	1.80
White	94	94	1.99
III. Age			
< 20	9	6	1.29
20–34	33	39	2.35
35–49	32	30	1.88
50+	26	25	1.90
IV. SES			
Lower	10	8	1.20
Middle	45	54	2.11
Upper	44	38	1.50
V. Role			
Serious	71	62	1.75
Comic	29	38	2.52

[3]This demographic analysis is based on the 1977–78 season data.

course, this age group included substantial numbers of children. Those 20–34 were likelier to be heavier drinkers, and those over 50 (16 percent of the TV characters) were more likely to be part of the user group.

In terms of the socioeconomic status of the characters, as categorized from their occupations, the lower SES characters (15 percent of the characters) were less likely to be users, and even the users in that SES group did less using. The middle-class characters did heavier drinking, and the upper-middle and upper-class characters (29 percent of the TV characters) were more likely to be users.

The coders also made a general judgment about each character, i.e., whether the character was portraying essentially a serious or comic role in the TV show. Although the serious characters outnumbered the less serious ones, the latter were more likely to be heavier drinkers.

Finally, one should note that the alcohol user group comprised slightly more than 6 percent of all the TV characters.

DISCUSSION

Before drawing any implications from these data, it is necessary to identify certain omissions in the analysis. Important descriptors relevant to the consumption of alcohol on television shows, as well as the other substances, remain to be determined. For one, any subsequent analysis should collect data with regard to the *effects* of consumption on the TV users. Knowing whether there are negative or positive social consequences is critical if one is interested in projecting possible impact on the viewer. If, for example, the typical drinking scene results in greater joy, or as a possible prelude to victory for the hero, then one would expect a positive impression from those scenes on viewers.

Second, one should examine the *context* of drinking scenes. Are such episodes typically carried out in a social, rather than private, context, among convivial folk? If so, one could anticipate that drinking would be associated with happy events and situations in the minds of viewers. Third, one might determine the *motives* which precede substance usage. How much drinking occurs for no apparent reason, or no necessary reason other than to give the characters something to do as they deal with the story situation? How much is done at the time that the serious characters set about solving this episode's problem? Such information would further identify for viewers just what the principal reasons seem to be for substance usage.

In contrast, if the consumption of illicit drugs is accompanied by suffering, or by legal punishment, or other negative consequences, one would posit a possible aversion toward such behavior by the viewer. For some substances, the consequences depicted typically may be positive and others negative. Thus, a more comprehensive analysis of substance use on television would provide more than conjecture about this issue.

One problem peculiar to descriptive content analyses is the temptation to label identified acts or occurrences as "a lot" or "too much" or "too few." Such statements attach values not inherent in the data, but superimposed by the researcher. Here, at least, we have been able to compare two seasons and say there is more or less; we have been able to compare three substances and can say one is found more or less often than the others. But how much is enough, or too much, is indeterminate. The lesser-found substances of tobacco and illegal drugs have not received the emphasis accorded alcohol in this presentation. Their incidence is much less. Yet, if one averages the two seasons of data and concludes that smoking and drugging are occurring about once every two hours of television, then one can begin to examine that incidence relative to other factors. For example, national surveys indicate that the typical elementary school age youngster watches television about four hours each day. So, that child sees two acts of smoking and drugging each day, or about 700 instances of each across a year's period of time. Thus, as one moves from a small figure of one-half act per hour, to reflect on how many acts that is in a year of viewing, there may be cause not to slough off the low incidence rates of the lesser-used substances as inconsequential. We don't know how many times something has to be seen to be liked, or imitated, or for certain types of beliefs to develop. Further, when one begins to deal with exposures of that magnitude, it perhaps becomes clearer why additional information about consequences, motives, etc., for these acts is imperative.

Even with that caveat, it is difficult to survey the data presented on alcohol portrayals and not conclude that the incidence rate is a high one. During no hour of the evening does the alcohol usage rate on fictional television series average less than 1½ acts per program hour. And during the later hours of prime time—9–11 p.m.—no hour goes by with an average of less than three instances of usage. One can find no program type, save on Saturday mornings, with less than one or two instances per hour. And the more heavily watched types of situation comedies and crime shows exceeded four acts per hour during the most recent season analyzed. Conservatively, a youngster, too young to drink, will be exposed to 10 drinking acts on television during a day's viewing; perhaps it is excessive to indicate that this can be projected to more than 3000 in a year's period.

This analysis was done in the context of a research project examining social learning among young people from television content. Social learning theory suggests that exposure to content stimuli which are consistent in theme and of considerable frequency can have an impact on a young viewer. Actually the theory does not delimit the age of the viewer, in terms of impact, but most tests of the theory have chosen young people as study groups. To the extent that social behaviors on television, such as acts of drinking, are performed by liked characters, in a positive context, without negative consequences, or with positive rewards, social learning is more likely to occur. Such learning can take several forms. It can affect the viewer's aspirations and expectations about the observed behaviors; it can impinge on the viewer's beliefs with regard to the acceptability or appropriateness of the behavior, it can teach the behavior, and it can induce either imitation or a desire for imitation. So far as the behavior is a common one, with the tools for performance easily accessible, the likelihood of such learning is further enhanced.

In addition to examining some content attributes of substance usage not yet analyzed, it would be appropriate to begin to determine what, if any, social learning accrues from the display of alcohol in fictional television programs. Coupling that question to the advertising of alcohol on television would also be in order.

IV
FAMILIES ON TELEVISION

11

FAMILY ROLE STRUCTURES
AND INTERACTIONS
ON COMMERCIAL TELEVISION

BRADLEY S. GREENBERG
MARY HINES
NANCY BUERKEL-ROTHFUSS
CHARLES K. ATKIN

The primary organizing unit in most societies and a common element in many television programs is the family. It may be a nuclear family consisting of two parents and some children; it may be a family with divorced parents; or it may be an extended family that includes a grandparent or more distant relatives. Such family types flourish in real life and on television. Most children have their first familial experiences with their own families and with those of their playmates. Yet, at the preschool age, a child begins vicariously to experience and watch families that are available on United States television, both in prime-time evening shows (e.g., "Good Times," "All in the Family") and in those afternoon periods when local stations lease syndicated series (e.g., "Brady Bunch," "Partridge Family"). One may wonder what a young viewer begins to extract from observing television families, their composition, and their family role interactions. This concern takes on cross-cultural implications when one considers two related issues—differential family roles in different subcultures, both domestic and international, and the large-scale export and popularity of United States television shows featuring family units.

The same social learning theories which have yielded testable propositions about the learning of aggression from television (Berkowitz, 1962; Atkin, et al., 1971; Liebert, et al., 1973), the learning of prosocial behaviors (Friedrich and Stein, 1973; Leifer, et al., 1974), and the learning of sex-role expectations (Atkin and Miller, 1975; Miller and Reeves, 1975) would also be applicable to the learning of family roles, attitudes, and behaviors. This work proceeds from two central propositions: (1) children can and do learn behaviors through observing models who perform those behaviors, without direct reinforcement; (2) children try to maximize benefits to themselves, usually in the form of reinforcement for imitating or identifying with a model (Aronfreed, 1969; Bandura, 1977). Learning, of course, depends in part on the developmental level of the child (Leifer, *et al.*, 1971; Wackman, *et al.*, 1973; Collins, 1975) and dispositional and environmental mediating factors (Greenberg, 1972; McLeod, *et al.*, 1972).

Family role structures and role interaction patterns on television constitute an abundant and potentially important class of environmental stimuli available for attitude formation and change and for behavioral modeling by a child. The observation of family role interaction patterns may lead directly to imitating behaviors displayed by television models or to behavioral change mediated by attitude change. Television family models could be expected to orient the child's responses to such issues as the predominance of certain types of family structures, the power associated with particular family roles, feelings of satisfaction with present family structure and interaction patterns in comparison to those observed, interaction patterns and structural relationships of families of differing racial and socioeconomic backgrounds, and expectations concerning parent and sibling behaviors.

Preliminary to assessing possible effects is the systematic identification of the predominant television themes and portrayals of family members and their interactions. Of particular interest are those shows which feature a family as the central unit of interest (e.g., "Family," "The Waltons"), since learning should be most facilitated by those shows which permit vicarious experiences with known characters over time. Despite a widespread interest in family contextual variables, no prior content analysis has systematically and comprehensively described television family role structures and family role interaction patterns.

METHODS

The present analytic scheme is a modification of one developed by Borke (1967) for the systematic description of normal family interaction in ordinary settings. She observed functioning families of parents and children performing a variety of family tasks in their homes. Verbal interactions were categorized according to their functional aspects from the speaker's point of view, and these categories were then reduced to a smaller number of primary and secondary *modes of interaction*, e.g., contributing information, giving support, resisting, retreating, directing. These were then subsumed under Horney's (1945) three classifications of interpersonal direction: going *toward* someone, going *against* someone, and going *away*.

The present content analysis consisted of a role-by-behavior description of verbal interactions among members of television families. The coding unit was any act or sequence of acts initiated by a family member and directed to another family member which was unitary with respect to direction, mode, and recipient. A coding unit could then consist of a single utterance or several comments or sentences. Whenever the initiator, recipient, direction, or mode changed, a new unit was coded.

Sample

One episode of each of 96 prime-time evening and Saturday morning fictional television series aired by the three major networks during 1975–76 was recorded on videotape. All shows containing verbal interactions among family members were included in this analysis; 53 of the shows met this criterion.

The Act Initiator and Recipient

The name and family role of the character initiating an act were recorded. *Family role* was defined as the role which the act initiator held with respect to the family member toward whom the act was directed. For example, if a woman directed an act toward her husband, her role for that act was recorded as wife. Coders were given a list of 40 family roles. The role list included all conceivable family roles which might occur in an extended family, ranging from the traditional nuclear roles to such roles as guardian, godparent, and stepchild.

Recipient character name and family role were recorded in the same manner as were initiator character name and family role. Recipient family role was determined by the relationship between the act receiver and act initiator.

Directions and Modes

Acts were coded into one of three directions: going *toward*, going *away*, or going *against*. Within each directional category, a series of modes was used to more precisely describe the manner in which characters were approaching, avoiding, or attacking. Both the modes and directions were adapted from Borke and Horney. After pretesting the content-analytic scheme, further refinements in operational definitions and categories were made. The categories which remained were expected to describe fully the quantity and quality of interactions among family members on commercial television programs.

Definitions of the three directions and their accompanying modes follow:

Going toward: These are positive acts which initiate, maintain, and/or build a family relationship. Operationally, nine modes were used:

1. Offering information—giving information or opinion in answer to a question, or spontaneously;

2. Seeking information—questions asked solely for the purpose of obtaining information;

3. Contributing and entertaining—miscellaneous behaviors intended solely to take part in or further an on-going interaction, including greetings exchanged as new characters enter interaction, nonhostile teasing and joking around;

4. Supporting—doing something to benefit another, showing approval for another, encouraging, protecting, pacifying, indulging, assisting, or helping another, supporting another's interests, attempting to reduce another's physical or emotional discomfort or pain;

5. Showing concern—behaviors which demonstrate concern for another's welfare or interests but which do not actively provide support for another;

6. Petitioning—attempts to obtain support, attention, or sources of gratification from another, actions which seek to obtain help, comfort, approval, encouragement, consolation, attention, or special favors for self;

7. Directing—positive attempts to manage or guide the behavior of another, giving instructions as to what to do, or how to do something, organizing family members in order to accomplish a task, directing plans, encouraging others to cooperate or behave harmoniously;

8. Accepting support—communicating to another recognition of attempts to provide support, accepting apologies from another;

9. Accepting direction—obeying, cooperating, or complying with another person's attempt to direct or manage one's behavior, this also includes accepting another's point of view and offering an apology in response to a request or demand that apology be given.

Going against: This is conflict-producing and conflict-maintaining behavior. Operationally, three modes were defined: (1) ignoring—this includes disregarding another, refusing to take notice of another, reacting coldly, or with obvious and/or persistent disinterest; (2) opposing—this includes protesting, disagreeing, refusing to accept direction or support, refusing to cooperate, disobeying, and justifying self and/or actions in a hostile manner; and (3) attacking—this includes initiating conflict with another, criticizing, belittling, challenging, provoking, teasing maliciously, and arguing.

Going away: These are behaviors which psychologically distance one family member from another and/or behaviors by means of which one family member physically withdraws from another. Operationally, two modes were used: (1) evading—to avoid dealing with another, to give evasive answers, to attempt to change topic or focus of interaction in order to evade issues or questions raised; (2) withdrawing—to terminate interaction or stop participating in interaction by physically leaving. This does not include natural termination of interaction such as when one party must leave to fulfill recognized and valid external obligations.

Family Structure Analysis

Key descriptors of family structure were also coded, in terms of size, i.e., sum of blood and marriage-related individuals; number of children; the patterns of family extendedness, e.g., childless, traditional nuclear, extended, broken, and other combinations; the parent structure in the family, i.e., two original parents, single parent, two parents but only one an original parent, no parents; and the marital status of the adult members of the family, i.e., never married, first marriage, divorced, widowed.

Reliabilities

Four undergraduate student coders were trained in two-person teams for approximately ten hours. Inter-rater reliability estimates were obtained across two coders for seven shows and across four coders for one show. *Inter-rater reliability* refers to the percentage agreement in categorization of acts for each of the descriptive dimensions. Average inter-rater reliability estimates for each dimension were: initiator family role, 95 percent; act direction, 92 percent; act mode, 88 percent; recipient family role, 95 percent; and age/sex code, 95 percent.

RESULTS

Fifty-three of the 96 shows analyzed from the composite week of prime-time and Saturday morning television contained a "family." In all, 73 family units were represented, encompassing 208 television characters. Of these characters, 79 were children of some other character; 52 of the 79 were under 18 years of age. This subset of 208 characters was obtained from a pool of 1212 speaking characters across all shows. Therefore, for each TV character with one or more relatives, there were five without relatives.

There were three basic types of television families: (1) the nuclear family, two parents with one or more children, was identified 28 times;

(2) in 19 instances, families consisted of one parent, plus children; (3) in 17 situations, a husband and wife without children constituted the family. The nine remaining family types were a miscellaneous collection of two cousins, an uncle and his niece, etc.

Among the adults (over 18) in these families, divorce was not found with any frequency. Thirty-four of the adults had never been married; 95 were in their first marriage; and eight were divorced. Most of the 19 single-parent families were headed by widows or widowers. In these families, the proportion of males to females was 55:45. Across all television fiction, three males have been located for each female (Simmons, *et al.*, 1977). This means, then, that in shows without family representation, males outnumber females four and five to one.

Family Roles. The original set of family roles included 40 different possibilities, ranging from former spouses to foster children. The actual occurrences of family roles were confined predominantly to nuclear roles—husband-wife, father-mother, son-daughter, and brother-sister. The male half of this reduced set comprised 76 percent of all observed male family roles; the female half accounted for 77 percent of all observed female family roles. No other single role category accounted for as much as 10 percent of the portrayed family roles. Table 11.1 presents the frequency obtained for each family role.

Initiators and Receivers of Family Role Interactions. Before turning to the actual content of the family role interaction analysis, the participation of family members as initiators and receivers of interactions was examined. In all, more than 5700 acts were identified and coded. Nuclear family males were the initiators of 50 percent of all family acts; nuclear family females accounted for 36 percent of all initiated family acts. In combination, these eight nuclear roles were sufficient to describe the initiators of the vast majority of the acts studied. As for receivers of these same acts, the four male roles in the nuclear family received 48 percent of all acts, and the four parallel female roles received 37 percent. In total, the men and women in the nuclear family roles accounted for more than 85 percent of all interactions and did so in the same manner in both initiator and receiver roles. Table 11.1 contains the basic data describing act recipients and initiators.

The roles featured within the nuclear subset occurred with considerably different frequencies for men and women, however. Among men, three nuclear roles were equally predominant: husband, father, and son. The role of brother was markedly lower in number of initiator or receiver interactions. In contrast, one female role—wife—stood out as the initiator or recipient of interactions. This role accounted for 12 percent of all acts initiated and 13 percent of all acts received.

TABLE 11.1
Family Roles Distribution and Initiators and Receivers of Family Role Acts

Male Roles	Role Frequency	Initiating Acts (%)	Receiving Acts (%)	Female Roles	Role Frequency	Initiating Acts (%)	Receiving Acts (%)
Husband	45	13	12	Wife	45	12	13
Father	33	14	12	Mother	29	8	7
Son	37	13	14	Daughter	29	7	8
Brother	32	10	10	Sister	25	9	9
Father-in-law	6	1	1	Mother-in-law	6	1	1
Son-in-law	4	1	1	Daughter-in-law	5	1	1
Brother-in-law	10	1	2	Sister-in-law	5	2	2
Uncle	5	1	1	Aunt	5	1	1
Nephew	8	2	2	Niece	3	0	<1
Cousin	1	<1	<1	Cousin	2	2	2
All others*	14	1	1	All others**	13	1	
		(n = 3247)	(n = 3138)			(n = 2485)	(n = 2567)

*All others, male, include grandfather, stepfather, foster father, stepson, foster son, grandson, stepbrother, exspouse, godfather, male guardian.
**All others, female, include grandmother, stepmother, foster mother, stepdaughter, foster daughter, granddaughter, stepsister, exspouse, godmother, female guardian.

A final analysis of the nuclear family interactions, without concern yet for the content of the interactions, paired the family members in their initiating and receiving roles. Table 11.2 presents this analysis.

Husbands and wives were the primary interactors, splitting 29 percent of all interactions in the nuclear family as receivers and initiators. The second largest set of behaviors occurred between fathers and sons (21 percent). This was twice the frequency of interaction between mothers and daughters (9 percent), mothers and sons (9 percent), or fathers and daughters (9 percent). In addition, brothers and sisters interacted with opposite-sex siblings in 14 percent of the interactions, while interacting with same-sex siblings in 9 percent of the acts.

TABLE 11.2
Nuclear Family Interacts

Initiator	Recipient	No. of Acts	% of Acts	Acts per Initiator	% of Acts Going Toward
Husband	Wife	723	15	16.1	86
Wife	Husband	666	14	14.8	88
Mother	Son	223	5	7.7	93
Son	Mother	215	4	5.8	87
Mother	Daughter	233	5	8.0	95
Daughter	Mother	195	4	6.7	88
Father	Son	556	11	16.8	91
Son	Father	503	10	13.6	90
Father	Daughter	229	5	6.9	95
Daughter	Father	192	4	6.6	93
Brother	Brother	234	5	7.3	84
Brother	Sister	336	7	10.5	85
Sister	Brother	344	7	13.8	85
Sister	Sister	191	4	7.6	96
		4840	100		

Direction and Mode of Family Role Interactions. Table 11.3 presents the overall distribution of interactions by direction and mode. One direction—*going away*—occurred only trivially in either the modes of evasion or withdrawal from the interactive situation. A second direction—*going against*—accounted for just under 11 percent of all family role interactions. The most frequently occurring mode of *going against* was verbal opposition (7 percent). Direct verbal attacks occurred less frequently (3 percent), the act of ignoring was virtually nil.

The most frequently observed direction of family role interactions was *going toward*, or approaching the other person in a positive, constructive fashion. Table 11.3 identifies *offering information* as the mode most often observed in television family interactions, accounting for 35 percent of all such behaviors. Two other modes also occurred with high frequency, *seeking information* and *directing others*. We note that more than half of the offers of information were not preceded by requests for such

TABLE 11.3
Direction and Mode of Family Role Interactions

Direction	Mode	f	(%)
Goes against	1. Ignores	8	(< 1)
	2. Opposes	403	(7)
	3. Attacks	193	(3)
Goes away	1. Evades	36	(1)
	2. Withdraws	9	(< 1)
Goes toward	1. Offers information	2012	(35)
	2. Seeks information	837	(15)
	3. Contributes	480	(8)
	4. Supports	376	(7)
	5. Shows concern	84	(2)
	6. Petitions	301	(5)
	7. Directs	790	(14)
	8. Accepts support	60	(1)
	9. Accepts direction	144	(3)
		5733	100

information. Three other modes of going toward others generated high behavior counts. These were *contributing* behaviors, which serve largely to continue the conversation, *supportive* or reinforcing behaviors, and *petitioning* behaviors. Three of the behaviors associated with this direction of interaction did not occur frequently, *showing concern* for others, *accepting support* from others, and *accepting directions* from others.

From the original scheme of family role interactions, acts of evasion and withdrawal were not observed with sufficient frequency to warrant further analysis. Acts of *going against* were primarily observed as acts of opposition and, secondarily, as verbal attacks. These two modes were retained for further analyses. The distinctions among modes of *going toward* were also maintained to facilitate description of differential use of these family interaction modes.

In Table 11.2 we presented the total frequency with which different role-role pairs of the nuclear family (e.g., father-mother) engaged in family interactions. The righthand column of Table 11.2 presents the proportion of all acts by these pairs which were acts of *going toward*. The complement to these proportions were acts of *going against*. All pairs predominantly engaged in acts of *going toward*. Some interesting differences appeared in these telvision families. Mothers were more affiliative toward their sons and daughters (94 percent) than the sons and daughters were toward mothers (87 percent). The father-child pairs did not show the same discrepancy.

Sister-brother and brother-brother relationships were more often in conflict (15 percent) than sister-sister relationships (4 percent). Table 11.2 also indicates that husbands and wives provided a disproportionate share of the available going against or conflictual interactions.

Table 11.4 presents each nuclear family role and the degree to which that role consists of the behaviors of *going against* and *going toward*. The following are conclusions from that table:

1. For all family role members, *offering of information* was the most frequently observed behavior. For some, the seeking of information was the second most frequent behavior (wife, son, daughter, brother, sister); for others it was giving directions (husband, father, mother).

2. TV mothers engaged in least opposing behaviors. They did least disagreeing or protesting of any role holder.

3. Mothers were most likely to give instructions on what to do or how to do it. They were the family directors, more so than anyone else. Fathers also did more of this than others, but less so than mothers. Children did the least, along with wives.

4. Sons and daughters did the most *petitioning*, or seeking of help and support. This *petitioning* was aimed at parents, who themselves did the least of this mode of behavior.

DISCUSSION

If children do learn and model role relationships they observe in television family interactions, what they observe are ways or modes of communicating with specific others in specific situations. In that sense, television portrayals of family interactions have the potential to provide information about how families *should* communicate. The implications of such learning are clearly more immediate than in many other social role content areas. For example, if a child learns about the role of the police in the cultural system, the opportunity for actual behavior or interaction with the police will probably be many years in the future. In the case of family interaction, the arena for testing newly acquired attitudes and behaviors is directly and pervasively accessible.

There are several implications for children's social learning of family roles from television from these results. First, there are not many preadolescent or even early adolescent role models available. Most children observed were either older teenagers or the adult children of other characters. As such, the role of the young child is vague and ambiguous. Finding young children largely absent from television families could lead a child to question his or her own role in the family system.

There is considerable impetus for anticipatory socialization for young children, however. Teen role models appear to joke around and oppose their parents a generous share of the time, indicative of the independence-seeking typically associated with adolescence. Given that many of these portrayals are humorous and on extremely popular shows ("Happy Days," "One Day at a Time"), they could increase the tendency for identification, and, as theory indicates, for imitation. Also

TABLE 11.4
Direction and Mode of Family Role Interactions by Family Role Initiators

Direction	Mode	Husband (%)	Wife (%)	Mother (%)	Father (%)	Son (%)	Daughter (%)	Brother (%)	Sister (%)
Goes against	1. Opposes	10	8	4	6	8	7	10	7
	2. Attacks	3	4	2	2	2	3	6	3
Goes toward	1. Offers information	36	36	31	31	34	35	34	40
	2. Seeks information	11	14	13	17	13	15	16	15
	3. Contributes	9	7	8	10	11	7	7	6
	4. Supports	6	7	9	8	4	7	5	5
	5. Petitions	4	5	3	2	8	11	4	6
	6. Directs	16	11	24	19	8	10	13	14

important to anticipatory socialization are the adult role models. The spouse/spouse portrayals support a stereotype common to several cultures: the husband directs the wife; the wife seeks support from the husband. As such, television portrayals may add strength to stereotypes already in the child's beliefs.

It is not possible to compare directly the data obtained from observation of televised interactions with "real world" interaction styles in typical nuclear households. First, we have little data taken from observations of normal families in typical interaction situations. Second, aggregation of the television data provides a description of available roles and interaction modes for possible social learning; it does not attempt to identify interaction styles that are normative in different types of families. Third, most empirical investigations of family interactions take a case study approach which does not attempt to generalize across families. What can be compared, however, is the similarity of televised interaction to commonly held standards and stereotypes. Television seems to support such views of family interaction.

The purpose of this analysis, beyond the descriptive aspects presented here, is to identify social learning which may originate with these content presentations. Sheer exposure to television seemingly is too crude an estimate of potential effects; adding specific content components to measures of exposure ought to yield more precise statements about the relationship between exposure and social learning. Here, an obvious next stage is to link content and exposure measures for programs viewed by young people to their expectations, beliefs, aspirations, values, and behaviors within their own family setting. The findings presented here are an antecedent for investigating the exposure–social learning relationship.

12

THREE SEASONS OF TELEVISION FAMILY ROLE INTERACTIONS

BRADLEY S. GREENBERG
NANCY BUERKEL-ROTHFUSS
KIMBERLY A. NEUENDORF
CHARLES K. ATKIN

This study describes the results of a content analysis of family role structures and interaction patterns within United States television families for each of three consecutive television seasons. It extends the basic paradigm of the last chapter to two additional seasons.

The contemporary United States family is a more ambiguous unit than in the past. Single-parent families abound; the extended family is more rare; unmarried "relationships" flourish, often accompanied by children and lawsuits. In this context, the role of the nuclear family—two original parents with their offspring—as the ideal family unit may be changing. Thus, information available from a variety of sources about the importance, structure, and operation of families may affect the kind and quality of family perceptions selected by today's youngsters. Further, information received about other families may influence a child's interactions within his or her own family unit.

The young child's primary experiences with family life come from its own family and that of playmates. This information is supplemented, however, by observation of fictional television families, both in prime-time shows and in those afternoon periods when local stations lease syndicated series featuring families.

Positing specific family role effects from these shows should follow the systematic identification of the predominant portrayals of family members and their interactions. Of particular interest are those shows which feature a family as the central unit of interest (e.g., "Family," "The

Waltons"), since learning should be most facilitated by those shows which permit vicarious experience with known and familiar characters over time.

METHODS

This content analysis constituted a role-by-behavior description of verbal interactions among members of television families. The coding unit was any act, or sequence of acts, initiated by a family member and directed to another family member which was unitary with respect to *direction, mode, initiator* and *recipient.* As such, a coding unit could vary from a single utterance to several comments or sentences.

Directions and Modes

Some modifications were made after the first season in the selection of modes, and these are explained in the definitions of the three directions and their accompanying modes which follow:

A. *Going toward:* Positive acts which initiate, maintain and/or build a family relationship. Operationally, eight modes were used in all three years; (1) offering in........ on—giving information or opinion in answer to a question, or spontaneously; (2) seeking information—questions asked solely in order to obtain information; (3) contributing and entertaining—miscellaneous behaviors intended solely to take part in or further on-going interaction, including greetings exchanged as new characters enter an interaction, nonhostile teasing and joking; (4) supporting—doing something to benefit another, showing approval for another, encouraging, protecting, pacifying, indulging, assisting or helping another, supporting another's interests, attempting to reduce another's physical or emotional discomfort or pain; (5) petitioning—attempts to obtain support, attention, or sources of gratification from another, actions which seek to obtain help, comfort, approval, encouragement, consolation, attention, or special favors for self; (6) directing—this includes positive attempts to manage or guide the behavior of another. Directing behavior includes giving instructions as to what to do, or how to do something, organizing family members in order to accomplish a task, directing plans, encouraging others to cooperate or behave harmoniously; (7) accepting support—this includes communicating to another recognition of their attempts to provide support, accepting support, showing gratitude and appreciation and accepting apologies from another; and (8) accepting direction—this includes obeying, cooperating or complying with another person's attempt to direct or manage one's behavior. This also includes accepting another's point of view and offering an apology in response to a request or demand that apology be given.

A ninth mode, showing concern, was omitted after year 1 because of low frequency of occurrence.

B. *Going against:* This is conflict-producing and conflict-maintaining behavior. Operationally, two modes were used consistently: (1) *opposing*—this includes protesting, disagreeing, refusing to accept direction or support, refusing to cooperate, disobeying, and justifying self and/or actions in a hostile manner; (2) *attacking*—this includes initiating conflict with another, criticizing, belittling, challenging, provoking, teasing maliciously, and arguing. Ignoring was deleted after the first season.

C. *Going away:* These are behaviors which psychologically distance one family member from another. Operationally, one mode was examined all three seasons: *evading*—to avoid dealing with another, to give evasive answers, to attempt to change topic or focus of interaction in order to evade issues or questions raised.

Two other modes—ignoring and withdrawing—were omitted after year 1 because of low frequency of occurrence.

Family Structure Analysis

Certain key descriptors of family structure were also coded. They were substantially the same as those identified for year 1: family size, extendedness, number of children, parental status, and marital status.

The Act Initiator and Recipient

The name and family role of the character initiating an act were recorded. *Family role* was defined as *the role which the act initiator held with respect to the family member toward whom the act was directed*, permitting each character to hold more than one family role. Coders were given an original list of 40 family roles. Low frequencies for many roles, however, yielded a primary set of 14, including eight nuclear family roles plus uncle, aunt, nephew, niece, and male and female in-laws. Roles such as grandparents, guardians, cousins, and stepchildren were included as "others" because they appeared in trivial numbers during the first season coded. Recipient character name and family role were recorded in the same manner as were initiator character name and family role.

Coding and Reliability

Undergraduate students were trained as coders. There was carryover each year in terms of coding team composition, and one of the coders during the first two seasons supervised the third year of coders. Each year, inter-rater reliability estimates were obtained; the *estimate* was the percentage of exact agreement among coders in categorizing acts along each of the identified dimensions. Thus, since even minor discrepancies count as disagreements, the estimation procedure is conservative. Across the three sets of data, the reliabilities ranged from .85 to .95 for both initiator and recipient family role identification, from .81 to .92 for act directions, and from .66 to .88 for act mode. Age/sex coding exceeded .90.

Sample

One episode of each weekly *family-centered* fictional series aired by the three major networks in the fall of 1975–76, 1976–77, and 1977–78 during evening prime time (8–11 p.m.) and Saturday morning was videotaped and coded. The year 1 data base also included family-role interactions occurring in shows which contained only casual, non-central or irregularly appearing family relationships. *In subsequent seasons, only series which regularly featured family units were used.* This change was made because only the latter provides a sufficient magnitude of regular family characters over time. In total, 53 shows were analyzed in the first year; 28 in year 2; 34, in year 3. Eleven shows were common to all three years analyzed.

RESULTS

Each season, the population of speaking television characters across all shows was about 1200. The vast majority had no relatives. For each character on television with one or more relatives, there were from six to seven speaking characters without relatives.

In the three seasons, 73, 40, and 47 families were identified. They reflected four basic types of TV families. First, there was the nuclear family with two parents and one or more children. For the first two seasons, this type accounted for 40 percent of the identified families, but dropped to 28 percent in the most recent season. The second family type was that of the single parent with children. In the first two seasons, this represented 25 percent of the TV families and increased to 34 percent in the third year. The third type was that of a married couple without children. This fluctuated from 23 percent to 15 percent to 19 percent, consecutively. The remaining type was a conglomerate of cousins, aunts, nephews, in-laws, and foster parents, etc., accounting for 12 percent, 20 percent, and 19 percent. Thus, the clear plurality of the nuclear family found in years 1 and 2 did not occur in the most recent season; family role types were more heterogeneously distributed.

There was considerable consistency in the marital status of adults in these families. First marriages accounted for 60 percent of the adults in years 1 and 2, and 50 percent in year 3. One-fourth of the adults in each season had never married; and about 12 percent were widows and widowers. Divorce, however, appears to be intruding further in TV families, accounting for 5 percent, 8 percent, and 10 percent of the adults in the three successive seasons. These families averaged slightly more than three persons per family each year, and about 40 percent of the family members were the children of some other TV character.

Across all of television fiction, the distribution of characters by sex has been three males for each female. In this subset of shows featuring family units, the sex distribution was virtually a 50-50 division. This is important for two reasons. First, it means that in shows without families, males outnumber females five or six to one. Second, it permits us to analyze family role interactions without accounting for an unequal distribution of the sexes.

Family Roles

The original list contained 40 different family roles, but the actual occurrence of family roles was much narrower. Table 12.1 shows that female nuclear roles (wife, mother, daughter, and sister) accounted for 76 percent, 79 percent, and 87 percent of all female roles in the three years; male nuclear role counterparts accounted for 75 percent, 74 percent, and 82 percent. The third-year increments for both sexes were located in children and sibling roles. The preeminence of husbands and wives in year 1 did not exist in the subsequent seasons when the subset of shows was reduced to those with regular family portrayals. By year 3, the children and sibling portrayals exceeded parent and marital roles for both sexes.

TABLE 12.1
Family Roles Distribution

Male Roles	75-76	76-77	77-78	Female Roles	75-76	76-77	77-78
Husband	23	21	19	Wife	27	21	20
Father	17	18	17	Mother	17	20	15
Son	19	20	24	Daughter	17	19	28
Brother	16	15	22	Sister	15	19	24
Male in-laws	10	7	4	Female in-laws	10	8	3
Uncle	3	3	1	Aunt	3	1	0
Nephew	4	4	1	Niece	2	1	0
All others*	8	11	13	All others**	9	11	9
	(n = 195)	(n = 123)	(n = 143)		(n = 167)	(n = 122)	(n = 137)

*All others, male, include grandfather, stepfather, foster father, stepson, foster son, grandson, stepbrother, exspouse, godfather, male guardian.
**All others, female, include grandmother, stepmother, foster mother, stepdaughter, foster daughter, granddaughter, stepsister, exspouse, godmother, female guardian.

Initiators and Receivers
of Family Role Interactions

Table 12.2 identifies the frequency of initiators of family role interactions, by sex. The same data for receivers do not vary in any cell for either sex by more than 2 percent, and have therefore been omitted.

Of all family role acts coded, nuclear males initiated 50 percent in year 1, and 43 percent and 42 percent in the subsequent seasons; for females, the parallel proportions were 36 percent, 46 percent, and 44 percent. Thus, in shows which regularly featured families, males and females showed the same degree of initiative; irregularly appearing family units were more likely to emphasize male roles. In conjunction with the Table 12.1 results, males and females appeared in equivalent numbers in these shows and demonstrated the same levels of initiation and reception of family role acts. Activity outside the nuclear family was infrequent and distributed across an extensive cluster of family roles.

Turning next to who interacted with whom, Table 12.3 identifies the frequency of paired-role interactions. For all three seasons, the most commonly interacting pair was the husband-wife team, accounting for from 27 percent to 36 percent of all interacts. The cluster of four different parent-child combinations accounted for nearly half of all interactions each season, but no particular parent-child combination predominated over any other. If anything, the mother-son pairing was least active across the full time period.

Table 12.3 further identifies the frequency of acts per initiator in the three righthand columns. For years 1 and 3, the high average frequency of husband and wife acts was matched by father and son activity. This version of the data indicates the relative paucity of mother-son interactions, and the comparative equity in the remaining transacting pairs.

TABLE 12.2
Initiators of Family Role Acts

Males	75–76 (%)	76–77 (%)	77–78 (%)	Females	75–76 (%)	76–77 (%)	77–78 (%)
Husband	13	16	12	Wife	12	16	11
Father	14	10	12	Mother	8	11	8
Son	13	11	8	Daughter	7	10	12
Brother	10	6	10	Sister	9	9	13
Male in-laws	3	3	1	Female in-laws	4	2	<1
Uncle	1	2	<1	Aunt	1	<1	0
Nephew	2	1	<1	Niece	0	1	0
All others, male	2	1	7	All others, female	3	2	4

For 1975–76, the percentages are based on 5732 acts, 3247 for males and 2485 for females; for 1976–77, the percentages are based on 3248 acts, 1618 for males and 1628 for females; for 1977–78, the percentages are based on 4191 acts; 2191 for males, 2000 for females.

TABLE 12.3
Nuclear Family Interacts

Initiator	Recipient	% of Acts 75-76	76-77	77-78	Acts per Initiator 75-76	76-77	77-78
Husband	Wife	15	18	14	16.1	20.1	16.2
Wife	Husband	14	18	13	14.8	20.2	16.1
Mother	Son	5	5	2	7.7	6.2	6.7
Son	Mother	4	5	2	5.8	5.7	4.7
Mother	Daughter	5	7	7	8.0	8.4	12.8
Daughter	Mother	4	7	8	6.7	9.0	9.8
Father	Son	11	7	8	16.8	9.2	17.4
Son	Father	10	7	7	13.6	8.5	11.3
Father	Daughter	5	4	6	6.9	5.2	13.7
Daughter	Father	4	4	6	6.6	4.5	8.0
Brother	Brother	5	2	6	7.3	3.0	9.3
Brother	Sister	7	5	6	10.5	7.1	9.0
Sister	Brother	7	5	7	13.8	6.4	10.5
Sister	Sister	4	5	8	7.6	6.1	14.6
		(n = 4840)	(n = 2874)	(n = 3644)			

Direction and Mode of Family Role Interactions

Table 12.4 presents the overall distribution of interactions by direction and mode. One direction, *going away*, did not occur with any frequency in any of the three years. The mode of withdrawal was dropped after year 1. A second major direction—*going against someone* accounted for just under 11 percent in Year 1, then 15 percent and 12 percent, with the mode of ignoring others dropped after the first season. In all three seasons, the most frequently occurring mode of going against someone was by verbally opposing others. This tended to be twice as likely as direct verbal attacks.

Going toward, or approaching another person in a positive, constructive fashion was the dominant direction of family role interaction. In year 1, the nine modes of this direction accounted for 88 percent of all family role interactions, and in years 2 and 3, the eight reexamined modes accounted for exactly the same proportion. Among these modes, offering information was persistently the most common interaction, yielding slightly more than one-third of all interaction content in each season. Two other modes occurred regularly: seeking information and giving directions to others. Relatively high behavior counts were also found for the modes of supportive acts toward others and contributing behaviors, which served largely to continue interpersonal interactions. The modes of asking for support, accepting support, and accepting directives were insubstantial.

Television family interactants performed largely in modes that were affiliative. Evasion was trivial, and disaffiliative or antagonistic behaviors ranged from 10 percent to 15 percent of all family interactions.

TABLE 12.4
Direction and Mode of Family Role Interactions

Direction	Mode	75–76 (%)	76–77 (%)	77–78 (%)
Goes against	1. Attacks	3	6	4
	2. Opposes	7	9	8
	3. Ignores	< 1	*	*
Goes away	1. Evades	1	< 1	< 1
	2. Withdraws	< 1	*	*
Goes toward	1. Offers information	35	37	35
	2. Seeks information	15	16	15
	3. Contributes	8	6	10
	4. Supports	7	9	11
	5. Shows concern	2	*	*
	6. Petitions	5	3	3
	7. Directs	14	11	12
	8. Accepts support	1	2	1
	9. Accepts direction	3	3	2
		(n = 5733)	(n = 3262)	(n = 4192)

*Not coded.

To examine further the instances of conflictual behavior in these settings, we paired each nuclear family role, e.g., husband-wife, mother-son, and computed the proportion of all acts between these pairs which were acts of going against. From Table 12.4 all pairs engaged in acts of going toward in the vast majority of instances. Two patterns, however, emerged from this analysis of conflict. First, more conflict occurred in husband-wife and in two sibling pairs (brothers and brothers-sisters). For these dyads, conflict occurred about 15 percent of the time. In contrast, parent-child pairs generated conflict about 10 percent of the time, with sister-sister relations even less conflictual than that. Spouses and brothers are more likely to be squabbling among themselves on these shows than other family members.

The final analysis examined the regularity with which different family role holders initiated these interactions. Table 12.5 contains the findings for the modes of going against and going toward, omitting modes which occurred with little frequency (i.e., evading, showing concern, accepting support, and accepting direction). The table supports the following conclusions:

1. For all family role members, offering information was the most frequent behavioral act. This mode did not vary in any significant fashion among seasons or among role holders. It encompassed one-third of the interactions.
2. The seeking of information was the next most consistent and prominent role behavior, again varying little among seasons or among role holders, accounting for about 15 percent of all interactions.
3. Giving directions was located most heavily in parents, least so among children; the mode accounted for about 15 percent of all interactions across all family role holders.

TABLE 12.5

Direction and Mode of Family Role Interactions by Family Role Initiators*

Direction	Mode	Husband	Wife	Mother	Father	Son	Daughter	Brother	Sister
Goes against	1. Opposes	10/14/6	8/11/9	4/6/6	6/9/8	8/8/8	7/12/12	10/12/9	7/3/8
	2. Attacks	3/5/4	4/9/7	2/8/4	2/3/3	2/5/2	3/3/1	6/8/5	3/7/5
Goes toward	1. Offers information	36/35/39	36/34/30	31/28/33	31/37/30	34/41/36	35/39/32	34/33/39	40/40/34
	2. Seeks information	11/15/14	14/15/15	13/20/17	17/18/17	13/22/17	15/12/15	16/14/17	15/14/13
	3. Contributes	9/5/8	7/4/6	8/5/9	10/5/10	11/6/12	7/6/12	7/9/8	6/6/10
	4. Supports	6/9/12	7/8/13	9/15/13	8/12/11	4/6/7	7/10/10	5/6/7	5/7/13
	5. Petitions	4/3/2	5/4/4	3/1/2	2/1/2	8/3/5	11/8/3	4/2/3	6/4/1
	6. Directs	16/9/13	11/13/10	24/16/13	19/13/18	8/6/8	10/4/10	13/11/11	14/13/13

*The first percentage is that obtained from 1975–76 shows; the second, for 1976–77 shows; the third, for 1977–78 shows.

4. Supportive behaviors tended to originate more with parents and spouses; least with sons and brothers; seeking support was identified more with children.

5. The origin of conflictual behaviors was focused more heavily among spouses and brothers for the first two seasons; by the third year, conflict origins were more variable.

DISCUSSION

The themes and behaviors identified in this content create a basis for projecting what viewers could be learning about families and family role communication behaviors. Young people in the process of developing and learning their myriad social roles have ample opportunity for real-life assessments and practice of this category of role information. This contrasts with social learning from TV about more remote roles, e.g., criminal justice roles, where the viewer has little opportunity to be plaintiff, defendant, lawyer, judge, or victim. Thus, there is the opportunity to move from this empirical approach to field assessments of the relationship between exposure to family roles information on television and the family role cognitions, attitudes, and behaviors of young viewers. These descriptive results become the conceptual fodder for creating testable propositions about social learning of family roles from television. The research evidence yields these propositions:

1. The vast majority of fictional television characters do not have relatives appearing in the stories with them.

2. No particular configuration of family structure dominates; most common are families headed by a single parent or two parents, plus children; childless couples are nearly as frequent.

3. Divorce has increased each season; it has become equivalent to widowhood, as a factor to account for single-parent families; first marriages account for half the adults, and one-fourth have never married.

4. Relatives outside the nuclear family are rare; nuclear family members account for 80 percent of all roleholders.

5. Males and females are equal in number in TV families.

6. Females and males are equal in initiating and receiving family role interactions.

7. Husbands and wives are the most active interacting TV family role pair.

8. Parents are more likely to interact with same-sex children, e.g., more father-son than father-daughter interactions.

9. Affiliative acts occur in TV families about eight times more often than conflictual acts.

10. Conflict is more heavily concentrated in husband-wife pairs and dyads that include a brother.

11. Offering information to others is the dominant mode of family interactions.

12. Parents are most likely to give directions; children least so.

13. Parents and spouses are more likely to give support or encouragement; children are most likely to seek it.

These statements yield a partial set of the major parameters of family role portrayals on television. One can posit that each statement is more likely to be accepted by the more avid viewer of the shows in which this content originates. The propositions derive solely from overall quantitative estimates and do not permit evaluation of individual programs; they also do not differentiate the quality of the acts themselves, i.e., all acts within a mode are nominally equivalent in the findings. Clearly, a further step is refining this method to permit differentiation among interactions within a mode in terms of such attributes as act duration, strength, or intensity.

Returning to potential social learning from TV's presentation of family roles, one would need to determine just how many of these propositions are already part of the viewer's cognitive map? When did they become so? Do they conflict or reinforce existing beliefs? In other words, can we determine baseline attitudes, beliefs, and practices in these areas, independent of the television stimulation, on which the impact of the additional television stimuli may be assessed. This content area would provide a particularly severe test of social learning effects from television because of the prominence of daily, alternative sources of information, and daily engagement in family interactions.

Further, one might compare the propositional offerings of TV content with normative family practices and with actuarial information about families. For example, how close a parallel to the TV increase in divorce is the real-world divorce rate? Are two-parent families a plurality and not a majority of existing family structures? In more complex informational areas, how would real-life interaction patterns between husband-wife and parent-children measure up against their TV counterparts?

Finally, there is a special linkage between family roles and minority characterizations on TV. In the past several seasons, nearly half of all regularly appearing black TV characters have been located on half a dozen situation comedies featuring family units, e.g., "Good Times," "The Jeffersons," "What's Happening?" (Fernandez-Collado *et al.*, 1979). This concentration within a small subset of shows suggests that young black viewers, eager to watch characters of their own race, may be especially susceptible to televised family role messages.

13

BLACK FAMILY INTERACTIONS ON TELEVISION

BRADLEY S. GREENBERG
KIMBERLY A. NEUENDORF

The final research question in the preceeding chapter can begin to be examined with our data set. Specifically, among those fictional black TV families who have been found in three different television seasons, how do their roles, family structures, and interactive behaviors compare with white TV families? This will not tell us whether young black viewers watching black families are especially susceptible to messages presented in a family context, but it would identify whether there are systematic differences and/or similarities between black and white family role presentations. For example, one would expect husbands and wives to engage in similar interaction patterns irrespective of race; one would expect parents to interact with their children to the same extent irrespective of race. To the degree one finds systematic differences in frequency, direction, and mode of interaction among black family members in contrast to white family members, at least two major implications result: first, a need to determine why such differences in characterization and portrayal were being created, whether there was an unconscious and/or deliberate bias in the creative depiction of black and white families; second, differential portrayals would permit the development of hypotheses with regard to social learning potential. This means that if black mothers were distinctly different in family role interaction from white mothers, the viewer might begin to sense and accept those differences as part of their real-life image of that particular role holder.

In order to find a large enough collection of black families to conduct this analysis, we collapsed the three sample weeks reflecting three different television seasons into a single pool. In those three sample weeks, there were 19 distinct black families out of 160 total families, or 12 percent. The dominant black family type—10 of the 19 families— consisted of a single parent plus children. Among white families, this type accounted for approximately one-fourth of their family structures. In contrast, the primary white family type was the nuclear family, with two parents and one or more children. This was found among only three of the 19 black families, including none at all in the most recent season analyzed, one in the season before that, and two in the season in which the sample also included irregularly appearing families. The dominant black TV family is the broken family; the dominant white group is the nuclear family. A third type that occurred with considerable regularity among white families was that of a married couple without children, accounting for approximately 20 percent of all families; this was found in three of the 19 black families.

As for marital status, equivalent proportions of white and black family members had been divorced, 8 percent. There were somewhat more unmarried black adults than white adults in family roles, and a larger proportion of whites who were in their first marriage. An equivalent proportion in each racial group consisted of widows and widowers. Marital status was not particularly different between black and white family role members although the tendency was for more of the white adults to be married and for more of the black adults to be unmarried.

Across all of the family units on television, there was an even split between male and female portrayals; of the total of 51 black characters in these families, 29 were male and 22 were female. In white families, slightly less than 40 percent of the family members were the children of some other TV character; in black families, slightly more than half of the family members were children of some other character.

The origin of these black families came from a very small number of television shows in each of the three seasons analyzed. For the record, let us give a capsule description here of the structure and origin of each of the shows.

> In the first sample week, the following shows contained the types of families described: On "Fat Albert," there were two preadult brothers; on "Good Times," there were two parents and three preadult children. On an episode of "The Invisible Man," there was a mother with an unmarried adult son; on an episode of "The Rookies," the black family consisted of two parents and an unmarried adult daughter. On "Sanford and Son," there was a widower with an unmarried adult son plus a husband-wife family; on "That's My Mama," there was one family consisting of a mother, her unmarried adult son, and another male relative, and a second family consisting of a father, with an unmarried adult son.
>
> In the second season's sample week, the black families consisted of a "Good Times" family, which had now been transformed into a widowed

mother, with two sons and an adult daughter; "The Jeffersons," with two families, one consisting of two parents and one unmarried adult son, and a second family with two parents (one white) with an unmarried adult daughter; "Sanford and Son," with the same widower and his adult son; and "What's Happening," with a divorced mother and two young children, plus an ex-husband.

The third season included these black families: "Good Times," now with two families, one of three siblings, and a second family consisting of a never-married mother and her preadult daughter; the same "Jeffersons" group; "Sanford Arms," which consisted of one husband-wife combination, and one widower with his unmarried adult daughter and relatively young son; and "What's Happening," which featured a divorced mother and two preadult children.

Given this general structural description of black families, we now move to a systematic analysis of their family role interactions and a direct comparison between their interactions and the distribution of the same behaviors in white television families. Although the number of black families (19) is small, and the number of individuals in those families is also not large (51), the frequencies of interactions they generated are substantial and qualify for an intensive empirical analysis. At the same time, the reader should realize that relatively few shows involve black family situations, and that there was some redundancy among those shows across seasons. Even that redundancy is misleading, however, because the composition of the family in "Good Times" changed in each of the three seasons, and the composition of the Sanford family was different in two of the three seasons.

FINDINGS

Table 13.1 contains the distribution of family roles for both white and black family members. There is a marked difference between the two distributions. Most different is the large proportion (22 percent) of white family members who are not part of the nuclear family. In contrast only 4 percent of the black family members were not either a spouse, a parent, a child, or a sibling. The black television family roles

TABLE 13.1
Family Roles by Race

| | Race | |
Role	White (%)	Black (%)
Spouse	23	16
Parent	17	26
Child	20	30
Sibling	18	24
Others	22	4
	(n = 817)	(n = 70)

were almost exclusively nuclear with no in-laws, cousins, nephews, or any other extended kin present. Typically, the black families had more children and that same fact accounted for the larger proportion of siblings present in black television families. White families more often consisted of husbands and wives without children than black families, which also tends to account for the greater proportion of blacks in parent roles. Black families, then, tended to consist of fewer types of families with the concentration being on parent-child-sibling roles, whereas white families were more evenly distributed among a wider range of both nuclear and nonnuclear family roles.

A further breakdown of these family roles by the sex of the role member (untabled) showed that within white families, the parallel male and female roles, e.g., husband and wife or mother and father, were present to the same extent. There were very similar proportions of each sex in each role within white families. This was less true for black families. Specifically, there was an overrepresentation of black mothers (32 percent) in contrast to black fathers (21 percent), and an overrepresentation of black brothers (28 percent) in contrast to black sisters (19 percent). This means that within the black families there were more likely to be black mothers than black fathers, and the young children were more likely to be males than females.

Table 13.2 displays three variables. These identify the extent to which black and white family role holders in both male and female roles were either the initiator or receiver of family role interactions. First, one can note that the distributions differ among the nonnuclear or "other" family members in each of the comparisons. The paucity of black nonnuclear role holders limits their opportunity to participate in family role interactions; thus, the proportion of role interactions by nonnuclear family members among whites is always greater in these comparisons

TABLE 13.2
Family Role Act Initiation and Reception by Race and Sex

	Initiation		Reception	
Role	Black (%)	White (%)	Black (%)	White (%)
Husband	13	13	12	13
Father	15	12	15	11
Son	17	10	20	11
Brother	10	9	10	10
Other male	4	9	3	9
Wife	12	13	13	14
Mother	13	8	9	8
Daughter	8	9	8	9
Sister	7	11	7	10
Other female	1	7	2	6
	(n = 1738)	(n = 11,564)	(n = 1729)	(n = 11,294)

than among blacks. The second major finding is the concentration of role interactions among black sons. In black families, both as initiators and receivers, the son is the most active among the family members. White sons are no more active than daughters, whereas black sons are more than twice as active in family role interactions as daughters. In the white television families, the spouses are most active, particularly among the females.

It is also interesting to note that black and white husbands and wives have the same degree of activity in all these comparisons, whereas black fathers and mothers are consistently more active than their white parent counterparts. The former exists despite a greater proportion of white spouses; the latter occurs among a greater proportion of black parents. Further, it can be seen that activity as an initiator of family role interactions is not very different by role than activity levels as receivers of family role interactions. Within race, the distributions of interactions as either initiators or receivers are not significantly different.

If one compares the distribution of white family roles in Table 13.1 with the distribution of their acts in Table 13.2, the proportions are very much alike. For example, 23 percent of the white family roles are as husband and wife, and these roles account for 26 percent of the initiated acts. Within white families, the major discrepancy between role and interaction distributions is among the nonnuclear family members, i.e., there are 22 percent of the nonnuclear roles in white families which account for 16 percent of the initiated interactions. By contrast, there are more substantial discrepancies in the interactive behavior of black family members. Most outstanding is the finding that 16 percent of black family roles as husband and wife account for 25 percent of all family interactions. Black siblings are less interactive than the number of roles they have might suggest. Although 24 percent of black family members are brothers or sisters, they account for only 17 percent of the interactions.

In summary from this portion of the data, nonnuclear members of white families provide a substantial part of the family interaction, whereas they are neither present nor active in black families. Black sons have been preeminent in black television families, accounting for the largest share of family interactions, exceeding even that of their parents. Black spouses are more interactive with each other proportionate to their frequency in television family structures than white spouses. Finally, if one examines the distribution of male and female interactions within these families, it can be concluded that the male role in general has been more energetic in black families than in white families in both initiation and reception of interactions. Approximately 60 percent of all the interactions have been among males in black families, whereas the comparable proportion in white families has been 53 percent.

Table 13.3 takes each possible role-pair in the nuclear family, and indicates their relative participation in family role interactions. It shows, separately within white and black families, how much of the interactive behavior is accounted for by wives-husbands, mothers-sons, etc. The original analysis of this data set separated each role-pair in terms of whether they were the initiator or the recipient of the family role interaction. That distinction showed no difference in amount of interaction whether, for example, the husband or the wife was the initiator or the recipient; hence we have omitted that distinction from Table 13.3. Let us look, then, at both similarities and contrasts between white and black family interactions within the nuclear family role-pairs. First, the most active role-pair in both white and black television families is the wife-husband pair, accounting for more than one-fourth of all the family interactions analyzed. Second, the largest disparity between white and black television families is the degree of interaction between parents and their children. Black mothers and fathers are far more active with their sons than are white parents. Forty percent of all of the interactions in black nuclear families were between either a mother or father and a son, in comparison with 23 percent of the interactions in white families. White mothers, however, are busier in these situations with their daughters than are black mothers. Finally, in both the black and white families, brother–sister interactions are at least double those of same sex sibling interactions. Among the black television families, however, there was a complete absence of any sister-sister interactions. Table 13.3 thus shows that black spouses are nearly as active in family role interactions as white spouses, that black parents are much more oriented to interacting with their sons than white parents, and that young females are more central in white families both in their roles as daughters and as sisters.

TABLE 13.3
Nuclear Family Interactions by Race

| | Race | |
| | White | Black |
Role-pair:	(%)	(%)
Wife-husband	31	26
Mother-son	6	17
Mother-daughter	14	7
Father-son	17	23
Father-daughter	10	10
Brother-brother	5	4
Brother-sister	12	14
Sister-sister	6	0
	(n = 9703)	(n = 1631)

Table 13.4 presents the first comparative findings on the specific content, both in terms of direction and mode, of family interactions by race. The first direction listed, that of one family member going "against" another family member yields a major racial difference. Black family interactions that were antagonistic comprised 17 percent of all their interactions, compared with 11 percent among white family members. Within black families there was a greater probability that family members would be in conflict with each other.

The remainder of the interactions fell within the "goes toward" direction, or acts that were primarily affiliative in content. Here there was only one significant discrepancy between the two types of families; white families were more likely to engage in the mode of offering information to other family members than were black family members, although this mode was the major one for both races. All other modes occurred with similar regularity; the two other major modes were seeking information and giving directions to others. Within this direction, the compatability of findings is more impressive than the discrepancy.

The most distinctive difference in content of family interactions was that black family members were more often portrayed in interpersonal conflict.

The final analysis within these families examined who was interacting with whom in what direction and modes. This meant extending the analysis of Table 13.4 to determine which role-holders were engaging in conflict behaviors and which in affiliative behaviors. A summary of this is

TABLE 13.4
Direction and Mode of Family Role Interactions by Race

Direction	Mode	Race Black (%)	White (%)
Goes against	1. Attacks	8	3
	2. Opposes	9	8
Goes away	1. Evades	< 1	< 1
Goes toward	1. Offers information	26	36
	2. Seeks information	14	15
	3. Contributes	11	8
	4. Supports	8	9
	5. Shows concern	1	1
	6. Petitions	3	4
	7. Directs	15	12
	8. Accepts support	1	1
	9. Accepts direction	3	3
		(n = 1751)	(n = 11,603)

in Table 13.5. For each nuclear family role, we present the proportion of antagonistic or conflictual behaviors, those in which one family member attacks or acts in opposition to another family member. Evasion interactions are omitted because of their lack of occurrence, and the complementary proportions to those in Table 13.5 are affiliative behaviors. For example, where 15 percent of the family interactions by white husbands were in the direction of "goes against," 85 percent of the white husband behaviors were in the direction of "goes toward."

First, among the white family members, all roles participated in conflictual behavior very similarly. The range was only from 10 percent to 16 percent. Thus, any white family nuclear member was as likely to engage in conflict interactions as any other white family role-holder, and for none of the white roles was the proportionate display of conflicting behaviors likely to be considered large. In contrast, the variances in conflictual behaviors among black family role-holders was considerable, ranging from 10 percent to 33 percent. In particular, two roles among black family members were substantial in conflict and deviated greatly from the overall display of this behavior. The black wife is the single largest performer of family conflict interactions. Fully one-third of her interactions were in opposition to, or attacking of, her husband, the only possible recipient of that role's interacts. Thus, the black wife is set up as a most active antagonist against her husband, who himself is below the black average for conflict behavior and is also less conflictual than his white counterpart.

Black siblings are also distinctly active in conflictual family role interactions. Among acts initiated by black brothers, 25 percent are in the direction of going against, and among black sisters, that figure is 28 percent. Both these proportions are significantly larger than their white counterparts, and are significantly larger than any other black family members, except for the black wife.

TABLE 13.5
Conflict in Nuclear Family Interactions by Race and Role

Role	Race Direction: Goes against	
	Black (%)	White (%)
Husband	12	15
Wife	33	14
Mother	10	10
Father	14	10
Son	14	11
Daughter	12	13
Brother	25	16
Sister	28	10

Therefore, this final comparative analysis identifies particular role holders in black families as more likely to be in conflict, whereas conflict is evenly distributed among white family members. The black wife is unusually attacking and opposing of her husband, and black siblings are frequently in conflict situations.

SUMMARY

Across a week of television, during three different but consecutive seasons, one could see a regularly appearing black family on four or five shows. Most typically, that family would have a single parent; a complete family of two parents plus children was a rarity, averaging one a season. White families were more often complete nuclear units.

Black family members were found almost entirely in nuclear roles—as fathers, sisters, wives, children; whereas, about one-fifth of white family members were part of extended families, e.g., cousins, uncles, in-laws. The distribution of roles by sex within white families was equivalent, whereas there were more black mothers than fathers.

In terms of family interactions, the black son played a more major role, larger than black daughters and larger than white children. Extended kin were minimally active in black families. Overall, black males were more active in family interactions than white males. The most active role-pair in both racial families was husbands and wives, and not differentially so.

Conflict as the content of family interactions was more prevalent in black family units on television, accounting for 17 percent of their interactions compared with 11 percent for white family members. The kinds of affiliative acts which occurred were quite similar for the two racial groups. The locus of conflict in family units was quite evenly distributed among white family role members. Among blacks, that conflict was more centralized in black wives and among siblings.

CONCLUSIONS

Television fiction provides a strong dose of tunnel vision. A steady ingestion of episodes from fictional series on the commercial networks would be as representative of life as a steady ingestion of the output of fast-food chains would be representative of the fare offered by American restaurants. Television characterizations and interactions are narrow, contagious, and persistent. Overdosing on hamburgers and french fries may lead to gagging or indigestion; the consequences of overdosing on television are less easily diagnosed. If one accepted the full litany of television content as isomorphic with the depiction of life, the ensuing beliefs and social expectations would be so distorted as to be laughable, pitied, or scorned. Given that no one (or few) would go that far, the critical question remains: What residue of beliefs and social attitudes may accumulate from allocating at least one-third of available leisure time to watching television?

The industry may rebut appropriately at this point. Television series are designed to entertain, to please; they are not designed to teach or, worse, to inform the viewer about life. Television fiction has no mandate to reflect life in its episodes. Indeed, programming with that mission might be intensely boring. So, let the viewer beware, lest he or she take away from the viewing experiences what is not intended as information. The viewer is expected to invoke the caveat that it's only a story, make believe, not true to life. Thus, the paradox is set as a relatively straightforward conflict between the industry's dual goals of entertainment and profit, with the possibility that viewers might bare parts of their mental systems to the intrusive and dominant themes and values in television programming that have been partly documented in this book's multiple content examinations.

The data presented here do not ascribe blame. There is no evidence or claim here of ill will or ill effects. There is a cataloging of what has been available to be heard and seen, and to be learned, whether it was so intended by the creators, and whether it was so received by many viewers or some significant subgrouping of them. Elsewhere, evidence has accumulated as to what effects oversubscribing to violent shows or obtaining primary racial experiences with television minorities have on consequent responses. But information is minimal or nil on equally important issues:

1. Whether the magnitude of social consumption of alcohol on TV increases susceptibility to drinking.

2. Whether attributes portrayed by a small set of elderly characters on television programs diminish respect for the aging.

3. Whether the large amount of prosocial activity is absorbed to nearly the same extent as the large amount of antisocial activity.

4. Whether visual, verbal, and physical references to sexual promiscuity intensify intimate sexual aspirations.

5. Whether the dominance of males retards the development of female independence.

6. Whether the invisibility of Hispanics hinders the development of stronger self-concepts among Hispanics.

7. How the preeminence of husband-wife conflict feeds into attitudes toward marriage.

These questions only partly reflect the content we have sampled, but they provide the basis for subsequent research inquiries.

Much remains. The content has not yet been exhausted. First, there are issues not examined at all and two examples can illustrate this. One deals with the portrayal of the criminal justice system. The dramatic portrayal of a variety of aspects of this system has been on television since its inception. These shows portray a streamlined and dramatic legal process with many portions omitted altogether and other aspects overemphasized. The television world of law, crime, and justice is likely to deviate sharply from reality. Nevertheless, for much of the viewing public, their first experiences with the criminal justice system are vicarious through television. At least eight different role types come to mind. There is the judge, typically a minor functionary presiding over criminal cases; the prosecutor, often abrasive and incompetent, harassing the witness and persecuting the defendant; the defense attorney, suave, capable, and successful; the criminal; the defendant; the witness, usually a passive observer of the crime and a reluctant testifier; the victim, often focused on during the criminal incident, but typically secondary in the legal process; and the apprehender, the honest, efficient, often law-ignoring hero. There is also the process of justice itself, its speed, its equity, its containment within the law. No systematic content analysis of this central portion of television fare has yet been made prominent. Such an analysis would better prepare social researchers to investigate the accuracy of information about the operation of the judicial system derived by viewers from these shows, e.g., rights of accused; stages in the judicial process; viewer beliefs formed from watching the interactions of lawyers and witnesses, or police and defendants; positive or negative attitudes created about the judicial process and its role-holders; or the aspirations of young viewers with regard to vocational tendencies in law-related fields. Surely, I would want to grow up to become a defense attorney rather than a prosecutor, but would I understand that I had to become a lawyer first?

A second content area example may be found in the instances of car driving on television. Abundant in all contemporary crime/adventure shows, the driving of cars on television parallels the national fetish for the automobile. Yet, it is hard to recall a television driving vignette that is not aberrant, discomfiting, or near-suicidal. The chase scene began with horses, but is more exciting and graphic with cars. What kinds of driving models appear on television systematically for would-be license holders to observe? Who are the drivers? Do they screech their brakes, burn rubber, speed, use the horn, or siren needlessly? What of driving and drinking, or using seat belts? What consequences are visible? Are there injuries, accidents, legal penalties? Are other motorists, pedestrians, or passengers in some peril? Are we driving in pursuit, for pleasure, or for business? From questions such as these, categories are formed, tried, refined, and subsequently filled with data. The portrayal of driving behaviors on network television series is another content area of no small mass in fictional programming. Its implications for social learning about driving, the formation of driving attitudes, expectations, and aspirations, as well as outright driving tendencies and practices are available for empirical study.

Second, the issues examined in this volume are clearly repeatable. Perhaps not much new is to be gained from overfrequent replication. But at least occasionally, the findings need confirming, particularly if changes are expected or promised. One good example of identifiable change, outside the current studies, stems from the rapid rise in black characterizations on television beginning in the late 1960s. From an immodest beginning of "Amos and Andy" roles, a steady influx of black actors was detailed in several content analyses. From a level of 3 or 4 percent of the television population, blacks rose to 10 percent within a five-year period, then tapered off, and have remained there for about a decade. But there was change and it was documented because a baseline had been established against which subsequent information could be assessed.

Third, we could derive much additional information from the present data through blending the several sets of data. Master data tapes are being created which would permit cross-cutting of the content areas now examined in separate chapters in this volume. For example, prosocial and antisocial behaviors could be compiled with the television family interaction materials. From that, one could begin to look at family roles in terms of who provides antisocial and prosocial behavior models within the family setting, and then contrast that setting with nonfamily ones. Or one could examine sexual intimacies as they may occur in the context of alcohol or drug use. Or one could compare minority with majority sex role behaviors. Some examples have been presented, e.g., contrasting minority family interactions with majority family behaviors, and crossing age groupings of television characters with pro- and antisocial behaviors.

The point is that although the present effort constitutes the most comprehensive work to date in examining multiple aspects of television content, it is not exhaustive. It is more than static information, given two or three points in time for each content area, but it remains suggestive rather than conclusive. It is a prelude to further content analyses, but more to the research which should determine whether these content themes, values, depictions, models, and regularities affect the viewing public.

Let us return now to the core findings and use them to characterize our introductory diagnosis of tunnel vision. We shall do so within the organizing units of the book.

People on television can be fitted into a relatively small one-way tunnel in terms of central attributes. There is the majority male, a white adult in his late 30s or early 40s. He is even more of a majority if he represents a new minority group on television. For example, it requires great effort to find a Hispanic female on television. And our analysis of the aging shows a parallel absence of older women. So any movement away from this modal Anglo male central-casting type even more strongly reemphasizes the male world. This ideal, mature man finds himself in the midst of very pretty, soft women, typically a decade younger. The pairing suggests that when he was a high school senior, she may have just started on long division in the fifth grade. But they are both now of age and therefore eligible for various types of liaisons. Thus far, only one other minority group, aside from the television minority of females, has reached perhaps a critical mass level on commercial television. That black television population has some curious features. It is especially young; the majority bloc of blacks is under 20 years of age, as compared with less than 20 percent of the non blacks. The racial discrepancies remain solid even on those programs that are heavily black-oriented. By contrast with whites on the same shows, blacks are younger, funnier, less employed, poorer, etc. And about half of the entire population of TV blacks was on virtually all-black shows. It will be interesting to see whether the new minority, the Hispanics, begins to be represented by large numbers of cute children. People also work on television, but the occupational diversity can fill two fingers of a glove. There are the professionals and the law-related service workers; a thumb can be added for managerial-level job-holders.

The sexes on television comport in a manner that supports the numerical supremacy of the male. The woman is dependent and in need of more nurturing than the strong, independent, succorance-giving macho man particularly in psycho-emotional areas. The female seeks more help, is offered more of it, gets more of it, and probably says, "Thank you, sir," more often, although we neglected to assess the last in this sequence. We were most surprised by the persistency of this pattern in Saturday morning programming. Surely, if there is some resistance to strengthening women's roles too greatly on prime-time shows for fear of upsetting large numbers of male and female viewers, that anxiety need not extend to Saturday morning. At that time, male and female adults do not watch, and male and female children are probably more open-minded about sex role assignments. But the emerging pattern has been for more female equity in the early evening sitcoms. There, one can perhaps discount or suspect the equity because it's mostly funny. But Saturday shows were getting at least as heavy a dose of male dominance as found in the action/crime shows late at night. And these social interactions between the sexes were not contradicted by looking at more manifest, physical behaviors. The internal cluster of female-predominant behaviors linked entertaining, food preparation, and housework; males drove cars, played sports, and drank and smoked at higher rates.

The examination of social behaviors made an objective effort to document prosocial as well as antisocial activity on television. There, the anomaly is that both occur about equally *en masse*, with very sharp distinctions among program types and broadcast times. If one wanted to orient preferences for one or the other type of behavior, a personal television schedule could be projected from the data set that would maximize either major grouping of social behaviors. Again, Saturday morning was of interest because of the audience's vulnerability to strong television messages. The cartoon/noncartoon distinction in social behaviors was most curious. Cartoons were dominated by antisocial acts and noncartoons by prosocial behaviors. Parental monitoring of programming in that time period ought to be an effective intervention strategy—provided that the noncartoons, a declining type in more recent seasons, are often enough available.

The findings on television and alcohol use illustrate one of the difficulties in working with content-analytic results. We have presented rate measures for most of the content attributes examined. But there is little objective basis for attaching such labels as "large rate" or "low rate" to whatever is obtained, unless some phenomenon is virtually absent. Until one can link the rates information to behavioral outcomes, the interpretation of how often something occurs remains relatively subjective. A case in point is drinking and drugging. For the most recent season in which these behaviors were assessed, alcohol drinking incidents occurred 2.7 times per hour, and the use of illegal drugs .8 times per hour. Clearly one is larger than the other. Furthermore, if we project across a season of watching television, then 2.7 drinking incidents become eight in a viewing evening and more than 2000 in a year. And that seems like a large amount. But take the drugging rate, call it only one incident an evening and more than 300 perhaps in a year. Is that not a substantial amount of content and potential exposure to a particular form of behavior?

Our venture into sexual intimacies on television suggests that references to intercourse are not infrequent, whether one cites the one per hour rate in the first sample, or one per two hours in the third sample. The vagaries of what constitutes a reference to intimate sexual activity will need further exploration. A recent paper dealing with "sexual euphimisms" on television suggests there is more to be heard than to be seen. For us, the most intriguing aspect is just how much of the coded activity in this content area is widely interpreted as intimate sex, beyond the trained coders. Note also that what has been examined thus far has specifically avoided attempts to deal with related sex material, primarily nonverbal, e.g., the wet T-shirt, the bikini, or the tight trousers. The effort to couple visual sexual stimuli with verbal references to sexual intimacy remains to be initiated.

Finally, the television family received its first intensive examination in these data. The first important conclusion is that family relationships occur on fictional television series in a comparative minority fashion. One out of seven or eight characters has an identifiable relative on the program, a proportion not much larger than the occurrence of blacks on television. Within that subset of characters with manifest relatives, the family structures are best characterized as heterogeneous rather than constant or stereotyped, and the family interactions are best characterized as affiliative rather than conflictual. The nuclear family, the single-parent family, and the childless family occur nearly equivalently. First marriages are the majority; divorce is increasing; the typical family has three members; virtually all are immediate, nuclear family relationships. And the television family is the only unit identified to date in which the sheer quantity of females is equal to that of males. More importantly, the activity of females within the family unit is nearly identical in content to that of the males. They are as active in both initiating and receiving interactions as males among the most regularly appearing television families. Interactions oriented to affiliative, helping behaviors were identified by an 8:1 margin over conflictual, antagonistic ones, with conflict concentrated in husband-wife pairings. Family units that appear weekly on television provide variety in composition, and positive behaviors toward each other far exceed negative ones. Although one can obtain census data about United States family structure, marital status, size, and other compositional attributes, more central would be real-life family interaction information. Perhaps the television family is not distinctly different on this dimension from real-life families.

Let us now back off from these portraitures of our findings and deal with some more general issues relevant to conclusions drawn from content analyses. We have presented here the sheer quantitative results across all prime-time and Saturday shows and have supplemented that with subanalyses by program type, broadcast time, and some other programming and character traits. We have already suggested additional analyses that might be undertaken from the same data set. There is in all this an overarching principle of treating all data segments as nominally equivalent. The form of the analysis and of the data therefore ignores potential qualitative differences. Each show has been treated like every other show, for purposes of analysis. Each characterization is like every other characterization in those same analyses. Several times in the individual chapters we have questioned the merits of those assumptions and wish to do so again here. Some qualities could themselves be quantified. For example, one could separate those shows which have a certain criterion audience rating and analyze behaviors and characterizations in those shows alone. That assumes that potential social consequences are more likely to be derived from shows with maximum audiences. For another, the major characters on these shows could be separated from secondary or minor ones and analyzed separately. That would assume that potential social consequences are more likely to originate with regular and strong characterizations than with lesser ones. Even further, one could identify "favorite" characters of television audiences and focus only on their behaviors. We do not know whether the basic findings would differ, but those approaches have not yet been tested.

Some major portions of television programming have generally been omitted from our sample weeks, most notably made-for-television movies and movies originally available in theaters. These now constitute a generous portion of the television schedule. Also absent is evidence for television miniseries, e.g., "Roots," "Behind Closed Doors," "Holocaust," or "79 Park Avenue." We focused on weekly series because we were interested in regularity of characterization and character behaviors. The lack of evidence from these alternative programming types limits what we know of television content. Furthermore, there may well be qualitative differences between the one-shot miniseries special, or movies, and the regeneration of situational problems for weekly series. There is reason to believe that the former are more stark and intense in their portrayals, as they need to wrestle an audience away from regular series viewing. They may deal with different issues, typically more controversial and often more violent. Primarily in these movies and miniseries do we recall lengthy examinations of suicide, genocide, prostitution, slavery, homosexuality, the problems of aging, divorce, retardation, etc. There may be topical distinctions, as well as stylistic ones; these may be accompanied by different role characterizations and different clusters of behaviors. Who is yet to say whether these impress the viewer more, make for more lasting images, convey different information, or change perspectives. How does one begin to equate exposure to the full series of "Roots" with exposure to multiple episodes of "The Jeffersons" in terms of potential impact on white viewers' feelings about blacks, or in terms of black viewers' self-concepts?

Life on television is abundant with conflict and conflict resolution. The characters come and go, we love them and eventually leave them, but the problems come again. Within the briefest of time spans, the problems are solved spiritedly, often miraculously, and always quickly. There is a perspective of hope that transcends individual presentations because the viewer has certainly learned that the problem will be resolved. What needs to be filled in is the who and the how. Some of the conflicts are trivial, others more fundamental to human survival.

In this milieu of television content, there remains the proposition that exposure to the consistent, persistent imagery of characters and their behaviors accumulates over time. That accumulation contributes to our mental and behavioral dispositions. How much it forms, and in what directions and intensities remains for scientists to discover and report. The present collection of information was designed to accelerate that discovery.

REFERENCES

Aaronfreed, J. The concept of internalization. In D. A. Goslin (Ed.), *Handbook of Socialization Theory and Research.* New York: Rand McNally, 1969.

Aronoff, C. Old age in prime time. *Journal of Communication,* 1974, *24,* 86–87.

Atkin, C. Mass media and the aging. In H. Oyer & J. Oyer (Eds.), *Aging and Communication.* Baltimore, Md.: University Park Press, 1976.

Atkin, C., Greenberg, B. S., & McDermott, S. *Television and racial socialization.* Paper presented at the convention of the Association for Education in Journalism, Seattle, 1978.

Atkin, C. K., & Miller, M. M. *Experimental effects of television advertising on children.* Paper presented at the convention of the International Communication Association, Chicago, 1975.

Atkin, C. K., Murray, J. P., & Nayman, O. The Surgeon General's research program on television and social behavior: A review of empirical findings. *Journal of Briadcasting,* 1971, *16,* 21–39.

Bandura, A. Influence of a model's reinforcement contingencies on the acquisition of imitative responses, *Journal of Personality and Social Psychology,* 1965, *1,* 589–595.

Bandura, A. *Aggression: a social learning analysis.* Englewood Cliffs, N.J.: Prentice-Hall, 1973.

Bandura, A. *Social learning theory.* Englewood Cliffs, N.J.: Prentice-Hall, 1977.

Bandura, A., & Walters, R. H. *Social learning and personality development.* New York: Holt, Rinehart, & Winston, 1963.

Baptista-Fernandez, P., Greenberg, B. S., & Atkin, C. K. The context, characteristics and communication behaviors of Blacks on television. East Lansing, Mich.: Department of Communication CASTLE Report No. 14, 1977.

Berelson, B., & Salter, P. Majority and minority Americans: An analysis of magazine fiction. *Public Opinion Quarterly,* October 1946, pp. 167–190.

Berkowitz, L. *Aggression: A social psychological analysis.* New York: McGraw-Hill, 1962.

Bochner, A. P. Conceptual frontiers in the study of communication in families: An introduction to the literature. *Human Communication Research,* 1976, 2, 381–397.

Bogatz, G., & Ball, S. *The second year of Sesame Street: A continuing evaluation.* Princeton, N.J.: Educational Testing Service, 1971.

Borke, H. The communication of intent: A systematic approach to the observation of family interaction. *Human Relations,* 1967, *20,* 13–28.

Broverman, J. K., Vogel, S. R., Broverman, D. M., Clark, F. E., & Rosenkrantz, P. S. Sex-role stereotypes: A current appraisal. *Journal of Social Issues*, 1972, *28*, 59–78.

Bryan, J., & London, P. Altruistic behavior by children. *Psychological Bulletin*, 1970, *73*, 200–211.

Bryan, J., & Walbeck, N. Preaching and practicing self-sacrifice: Children's actions and reactions. *Child Development*, 1970, *41*, 329–359.

Bryan, J., & Walbeck, N. The impact of words and deeds concerning altruism upon children. *Child Development*, 1970, *41*, 744–757.

Burton, R. V. Honesty and dishonesty. In T. Lickona (Ed.), *Moral development and behavior: Theory, research and social issues*. New York: Holt, Rinehart & Winston, 1976,

Busby, L. Defining the sex role standard in commercial network television programs directed toward children. *Journalism Quarterly*, 1974, *51*, 690–696.

Busby, L. Sex role research on the mass media. *Journal of Communication*, 1975, *25* (4), 107–131.

Buss, A. H., & Durkee, A. An inventory for assessing hostility. *Journal of Counseling Psychology*, 1963, *53*, 417–424.

Clark, C. C. Television and social controls: Some observations on the portrayal of ethnic minorities. *Television Quarterly*, 1969, *8*, 18–22.

Collins, W. A. Learning of media content: A developmental study. *Child Development*, 1970, *41*, 1133–1142.

Courtney, A. E., & Whipple, T. W. Women in TV commercials. *Journal of Communication*, 1974, *24* (2), 110–118.

Deaux, K. *The behavior of men and women*. Monterey, Cal.: Brooks/Cole Publishing Co., 1976.

Dillin, J. TV continues to emphasize liquor. *Christian Science Monitor*, December 26, 1975.

Dominick, J. R., & Greenberg, B. S. Three seasons of Blacks on television. *Journal of Advertising Research*, 1970, 10 (2), 21–27.

Dominick, J. R. & Rauch, G. E. The image of women in network TV commercials. *Journal of Broadcasting*, 1972, *16*, pp. 3, 259, 265.

Donelson, E. *Sex differences in developmental perspective*. Homewood, Ill.: Learning Systems Company, 1975.

Downing, M. Heroine of the daytime serial. *Journal of Communication*, 1974, *24* (2), 130–137.

Ellis, G. T., & Sekyra, F. The effect of aggressive cartoons on the behavior of first-grade children. *Journal of Psychology*, 1972, *81*, 37–43.

Fernandez-Collado, C., Greenberg, B. S., Atkin, C., & Korzenny, F. Sexual intimacy and drug use in TV series. *Journal of Communication*, 1978, *8*, 18–22.

Flanders, J. P. A review of research on imitative behavior. *Psychological Bulletin*, 1968, *69*, 316–337.

Francher, J., It's the Pepsi-generation . . . . accelerated aging and the television commercial. *International Journal of Aging and Human Development*, 1973, *4*, 245–255.

Franzblau, S., Sprafkin, J., & Rubenstein, E. Sex on TV: A content analysis. *Journal of Communication*, 1977, *27* (2), 164–170.

Friedrich, L. K., & Stein, A. H. Aggressive and pro-social television programs and the natural behavior of pre-school children. *Society for Research in Child Development*, 1973, *41*, 1133–1142.

Garlington, W. Drinking on television: A preliminary study with emphasis on method. *Journal of Studies on Alcohol*, 1977, *38*, 2199–2205.

Gerbner, G. Cultural indicators project: TV message analysis, recording instrument (Rev. ed.). Philadelphia: The Annenberg School of Communications, University of Pennsylvania, July 31, 1974.

Gerbner, G., & Gross, L. *Violence profile no. 6: Trends in network television drama and viewer conceptions of social reality, 1967–73*. Philadelphia: Report of the Annenberg School of Communications, University of Pennsylvania, December, 1974.

Gerbner, G., & Gross, L. Living with television: The violence profile. *Journal of Communication*, 1976, *26* (2), 172–199.

Gerbner, G., & Gross, L., with Eleey, M. F., Fox, S. K., Jackson-Beeck, M., & Signorielli, N. *Violence profile no. 7: A technical report.* Philadelphia: The Annenberg School of Communications, University of Pennsylvania, 1976.

Gerbner, G., Gross, L., Signorelli, N., Morgan, M., & Jackson-Beeck, M. The demonstration of power: Violence profile no. 10. *Journal of Communication*, 1979, *29* (3).

Gorn, G., Goldberg, M., & Kanungo, R. The role of educational television in changing the intergroup attitudes of children. *Child Development*, 1976, *47*, 277–280.

Gottschalk, L., Gleser, G., & Springer, K. Three hostility scales applicable to verbal samples. *A.M.A. Archives of General Psychiatry*, 1963, *9*, 254–279.

Greenberg, B. S. Children's reactions to TV Blacks. *Journalism Quarterly*, 1972, *49*, 5–14.

Greenberg, B. S. British children and televised violence. *Public Opinion Quarterly*, 1974, *38*, 531–547.

Greenberg, B. S., & Atkin, C. *Learning about minorities from television.* Paper presented at the conference on Television and the Socialization of the Minority Child at the UCLA Center for Afro-American Studies, Los Angeles, 1978.

Greenberg, B. S., Atkin, C. K., Edison, N. G., & Korzenny, F., with Heald, G. R., & Wakshlag, J. J. Pro-social and anti-social behavior on commercial television in 1975–76. East Lansing, Mich.: Department of Communication CASTLE Report, No. 1, 1977.

Greenberg, B. S., & Reeves, B. Children and the perceived reality of television. *Journal of Social Issues*, 1976, *32* (4), 86–97.

Hanneman, G., & McEwen, W. The use and abuse of drugs: An analysis of mass media content. In R. Ostman (Ed.), *Communication Research and Drug Education.* Beverly Hills, Calif.: Sage Publications, 1976.

Hartup, W., & Coates, B. The role of imitation in childhood socialization. In G. A. Hoppe, R. A. Milton, & E. C. Simmel (Eds.), *Early Experiences and the Process of Socialization.* New York: Academic Press, 1970.

Hays, W. L. *Statistics.* New York: Holt, Rinehart, & Winston, 1963.

Head, S. W. Content analysis of television drama programs. *Quarterly of Film, Radio and Television*, 1954, *9*, 175–194.

Henderson, L. Sex-role portrayals on commercial broadcast television. Unpublished M.A. thesis, Michigan State University, 1978.

Hicks, D. J. Imitation and retention of film-mediated aggressive peer and adult models. *Journal of Personality and Social Psychology*, 1965, *2*, 95–100.

Hicks, D. J. Short and long-term retention of affectively varied modeled behavior. *Psychonomic Science*, 1968, *11*, 369–370.

Hinton, J., Seggar, J., Northcott, H., & Fontes, B. Tokenism and improving imagery of Blacks in TV drama and comedy: 1973. *Journal of Broadcasting*, 1974, *18*, 423–432.

Horney, K. *Our inner conflicts.* New York: Norton, 1945.

Johnson, D. K., & Satow, K. Getting down to specifics about sex on television. *Broadcasting*, May 22, 1978, *24*.

Katzman, N. Television soap operas: What's been going on anyway? *Public Opinion Quarterly*, 1972, *36* (2), 200–212.

Krebs, D. Altruism: An examination of the concept and a review of the literature. *Psychological Bulletin*, 1970, *73*, 258–302.

Leifer, A. D., Collins, W. A., Gross, B. M., Taylor, P. H., Andrews, L., & Blackmer, E. R. Development aspects of variables relevant to observational learning. *Child Development*, 1971, *42*, 1509–1516.

Leifer, A. D., Gordon, N. J., & Graves, S. B. Children's television: More than mere entertainment. *Harvard Educational Review*, 1974, *44*, 213–245.

Lemon, J. Women and blacks on prime-time television. *Journal of Communication*, 1977, *27* (1), 70–79.

Levinson, R. M. *From Olive Oyl to Sweet Polly Purebread: Sex role stereotypes and televised cartoons.* Paper presented at the meeting of the Georgia Sociological Society, Atlanta, 1973.

Liebert, R. M., Davidson, E. S., & Neale, J. M. *The early window: Effects of television on children and youth.* New York: Pergamon Press, Inc., 1973.

Long, M., & Simon, R. J. The roles and statuses of women on children and family TV programs. *Journalism Quarterly,* 1974, *51,* 107–110.

Lyle, J., & Hoffman, H. R. Children's use of television and other media. In E. A. Rubinstein, G. A. Comstock, & J. P. Murray (Eds.), *Television and Social Behavior, Television in day-to-day life: Patterns of use.* Washington, D.C.: Government Printing Office, 1973, *4,* 129–256.

Martinez, T. M. Advertising and racism: The case of the Mexican-American. *El Grito* (2), 1968–69.

McArthur, L. Z., & Resko, B. G. The portrayal of men and women in American television commercials. *Journal of Social Psychology,* 1976.

McEwen, W., & Hanneman, G. The depiction of drug use in television programming. *Journal of Drug Education,* 1974, *4* (3), 281–293.

McLeod, J., Atkin, C., & Chaffee, S. Adolescents, parents and television use: Adolescent self-report measures from a Maryland and Wisconsin sample. In E. A. Rubinstein, G. A. Comstock, & J. P. Murray (Eds.), *Television and Social Behavior* (Vol. III). U.S. Department of Health, Education, and Welfare, 1972.

McNemar, Q. *Psychological Statistics.* Wiley, New York, 1955.

Midlarsky, E. Aiding responses: An analysis and review. *Merrill-Palmer Quarterly,* 1968, *14,* 229–260

Miller, M. M., & Reeves, B. *Children's occupational sex role stereotypes: The linkage between television content and perception.* Paper presented at the convention of the International Communication Association, Chicago, 1975.

Miller, M. M., & Reeves, B. Dramatic TV content and children's sex-role stereotypes. *Journal of Broadcasting,* 1976, *20* (1), 35–50.

Mischel, W. A social learning view of sex differences in behavior. In Maccoby, E. E. (Ed.), *The Development of Sex Differences.* Stanford, Calif.: Stanford University Press, 1966.

Northcott, H., Seggar, J., & Hinton, J. Trends in TV portrayal of Blacks and women. *Journalism Quarterly,* 1975, *52,* 741–744.

Petersen, M. The visibility and image of old people on television. *Journalism Quarterly,* 1973, *50,* 569–573.

Poulos, R., Harvey, S., & Liebert, R. Saturday morning television: A profile of the 1974–1975 children's season. *Psychological Reports, 1976, 39,* 1047–1057.

Richards, M. Trends in sex-role portrayals on television. Unpublished M.A. thesis, Michigan State University, 1980.

Roberts, D. Communication and children: A developmental approach. In I. Pool *et al.* (Eds.), *Handbook of Communication.* Chicago: Rand-McNally, 1973.

Roberts, D., & Schramm, W. Children's learning from the mass media. In W. Schramm and D. Roberts (Eds.), *The process and effects of mass communication.* University of Illinois Press, 1971.

Robinson, J. P., Athanasiou, R., & Head, K. B. *Measures of occupational attitudes and occupational characteristics.* Ann Arbor, Mich.: Institute for Social Research, 1969.

Rogers, L. E., & Farace, R. V. Analysis of relational communication in dyads: New measurement procedures. *Human Communication Research,* 1975 (Spring), 222–239.

Rosenkoetter, L. I. Resistance to temptation: Inhibitory and disinhibitory effects of models. *Developmental Psychology,* 1973, *8,* 80–84.

Ross, S. A. A test of the generality of the effects of deviant preschool models. *Developmental Psychology,* 1971, *4,* 262–267.

Seggar, J. Television's portrayal of minorities and women, 1971–1975. *Journal of Broadcasting,* 1977, *21,* 435–446.

Seggar, J. F., & Wheeler, P. World of work on TV: Ethnic and sex representation in tv drama. *Journal of Broadcasting*, 1973, *17*, 201–214.

Simmons, K., Greenberg, B., Atkin, C., & Heeter, C. The demography of fictional television characters in 1975–76. East Lansing, Mich.: Department of Communication CASTLE Report No. 2, 1977.

Smythe, D. W. Reality as presented by television. *Public Opinion Quarterly*, 1954, *18*, 143–156.

Stein, A. H. Imitation of resistance to temptation. *Child Development*, 1967, *38*, 159–169.

Stein, A. H., & Friedrich, L. K. Television content and young children's behavior. In J. P. Murray, E. A. Rubinstein, & G. A. Comstock (Eds.), *Television and Social Behavior, Vol. II: Television and Social Learning.* Washington, D.C.: Government Printing Office, 1972.

Sternglanz, S. H., & Serbin, L. A. Sex role stereotyping in children's television programs. *Developmental Psychology*, 1974, *10* (5), 710–715.

Steur, F. B., Applefield, J. M., & Smith, R. Televised aggression and the interpersonal aggression of preschool children. *Journal of Experimental and Child Psychology*, 1971, *11*, 442–447.

Tedesco, N. Patterns in prime time. *Journal of Communication*, 1974, *24* (2), 119–124.

Turow, J., Advising and ordering: Daytime, prime time. *Journal of Communication*, 1974, *24* (2), 138–141.

U.S. Commission on Civil Rights. *Window dressing on the set: Women and minorities on television.* Washington, D.C., August 1977.

Wackman, D. B., Collins, W. A., & Wartella, E. A. Children's social learning from family-oriented television programs. Report to the John and Mary R. Markle Foundation, 1976.

Wackman, D. B., Ward, S., Wartella, E., & Ettema, J. S. Children's information processing of television commercial messages. Paper presented at a Symposium in Division 23, American Psychological Association Convention, Montreal, 1973.

Whitney, J. Image-making in the land of fantasy. *Agenda*, January–February 1978.

Winick, C., & Winick, M. Drug education and the content of mass media dealing with dangerous drugs and alcohol. In R. Ostman (Ed.), *Communication Research and Drug Education.* Beverly Hills, Calif.: Sage Publications, 1976, 15–37.

Wolf, T. M., & Cheyne, J. A. Persistence of effects of live behavioral, televised behavioral, and live verbal models on resistance to deviation. *Child Development*, 1972, *43*, 1429–1436.

Wotring, C. W., & Greenberg, B. S. Experiments in televised violence and verbal aggression: Two exploratory studies. *Journal of Communication*, December 1973, *23*, 446–460.

AUTHOR INDEX

Page numbers in *italics* indicate where complete references are listed.

SUBJECT INDEX

A

Affection, *see* Prosocial behavior
Age
  behavior
    alcohol use, 143–144
    antisocial behavior, 29, 30, 120
    prosocial behavior, 30, 125
    sexual intimacy, 134
  demographics, 42–44
    race, 17, 40, 28–29
    sex, 28–29, 41
  distribution, 26–27, 31, 38–39
  effects, 23, 31–33
  history of portrayal, 24
  occupation
    lawbreakers, 28–29
    socioeconomic status, 28–29
  program attributes
    program time, 27
    program type, 27–28
Alcohol use, *see also* Substance use
  demographics
    age, 143–144
    race, 143
    sex, 143
    socioeconomic status, 144
  distribution, 140
  effects, 137–138

Alcohol use *(cont.)*
  history of portrayal, 138–139
  program attributes
    network, 141–142
    program time, 140–141
    program type, 141
  role attributes
    serious/comic role, 144
Altruism, *see* Prosocial behavior
Antisocial behavior
  demographics
    age, 30, 121
    race, 120
    sex, 120
  distribution
    deceit, 114, 115
    physical aggression, 114, 115
    verbal aggression, 113–114, 115
  effects, 102, 126–128
  history of portrayal, 100–104
  program attributes
    network, 119–120
    program time, 115–117
    program type, 117–119
  role attributes
    hero/villain roles, 121–122
    regularity, 121
    role importance, 121

201